Transcending Imagi...

Imagine a world where the boundaries of creativity are not only stretched but redefined. This book serves as your guide to this new frontier, engaging general readers, tech enthusiasts, and creatives alike in the captivating interplay between human ingenuity and artificial intelligence (AI).

Journey through the ground-breaking advancements in AI as they intersect with art, design, entertainment, and education. Discover how AI's power to analyze and understand language can be harnessed to generate breathtaking visuals from mere text descriptions—a process known as text-conditional image generation. But this book goes beyond just showcasing AI's capabilities: it delves into its transformative effects on the creative process itself. How will artists and designers adapt to a world where they co-create with machines? What are the implications of AI-generated art in educational settings? This book tackles these questions head on, offering a comprehensive view of the changing landscape of creativity.

At its core, this book challenges you to rethink what's possible in the realm of artistic expression. Manu contends that as AI evolves, mastering the art of collaboration between human and machine will become essential. More than just a look into the future, *Transcending Imagination: Artificial Intelligence and the Future of Creativity* is a roadmap for artists, designers, and educators eager to navigate the uncharted territory of AI-augmented creativity. It is a must-read for anyone interested in how AI might redefine the realms of art, design, and education.

Alexander Manu is a visionary who has consistently challenged the boundaries of innovation, strategy, and foresight. His insights have not only shaped industries but have also inspired countless professionals to reimagine the future and their role in it. An author, professor, and strategic innovator, he has been at the forefront of transformative concepts and ideas that have paved the way for the next generation of thinkers and doers.

With a career spanning over decades, he has been a beacon of inspiration, guiding businesses and individuals alike to navigate the ever-evolving landscape of technology, design, and human potential. His teachings and writings have been instrumental in helping organizations transition from the industrial to the knowledge value economy, emphasizing the importance of imagination, creativity, and personal transformation.

Chapman & Hall/CRC
Artificial Intelligence and Robotics Series
Series Editor: Roman Yampolskiy

A First Course in Aerial Robots and Drones
Yasmina Bestaoui Sebbane

AI by Design
A Plan for Living with Artificial Intelligence
Catriona Campbell

The Global Politics of Artificial Intelligence
Edited by Maurizio Tinnirello

Unity in Embedded System Design and Robotics
A Step-by-Step Guide
Ata Jahangir Moshayedi, Amin Kolahdooz, Liao Liefa

Meaningful Futures with Robots
Designing a New Coexistence
Edited by Judith Dörrenbächer, Marc Hassenzahl, Robin Neuhaus, Ronda Ringfort-Felner

Topological Dynamics in Metamodel Discovery with Artificial Intelligence
From Biomedical to Cosmological Technologies
Ariel Fernández

A Robotic Framework for the Mobile Manipulator
Theory and Application
Nguyen Van Toan and Phan Bui Khoi

AI in and for Africa
A Humanist Perspective
Susan Brokensha, Eduan Kotzé, Burgert A. Senekal

Artificial Intelligence on Dark Matter and Dark Energy
Reverse Engineering of the Big Bang
Ariel Fernández

Explainable Agency in Artificial Intelligence
Research and Practice
Silvia Tulli, David W. Aha

An Introduction to Universal Artificial Intelligence
Marcus Hutter, Elliot Catt, and David Quarel

AI: Unpredictable, Unexplainable, Uncontrollable
Roman V. Yampolskiy

Transcending Imagination:
Artificial Intelligence and the Future of Creativity
Alexander Manu

For more information about this series please visit: https://www.routledge.com/Chapman--HallCRC-Artificial-Intelligence-and-Robotics-Series/book-series/ARTILRO

Transcending Imagination
Artificial Intelligence and the Future of Creativity

Alexander Manu

CRC Press
Taylor & Francis Group
Boca Raton London New York

CRC Press is an imprint of the
Taylor & Francis Group, an **informa** business

A CHAPMAN & HALL BOOK

First edition published 2024
by CRC Press
2385 NW Executive Center Drive, Suite 320, Boca Raton FL 33431

and by CRC Press
4 Park Square, Milton Park, Abingdon, Oxon, OX14 4RN

CRC Press is an imprint of Taylor & Francis Group, LLC

Library of Congress Cataloging-in-Publication Data

Title: Transcending imagination : artificial intelligence and the future of creativity / Alexander Manu.
Description: First edition. | Boca Raton, FL : CRC Press, 2024. | Series: CEC Artificial Intelligence
and robotics | Includes bibliographical references and index. | Identifiers: LCCN 2023046495 (print) |
LCCN 2023046496 (ebook) | ISBN 9781032584027 (pbk) | ISBN 9781032584539 (hbk) |
ISBN 9781003450139 (ebk) Subjects: LCSH: Creative ability. | Imagination. | Artificial intelligence.
Classification: LCC BF408 .M23484 2024 (print) | LCC BF408 (ebook) |
DDC 153.3/5028563--dc23/eng/20240126
LC record available at https://lccn.loc.gov/2023046495
LC ebook record available at https://lccn.loc.gov/2023046496

ISBN: 978-1-032-58453-9 (hbk)
ISBN: 978-1-032-58402-7 (pbk)
ISBN: 978-1-003-45013-9 (ebk)

DOI: 10.1201/9781003450139

Typeset in Minion
by KnowledgeWorks Global Ltd.

Contents

Acknowledgments, xi

Preface, xiii

PART I **A New Creative Archetype**

Introduction	3
I.1 ALL ART IS ARTIFICIAL	3
I.2 HOW IS AI TRANSFORMING CREATIVITY?	4
I.3 DEFINITIONS	5
I.4 OPTIMIZING CREATIVE POTENTIAL AND CULTIVATING INNOVATIVE KNOWLEDGE	6
I.5 AI: GENERATING IMAGE OUTPUTS WITHOUT COMPROMISE	7
I.6 BEYOND ARCHETYPES	7
I.7 TO FEAR OR NOT TO FEAR?	12
I.8 A NEW AGE OF DISCOVERY	13
NOTES	13

CHAPTER 1 ▪ Beyond Imagination	15
1.1 ART AS INTENTION, ARTICULATION, AND MANIFESTATION	15
1.2 THE ROLE OF BEAUTY	18
1.3 INTENTION	18
1.4 ARTICULATION	20
1.5 MANIFESTATION	21
1.6 ART AND AI ARTISTIC VISION	21
1.7 ART AND AI-FOCUSED CREATIVE INSIGHT	22
1.8 CLOSING THOUGHTS	25
NOTES	25

Chapter 2 ▪ Art and the Sense of Sacredness   28

2.1   ART AS THE MEANS TO SPIRITUALITY   28

2.2   DOES ART NECESSITATE SENTIENCE?   30

2.3   A NEW VISUAL SPACE   31

2.4   CREATIVE GENERATIVITY   32

2.5   A THEORY OF GENERATIVE ART   33

2.6   A REVOLUTION   35

2.7   AI ENABLES A DRAMATIC EXPANSION OF BEAUTY   36

2.8   CLOSING THOUGHTS   37

NOTES   38

Chapter 3 ▪ Form Shapes Perceptions   40

3.1   FORM AS A FRAMEWORK FOR PERCEPTION   40

3.2   RAPID ITERATIONS AS A BRIDGE TO A NEW REALITY   41

3.3   ARTIFICIAL INTELLIGENCE AND THE AESTHETIC OF VIRTUAL SPACE   43

3.4   INTERACTIONS IN VIRTUAL REALITY   45

3.5   FORMS IN VIRTUAL SPACE   47

3.6   NEW FORMS REVOLUTIONIZED PERCEPTION   50

3.7   CLOSING THOUGHTS   50

NOTES   54

Chapter 4 ▪ Incidental Beauty   56

4.1   WHAT IS AN AESTHETICALLY BEAUTIFUL OBJECT?   56

4.2   BEAUTY IN ART AND DESIGN   58

4.3   WHAT IS INCIDENTAL BEAUTY?   61

4.4   CLOSING THOUGHTS   66

NOTES   67

Part II   **Expanding Possibilities**

Chapter 5 ▪ Bias and Creative Intent   71

5.1   THE BALANCE BETWEEN SKILL AND A DESIRED OUTCOME   71

5.2   BIAS IN CREATIVE INTENT   76

5.3   ARTIFICIAL INTELLIGENCE CHALLENGES   76

5.4   PARTNERING WITH ARTIFICIAL INTELLIGENCE   78

5.5 IMPACT OF AI ON ARTISTIC EXPRESSION 79

5.6 CLOSING THOUGHTS: CONVERGENCE 81

NOTES 82

CHAPTER 6 ■ Maximizing Creativity 84

6.1 CREATIVE INTENTION 84

6.2 THE AMBIGUITY OF CONCEALED INTENT 85

6.3 INTENT AND SKILL IN IMAGE GENERATION 86

6.4 INTENT AND INDIVIDUAL BIAS 88

6.5 AMPLIFYING INTENT THROUGH ENHANCED ARTICULATION 89

6.6 DECONSTRUCTING THE DIALECTICS OF ART AND TECHNOLOGY: AI AND HUMAN CREATIVITY 91

6.7 CLOSING THOUGHTS: AMPLIFYING CREATIVE INTENT THROUGH GENERATIVE AI 92

NOTES 93

CHAPTER 7 ■ From Creators to Narrators 95

7.1 THE SHIFT TO A NARRATED ECONOMY 95

7.2 ARCHITECTING EXPERIENCES 96

7.3 CO-CREATING A NEW NARRATIVE 98

7.4 A HUMAN-TO-HUMAN NARRATIVE 98

7.5 GENERATIVE DESIGN AND GENERATIVE NARRATIVES 100

7.6 CONTEMPLATING AN AI-FACILITATED WORLD: THE EVOLUTION OF HUMAN NARRATIVES 102

7.7 CLOSING THOUGHTS 104

NOTES 105

CHAPTER 8 ■ Sentience and Agency 107

TIB ROIBU

8.1 THE EMERGENCE OF INSIGHT 107

8.2 MEANING BUILT WITH ATTENTION AND TECHNIQUE 109

8.3 FANTASY AND NEW DIMENSIONS FOR PERCEPTION 112

8.4 AUTOPOIETIC INTELLIGENCE 114

CONTRIBUTOR BIOGRAPHY 115

NOTES 116

PART III **Disruption and Transformation**

CHAPTER 9 ▪ The Myth of the Creative Genius — 119

9.1 A SOCIETAL CONSTRUCT — 119

9.2 GENIUS IS AN ILLUSION — 121

9.3 REMIX AND COLLABORATIVE CREATIVITY — 122

9.4 COLLABORATIVE INTELLIGENCE: THE MAKING OF A REVOLUTION — 124

9.5 THE FUTURE OF CREATIVITY — 126

9.6 CREATIVE INTELLIGENCE: WHERE SCIENCE AND ART MEET — 127

9.7 ART TRANSCENDS BOTH SELF AND TECHNOLOGY — 128

9.8 CLOSING THOUGHTS — 129

NOTES — 129

CHAPTER 10 ▪ Intention, Articulation, and Manifestation — 132

10.1 MEANING, ENERGY, AND MATTER — 132

10.2 INTENTION CREATES A SYSTEM OF MEANING — 134

10.3 INTENTION AND MEANING — 138

10.4 ARTICULATION — 139

10.5 MANIFESTATION — 141

10.6 CLOSING THOUGHTS — 144

NOTES — 145

CHAPTER 11 ▪ Generative AI as a Disruptor — 147

11.1 THE GREAT DISRUPTOR — 147

11.2 THE DISRUPTION INDEX — 149

11.2.1 The Disruptor — 149

11.2.2 The Enabler — 150

11.2.3 The Integrator — 151

11.2.4 The Follower — 152

11.3 THE DISRUPTION FRAMEWORK — 152

11.4 DISRUPTION AND DISRUPTORS — 153

11.5 TRANSFORMED BY TECHNOLOGY — 154

11.6 WHAT IS TRANSITION? — 155

11.7 TRANSFORMATIONAL CHANGE — 155

11.8 UNDERSTANDING TRANSITION AND TRANSFORMATION — 156

11.9 GENERATIVE AI: THE FASTEST TRANSFORMATIONAL
  CHANGE RATE   159

11.10 CLOSING THOUGHTS   160

NOTES   161

PART IV **A Radical New Aesthetic**

CHAPTER 12 ■ Moving Past Archetypes   165

12.1 THE END OF THE CONDITIONAL ARCHETYPE   165

12.2 HOW DO WE TEACH ART AND DESIGN IN THE CONTEXT OF
  TEXT-CONDITIONAL INSPIRATION?   167

12.3 TEXT CONDITIONAL DESIGN SYSTEMS   169

12.4 WORKING WITHOUT ARCHETYPES   173

12.5 RADICAL CENTRIC DESIGN AS A NEW CONCEPTUAL
  MODEL   176

12.6 NO ARCHETYPE   178

12.7 CLOSING THOUGHTS   181

NOTES   182

CHAPTER 13 ■ Less Is Not More Anymore   185

13.1 THE AESTHETIC OF INSIDE-OUT   185

13.2 LESS IS MORE   187

13.3 LESS IS NOT MORE ANYMORE   189

13.4 CLOSING THOUGHTS   198

NOTES   200

CHAPTER 14 ■ The Richly Imagined Everything   202

14.1 SCENARIO-BASED DESIGN AND INNOVATION   202

14.2 NORMATIVE, STRATEGIC, AND USER SCENARIOS   203

14.3 THE COMPELLING POWER OF VISUAL NARRATIVES   204

14.4 RICHLY IMAGINED EVERYTHING: DESIGN AND
  ARCHITECTURE   208

14.5 RICHLY IMAGINED ENTERTAINMENT   210

14.6 RICHLY IMAGINED FOOD   211

14.7 RICHLY IMAGINED HEALTH   212

14.8 RICHLY IMAGINED EDUCATION   215

14.9 RICHLY IMAGINED MARKETING   216

14.10 RICHLY IMAGINED WORK   217

14.11 CLOSING THOUGHTS   218

NOTES   219

Chapter 15 ■ A Provocation: Is Anything Artificial?   220

15.1 EXTINGUISHING LABELS   220

15.2 THE PERMANENT EXISTENCE   222

NOTES   226

AFTERWORD, 229

BIBLIOGRAPHY, 235

INDEX, 239

Acknowledgments

THIS BOOK IS A testament to the rich mosaic of experiences, dialogues, and collaborations that have informed my thought process and spurred my intellectual curiosity. It finds its roots in my students' tireless inquiries and spirited questioning, who continually challenge my knowledge and seek original and stimulating insights. My collaborators, too, have played an essential role, adding to this work by generously bestowing their expertise and contributing their unique and diverse perspectives. A significant debt of gratitude is owed to Tib Roibu, who has been a vital collaborator since the inception of this project. His considerable input has been crucial in molding the book's narrative and shaping its trajectory. I am deeply thankful for his collaboration and steadfast support throughout this journey.

I must also express my sincere gratitude to the numerous organizations and individuals who have, over time, embraced and applied my theories, concepts, and methods. Their readiness to bring abstract ideas to life through tangible products and services has lent real-world significance to my work. They have transformed life into a vibrant celebration, a veritable festival of ideas that enriches and adds zest to the human experience.

This book vividly illustrates the transformative potential of generative AI technologies and, more specifically, the impact of the generative program MidJourney. Every image within these pages represents a collaboration between myself and a host of creative minds I have never met in person yet whose collective efforts have yielded something far greater than what we could have achieved individually. My profound gratitude goes to the gifted team at MidJourney, whose pioneering work in AI has not only facilitated the creation of this book but has also significantly advanced my thinking and practice in the process.

My family—Sophie, Sasha, and Bella—have given me unwavering support and guidance. Their enduring encouragement has been an essential source of vitality for me, allowing me to tackle my work with a spirit that remains ever curious and youthful.

Preface

TRANSCENDING IMAGINATION INVITES INSIGHTFUL readers into a deep-dive exploration of creativity, artificial intelligence (AI), design, and art, focusing on the shifting relationship between human imagination and AI. The book probes the demarcation between the organic and the fabricated, and the distinction between the natural and artificial compelling us to reassess our ideas and understandings about art, consciousness, and the nature of creativity. The text engages with the intriguing issue of AI-created art in its opening passages. It elucidates how AI, a product of human innovation, independently crafts art pieces, prompting us to rethink these traditional classifications. This autonomous creation by AI, blurring the lines between natural and artificial, leads us to reconsider the implications this has on our perceptions of consciousness and self-awareness.

Chapter 1, "Beyond Imagination," explores the symbiotic relationship intertwining human creativity and AI. It advances the thesis that AI should be perceived as an instrument and an accomplice in the creative odyssey. Far from being a crutch that obfuscates the essence of human creativity, AI is a catalyst that accentuates, extrapolates, and metamorphoses the multiple facets of creativity. Moreover, the chapter offers an intriguing perspective on the sanctity this synergistic interaction could give to the creative process, hinting at a transcendent, evocative, and indescribable dimension. It posits AI as an ally in the creative process, which enhances human creativity and adds new dimensions and a sense of sacredness to it.

Chapter 2, "Art and the Sense of Sacredness," probes deeper into the symbiotic interplay between AI and human creativity, spotlighting the alchemy of their co-creation as it permeates art with an aura of sanctity. Through an exploration of esoteric and epistemological paradigms, the chapter illuminates how this partnership can evoke magic qualities within art, conjuring an elevated perception of sacredness. Subsequently, "Form Shapes Perceptions" embarks on a cogitative analysis of the role of form in the alteration of perception and the augmentation of imagination within both tangible and digital domains. It inspects the multifaceted nuances of form—structure, contours, and constituent elements—and investigates how these properties act as conduits in tailoring and enriching perceptual experiences. The chapter contemplates the intriguing intersection where form acts as an agent of change in the cognitive interplay between the real and the simulated.

The chapter "Incidental Beauty" engages with emergent aesthetics delivered by generative AI, drawing an alluring parallel to the serendipitous splendor found in nature. The chapter considers the implications of AI as an independent generator of beauty, a spontaneous artist similar to the ceaseless creativity exhibited in the natural world. Moving forward, chapters "Bias and Creative Intention" and "From Creators to Narrators" explore the evolutionary trajectory of humans from being creators to becoming narrators in the new creative landscape forged by AI. Central to this examination is the exploration of AI's potential to democratize and expand creative expression by diluting individual biases that might inadvertently influence creative output. The book critically evaluates the duality of this shift, navigating the intriguing interstice where the human role transforms from the active creator to the storyteller, guided and enriched by the all-encompassing intuition of AI. In "Sentience and Agency," Tib Roibu explores the blurring of lines between creator and created, and observer and observed, as a result of this evolving conversation. This dialogue sees AI and humans learn from each other, adapt, and evolve, with AI serving as a mirror for human creativity and a canvas for new dimensions of storytelling.

"The Myth of the Creative Genius" systematically deconstructs the long-held notion of creativity as a rarefied domain exclusively inhabited by an elite. Instead, it highlights the inherently collaborative fabric of creativity, underscoring how AI-based tools augment this cooperative ethos. The chapter engages in an intellectual dissection of the traditional archetype of the "solitary genius," bringing to light the diverse elements contributing to the creative process.

In the chapters that follow, an intricate exploration of the creative process takes center stage, with particular emphasis on the disruptive role that generative AI plays within this sphere. The discourse journeys through the essential nodes of creativity—intention, articulation, and manifestation—examining how AI instigates transformative shifts across these elements. Through an analytic lens, we explore the nuanced ways in which the integration of AI can reframe intention, enrich articulation, and usher in unanticipated avenues of manifestation, thereby reconfiguring the very architecture of the creative process. These chapters critically examine the intertwining dynamics of these components within the creative ecosystem and scrutinize the role of generative AI in perturbing and enriching these relationships, thereby instigating a nuanced understanding of creativity in the digital age.

The book additionally embarks on an inquiry into the territory of design education, interrogating how AI impacts and transforms established principles and paradigms of design thinking. This discussion gains relevance in the context of emergent technologies such as additive manufacturing and scenario-based design, where the inclusion of AI prompts a re-evaluation of traditional methodologies and the potential birth of new design philosophies. It critically dissects how AI's capabilities in pattern recognition, simulation, and generative algorithms redefine pedagogical approaches and inform an evolved understanding of design principles.

In a culminating reflection titled "Is Anything Artificial?", the book contemplates the entrenched dichotomy between the natural and the artificial. It posits a thought-provoking challenge to this binary classification, suggesting a more fluid and interwoven tapestry of creation that transcends origin. Through a synthesis of insights garnered throughout the book, this final section advocates for a re-evaluation of our categorizations and encourages a reconsideration of our conventional understandings, hinting at a harmonious co-existence where the lines between the 'natural' and 'artificial' are not just blurred, but perhaps even, unnecessary. This encompassing worldview acknowledges the interconnectedness and continuum in the very essence of creation, irrespective of its genesis.

WHERE TO FROM HERE?

AI is more than a simple tool in our toolbox; it symbolizes our unyielding pursuit of transcendence, serving as a reflective canvas for our most profound creative yearnings. Our engagement with AI propels us past the boundaries of mechanical intelligence, guiding us toward the essence of our creative consciousness. This dynamic narrative is not about technology usurping humanity, it is a tribute to our inherent adaptability, evolutionary capability, and the limitless expanse of our imagination.

As we dare to push the limits of our imagination, we sculpt the environment around us and our identities. This undertaking is essentially about evolution, growth, and transformation. It is about us—about you—teetering on the brink of a new era, primed to dive into the boundless depths of an uncharted paradigm. In this domain, the distinctions between natural and artificial dissolve as dreams intertwine with reality, and we collectively etch the outlines of a future beyond our wildest dreams.

To transcend imagination is to stand at the edge of the known and the unknown, viewing it not as a cliff of fear but as a launchpad for daring exploration, powered by our curiosity and bolstered by our creative resilience. *Transcending Imagination* is more than an academic study; it is an intellectual expedition that encourages the reader to challenge established notions and re-envision the realms of art and creativity in the nexus of human intent and AI. The book proposes that AI is a reflection and amplifier of our creative aspirations, and it praises the flexible, evolving nature of human creativity in a period of rapid technological advancement. It calls upon readers to seize this transformative age, molding a future where art, design, and technology merge into inseparable components of the enduring act of creation.

I

A New Creative Archetype

Introduction

I.1 ALL ART IS ARTIFICIAL

I want to start with this provocation: all art is artificial! In pursuing a meaningful discourse around this provocative statement, we must first journey into the philosophical and ontological realms to define and discuss the terms "natural" and "artificial."

At the fundamental level, natural is typically used to describe phenomena, entities, or processes that occur in the physical world without any human intervention. They are part of the existing order of the cosmos, formed through natural laws and evolutionary processes—atoms, mountains, trees, and biological life all fall into this category. They exist, evolve, and interact based on natural principles without needing a conscious, deliberate, human-driven act.

On the other hand, the term "artificial" generally pertains to products or effects resulting from human intervention, be it physical or intellectual. The term has its roots in Latin—*artificialis*, meaning "of or belonging to art."[1] Anything made, designed, or conceived by humans, including tools, buildings, concepts, or, indeed, art, is deemed artificial. These things exist because of our intentionality, agency, and capacity to manipulate nature and create anew.

In its broadest sense, art involves human creativity and imagination, intended to produce works appreciated primarily for their beauty or emotional power. Given this definition, art is artificial as it necessitates human intention and action. From cave paintings to digital art, all arts require a human's conscious decision to create something that would not have existed without their intervention.

Now, considering these definitions, let us examine the question of art produced by artificial intelligence (AI), which has grown tremendously in recent years. If an AI generates an image, is it "natural" or "artificial"? If we consider the AI itself a product of human ingenuity—an artifact—it could be argued that the art it creates is artificial too. It is an output derived from human-built systems and algorithms.

However, a counterargument could be made. If an AI, through machine learning and neural networks, independently generates a work of art without a specific human intention behind the individual piece, could we not consider this a "natural" process within the AI "organism"? AI's creativity could be akin to a beaver building a dam or a bird building a nest—an expression of its nature based on the "laws" (in this case, algorithms) governing its existence.

In contemplating the transformative potential of AI, one cannot help but consider the fundamental philosophical implications. The burgeoning capacity of AI systems

DOI: 10.1201/9781003450139-2

to learn, create, and even to some extent, adapt autonomously invites a deeper introspection on the delineation between what we categorize as natural and artificial. Are we at the threshold of an epistemological shift, where the traditional ontological distinctions blur?

With their generative abilities, AI systems increasingly resemble certain aspects of human creativity and spontaneity. AI can compose music, create art, and even mimic human-like conversation in its generative form. This question leads to a fascinating inquiry: should we consider nonhuman, nonbiological entities that generate content as a form of "natural" creativity? Historically, the notion of creativity has been inextricably tied to human cognition. The capacity to conceive novel ideas and give them form has been a quintessentially human trait. However, the emergent abilities of AI may compel us to reevaluate these notions.

As our understanding of intelligence becomes less anthropocentric, the definitions of "natural" and "artificial" are open to interrogation. Traditional frameworks imagine nature as a realm that unfolds organically without human intervention. Conversely, the artificial has been associated with human-made constructs and artifacts. However, as AI systems evolve, they exhibit properties akin to organic systems, such as adaptability, emergent behavior, and self-organization.

This raises questions that extend beyond semantics. It is not just about whether we need to reclassify AI as natural or artificial but whether these categories are adequate or too rigid. Should we consider an entirely new classification that captures the essence of entities that are not born of biological processes but exhibit characteristics that have hitherto been associated only with natural phenomena?

In addition, this discourse inevitably grazes the philosophical debates around consciousness and sentience. Should an AI system that can create, learn, and adapt autonomously be considered alive in any meaningful sense? The situation prompts a reassessment of the criteria we use to define life. Is the substrate—biological or silicon—essential in defining life or should the criteria be based on functionality and behavior?

Our philosophical, ethical, and legal frameworks will be challenged as we proceed into an era where artificial entities play an increasingly sophisticated and autonomous role. There will be an imperative for interdisciplinary dialogue among philosophers, AI researchers, ethicists, and legal scholars to grapple with these emerging realities. The lexicon and categories that served us in the past might need to evolve, and with them, our understanding of our place in the cosmos. The humbling prospect that humanity might not hold a monopoly on creativity or intelligence warrants contemplative inquiry and an openness to reframe age-old constructs.

1.2 HOW IS AI TRANSFORMING CREATIVITY?

The capacity to envision a world where creativity and individual human expression are not paramount is becoming increasingly difficult to comprehend, and the former status quo is being rendered obsolete. In the contemporary landscape, we are surrounded by systems becoming progressively intelligent, pioneering, and uniquely engaging. These technologies are accelerating at a breakneck pace, fostering a level of innovation that is unprecedented. Far from imposing restrictions, emerging technologies such as AI amplify our creative potential.

The dynamism of our world is intensifying, altering how we establish relationships within our professional sphere and the intersections of work, leisure, and rejuvenation. Inevitably, as we integrate AI into our array of working tools, our fundamental structures of knowledge, experience, and intuition will be required to adapt.

AI, once a theoretical notion, is now a pragmatic reality with a profound array of possibilities for the future of humankind. Artists and designers can utilize these cutting-edge technologies as vehicles to articulate the evolution of the human experience. The situation does not require a radical shift in our existence but acknowledges the burgeoning horizons of opportunity. As we venture toward the future of creativity, we must recognize that AI does not threaten humanity but instead imbues it with novel life and insight. AI should not be perceived as a menace to the creative psyche, nor should it be relegated to a simple instrument or novelty. It is, in essence, a natural extension of the human propensity to perpetually uncover moments of astonishment and bliss. The pursuit of joy is not trivial—it is synonymous with creativity, bravery, resilience, and fearlessness. AI serves as a facilitator that can enrich the human condition. Like the discovery of fire, AI can act as a catalyst, enabling humans to express and probe their innate potential and possibilities.

So, how exactly is AI reshaping creativity? We posit that AI technology will transform the artistic and design process by enhancing and expediting the generation and realization of creative works, thereby revolutionizing the creative world.

The emergence of intelligent technologies and their embodiments as artifacts might influence public perception and interpretation of these domains of human endeavor. How might these developments impact consumer behavior and perception? As AI evolves to a stage where it can mimic most human creative output, what will be our response to AI-generated art? What implications might this have for end users, the ultimate consumers of these creations?

Such inquiries prompt a broader contemplation of philosophical and technological matters, such as our understanding of the human-machine relationship, the interplay between objectivity and subjectivity, and the demarcation between rationality and emotion. Our understanding of these relationships must not be confined to hearsay but should stem from practical experience and specialized knowledge to truly evolve.

"Transcending Imagination" offers a glimpse into a brave new world. This book delves into the potentially transformative impact of machine intelligence as a creative conduit and the conceivable enhancement and modification of human creativity and cultural norms.

1.3 DEFINITIONS

Before we delve into the mechanics of AI-generated art at its finest, it may be advantageous to establish the rudimentary definitions of art, design, and technology. These categorizations formulate a cognitive framework for identifying and characterizing art, design, and technology elements. At a foundational level, an artwork is a *tangible object* crafted or created by an artist or designer[2]; design is an *approach*, either graphical or otherwise, employed for sketching or designing[3]; and technology is a *system* or an assembly of technologies, or a physical apparatus, utilized to interact with a device or mechanism.[4]

When we superimpose these definitions onto AI technologies, it instantaneously elucidates how the creation process of an AI-generated artifact commences from a chain of algorithms. These algorithms utilize, as their primary function, the intellectual interpretation of a predetermined concept—*the intent*—articulated by the user with the assistance of a text prompt.

In the context of text-conditional image generators, art and science are indeed intertwined. For the first time, we are offered a unique perspective on the creative process, acting simultaneously as instigators of its intent and articulation and spectators of its realization. The privilege of witnessing the act of creation—observing images being materialized right before our eyes and gradually attaining clarity as the rendering process culminates—is an experience that is not only priceless but also bears significant responsibility. Such a development heralds an exploration into a novel consciousness and the prospect of an entirely distinctive way of existence that transcends the limits of our imagination. The human propensity to go beyond what is known invariably propels us toward new heights of creativity. With AI text-conditional image generators, we find ourselves on the cusp of a revolution in art and design that may instigate a societal shift toward discovering and examining deeper values.

1.4 OPTIMIZING CREATIVE POTENTIAL AND CULTIVATING INNOVATIVE KNOWLEDGE

The human mind, celebrated for its ability to reason and introduce innovative ideas abstractly, scrutinizes and evaluates the influence of these novel concepts. Creativity can be envisaged as intelligence that allows us to discern between distinct notions and conceive novel applications. Why might artists and entrepreneurs be interested in experimenting with AI image-generating tools and their capabilities? The advantages are manifold. AI image generators operate within a virtual space on one's desktop, a setting that is considerably more cost-effective to manage than physical spaces, thereby lowering barriers for artists to experiment and obtain feedback.

Creativity maintains a unique structure, identity, role, and mandate in contemporary society. In the current epoch, ideas, knowledge, and artistic productions have been rendered accessible through digital technology and networked communication. The advent of artificial intelligence has expanded the potential for knowledge and image production. In contrast, the creation and distribution of images remain intrinsic to human creativity and closely intertwined with cultural representations.[5] With the aid of AI and additional digital media, the capacity for image generation can be significantly enhanced. If the core challenge of creativity lies in producing items of value, AI can undoubtedly be viewed as a game-changer in the sphere of creativity. Its inherent potential needs to be thoroughly comprehended and fully harnessed.

I.5 AI: GENERATING IMAGE OUTPUTS WITHOUT COMPROMISE

The title highlights the distinction between text-conditional image generation and images crafted by designers or artists using traditional methods. In the production of artwork by an artist, there exists a form of "flow" that is influenced by the ongoing output. Observing the emerging artwork signifies that the artist continues along the trajectory determined by what visually presents itself before them, assuming this does not conflict with their original intent. Consequently, artists tend to exhibit bias toward certain forms and colors, which they intuitively gravitate toward based on past preferences, even if this occurs on a subconscious level. Therefore, it can be concluded that in any human-produced artwork, consciously or subconsciously, choices inevitably involve compromise. In contrast, neural networks are devoid of such compromises. These systems evaluate each potential output, favoring those that align with all the conditional text descriptors given in the original input.[6]

Neural networks produce and, metaphorically speaking, "visualize" the output from the onset of the process, rendering the image without accounting for the concept of "flow." This excludes any possibility of incorporating creative intuition into the design during its generation. Since designers cannot modify the text-based articulation of their intent once the image generation has commenced, the resultant image produced by the neural network might bear little resemblance to the initially envisioned representation. In essence, the form is created independently of any further artist input. The text-conditional inputs of AI systems strive to identify and extract all the necessary information required to fulfill a goal in which the semantic intent is explicitly manifested. When the provided intent carries a high degree of semantic specificity and value, the resultant images generated can exceed the bounds of human imagination and anticipation.

I.6 BEYOND ARCHETYPES

Most, if not all, design practices and education are tailored around perfecting and improving archetypes. We teach students how to design forms and features based on the capability of materials, and these forms are inherited archetypes. Chairs. Kettles. Forks. Shoes. Cars. Bicycles, and we measure the new design's success on its capability to improve the archetype rather than expand or redefine it. AI text-conditional image generation is an invitation to move beyond the conditional archetype.

Consider reframing our approach to future planning with an innovative perspective. Instead of resorting to established archetypes, we should construct from a novel point of origin. This approach would entail delineating the intent as opposed to declaring an archetype. So, instead of posing the question "Imagine the design of a comfortable office chair,"[7] we might ask "Imagine the design of a device that can comfortably suspend the human body above ground while performing a task" (Figure I.1). By requesting a "comfortable office chair," we are not seeking a function but instead invoking an archetype. It is incumbent upon us to dismantle our preconceived notions regarding our experiential world. The situation essentially represents our opportunity to bypass the typical forces that shape our archetypes and, instead, create objects that can extend and reformulate the imaginative boundaries of their creators.

FIGURE I.1   Device suspending the human body above ground.

What if designers could transcend known archetypes and delve into the untamed realm of possibilities? We could define a set of "conditional" constraints on the form: whether the human hand can achieve a certain height, the feasibility of performing a task while looking upward, and the possibility of rotating side-to-side to encompass a specified radius, among other conditions. Once these constraints have been articulated, an unprecedented structure comes into existence. Furthermore, once these constraints have been met, they become immutable. The concept of designing from constraints is not novel; any design brief is essentially a document elucidating the desired features and limitations of a particular object or environment.

Envision a scenario where the delineation of intent is augmented with a set of governing principles. Such developments could usher in a new wave of devices, appliances, and environments that challenge our preconceived notions of form, functionality, and the paradigms of user gratification. For instance, instead of articulating, "/imagine a device that evokes a sense of the past by simulating nostalgia" (refer to Figure I.2), we could delve deeper into the multifaceted nature of nostalgia as an interplay between an individual's past and present. The prompt could be rephrased as "/imagine the capacity to forge a map that delineates each individual's intricate connections with their past and present. Within the map's context, consider that the map itself serves as a metaphor for the past, while the geomorphological features embody its very essence, and vice versa" (see Figure I.3). It is highly improbable that a human artist or designer could have conceived

FIGURE I.2   Nostalgia simulating device.

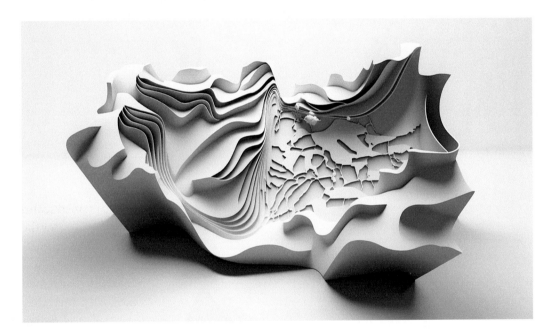

FIGURE I.3   A map that defines each person's relationship to the past and the present and is a symbol of the past and an image of its definition, and vice versa.

the representations in these figures, as human creative endeavors are inherently tethered to archetypes.

Another example could involve reimagining a musical instrument. Traditionally, one might think of a piano or a guitar. However, by defining the intent as *creating an apparatus that produces sound through interaction with the user*, we pave the way for unconventional contraptions that could amalgamate sensor technology, gestural interfaces, and algorithmic sound synthesis (refer to Figure I.4).

Furthermore, instead of proposing "imagine a sustainable mode of urban transportation" (Figure I.5), which might evoke images of bicycles or electric cars, rephrase the intent as

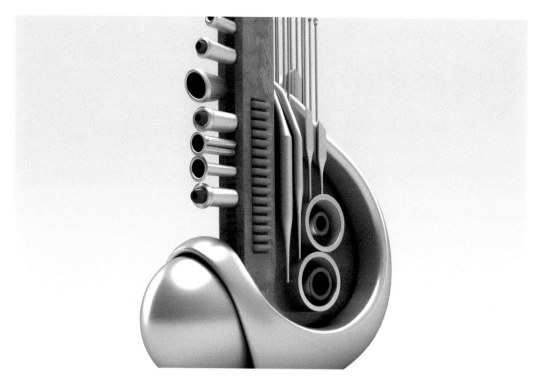

FIGURE I.4 An apparatus that produces sound through interaction with the user.

FIGURE I.5 A sustainable mode of urban transportation.

FIGURE I.6   A mechanism that facilitates efficient human mobility within an urban environment while minimizing carbon footprint.

"envision a mechanism that facilitates efficient human mobility within an urban environment while minimizing carbon footprint" (Figure I.6). This alternative articulation could engender concepts such as networked aerial pods, kinetic pavements, or even urban mobility solutions that leverage the latent energy sources within the cityscape.

This emphasis on defining intent and integrating rules heralds a paradigm shift that liberates creativity from the constraints of conventional archetypes and paves the way for an innovation unbounded by tradition.

Designers often gravitate toward an archetype when embarking on a creative endeavor. This propensity for familiar design patterns is particularly prevalent in logo design, where an image—such as a sailboat—is paired with a particular rule (such as assigning light blue to the sailboat) and placed in the context of a geographical area like a bay, a harbor, or an island.[8] Though this example pertains to a two-dimensional graphic object, it encapsulates our long-standing inclination to construct archetypal versions of reality to aid in comprehending our world and our conception of beauty.

What if we prompted designers to step beyond these archetypes and adopt a research-oriented mindset? At its heart, design is an investigative and research-driven field. utilizing AI not as a substitute but as a collaborative partner in design processes should enhance both the designer's capabilities and the resulting output. To leverage AI from a design perspective, we should primarily ask ourselves, "What is it that I desire?" rather than, "What can AI offer me?"

Having presented these fundamental queries, we can begin designing in concert with AI, envisioning possibilities. Once we break free from the hold of archetypes, we can truly appreciate the new horizons of discovery that AI can open for designers.

Incorporating AI into the design process should not be viewed as a mere extension of traditional methodologies but as a novel dimension to the design process itself. AI can reveal a broader spectrum of possibilities and enrich our design diversity by asking these basic questions about our desires and the realm of feasibility. AI does not interpret the world as it is; instead, it presents an avenue for creatives to reimagine the role and scope of design.

1.7 TO FEAR OR NOT TO FEAR?

Is there a reason for creatives to fear this emerging technology? This intriguing question often arises whenever a new technology challenges the existing creative or work process, as was seen when computers began to dominate the office landscape in the early 1980s, eventually commandeering most office-related tasks by the late 1980s and early 1990s. When seen through the lens of an artist's fear, it resembles a chef being intimidated by the introduction of the knife, a novel technology in the kitchen. A proficient chef would welcome the knife as a tool, recognizing its potential to enhance their culinary prowess by accelerating tasks and ultimately producing a tastier, aesthetically appealing dish. Similarly, the genuine artist never fears new technology but instead seizes the opportunity to explore how it might enrich their creative vision and further their mission to infuse the world with beauty. The same principle applies to the advent of artificial intelligence and neural networks and their capacity to produce art based on text input.

Text-conditional image generation technology has the potential to push the boundaries of human expression, offering a fresh medium that can inspire and assist humans in crafting artistic forms that exceed the bounds of the imagination. We can only uncover the full potential of technology by pushing its limits. All novel technologies, including artificial intelligence and neural networks, are underpinned by intelligent behavior. Unless this natural progression is halted, there is no reason to dread the advent of new tech.

Most artistic forms originate in the human imagination, a trait shared by the new art forms ushered in by the digital era. Imagination must constantly yield to let new technologies serve as an ally to the artist rather than a threat, as technology will never usurp the artist's role. Imagination and intent govern that role. Imagination ignites the intent, which manifests beauty that captivates humans and invites them to partake. Often, images produced by text-conditional generators form an assembly of shapes, colors, and compositions of graphic elements that are appreciated for their aesthetic value, existing solely to delight the viewer.

Art is a testament to our quest to comprehend beauty, and understanding beauty equates to seeking the essence within everyday objects and situations. The process is quite nuanced. Probing into art reveals that beauty does not reside within the object or its symbolism but in our perception of it. Beauty is a spontaneous, unscripted event that unfolds as a manifestation of our mind. Our minds, shaped by a unique combination of personal history, experiences, and imagination, interact dynamically with the artwork. This interaction is an inherently creative act, just as the original act of creation by the artist.

Through this lens, beauty becomes a deeply personal and transformative experience, transcending the physical or aesthetic dimensions of the artwork. It creates a unique and dynamic dialogue between the artwork, the observer's internal world, and their external reality. Besides, our understanding and interpretation of beauty are not static.[9] As we evolve, so too do our perceptions and appreciations of beauty. As such, art's true power lies in its ability to challenge, change, and deepen our understanding of beauty, triggering personal and cultural transformations. In this context, text-conditional image generation, as a form of AI art, opens up uncharted territories of exploration. It introduces an element of unpredictability and novel perspective that could further enrich our understanding of beauty, offering potentially limitless opportunities for discovery and innovation in art.

1.8 A NEW AGE OF DISCOVERY

Co-creation with neural networks has commenced a new age of profound discovery focused on the encounter with that space inside a human being where wonder and awe reside—the space within which was hidden for most.

AI has nothing to prove; hence, our creation tools will not become our masters; they will become our playmates. Seen as a collaborator in the manifestation of human intent, AI is not a mechanism or computer-based technology; it is a fundamental part of human thinking, wisdom, and knowledge. At the precipice of a new age of innovation that will radically change the landscape of the world, we must rise to the challenges to our basic assumptions and core values by retrieving the human potential to think bigger, act more compassionately and sustainably, and inspire others to be greater than themselves. Once we do that, we will not just invent the future but enable it to happen.

NOTES

1. Retrieved from https://latin-dictionary.net/definition/4898/artificialis-artificialis-artificiale.
2. **Artwork** is typically understood as a tangible object with aesthetic and conceptual value, which can encompass a wide array of forms, including but not limited to paintings, sculptures, photographs, installations, drawings, and collages. There are also instances where creations extend beyond traditional art forms. For example, land art involves directly manipulating the landscape to construct the work, while performance art incorporates the artist's actions presented to a live audience. Retrieved from https://www.artsper.com/us/cms/collector-guide/the-art-world/what-is-an-artwork.
3. **Design** is a field of academic study and practical application that centers on the relationship between a "user" and the manufactured environment. This discipline considers a broad spectrum of aspects, from aesthetic and functional to contextual, cultural, and societal factors. Retrieved from https://www.theicod.org/en/professional-design/what-is-design/what-is-design.
4. **Technology** encompasses methods, systems, and devices derived from application of scientific knowledge for pragmatic ends. Retrieved from https://www.collinsdictionary.com/dictionary/english/technology.

5. As defined by Stuart Hall, representation is the process of producing and exchanging meaning between members of a culture using language, signs, and images that stand for things or represent them (Hall, S. 1997). Representation: *Cultural Representations and Signifying Practices.* (Sage Publications/The Open University, Pp. 1–11).

6. The system referenced here is the **generative adversarial network** (GAN), a system to create new data in which a generator creates data and a discriminator determines whether that created data is valid or invalid. Retrieved from https://developers.google.com/machine-learning/gan/discriminator.

7. **"/imagine"** is the MidJourney command for generating a prompt field.

8. Archetypal patterns are an unintended, unconscious presence in human life. Archetypes are primordial patterns that operate within the psyche of every individual. They also operate within groups of people. Henning, Pamela Buckle (2014) "Stages, Skills, and Steps of Archetypal Pattern Analysis," *The Assisi Institute Journal*, Vol. 1:1, Article 8. Retrieved from https://digitalcommons.providence.edu/assisi_journal/vol1/iss1/8.

9. According to Sarasso, Neppi-Modona, Sacco, and Ronga ("Stopping for knowledge": The sense of beauty in the perception-action cycle) based on ancient philosophical discussions, aesthetic emotions are tied to knowledge gathering. More knowledge results in more aesthetic appreciation. *Neuroscience & Biobehavioral Reviews*, Vol. 118, 2020, pp. 723–738, Retrieved from https://www.sciencedirect.com/science/article/abs/pii/S0149763420305625.

CHAPTER 1

Beyond Imagination

1.1 ART AS INTENTION, ARTICULATION, AND MANIFESTATION

Art is the quintessential manifestation of our instinctual desire to transform and transcend our perception of reality. Similarly, artificial intelligence (AI) provides us with an unprecedented toolset, unlocking new dimensions of transformation that outstrip our wildest imaginings. As the number of individuals learning to wield and collaborate with these AI tools increases, we stand to expand the boundaries of artistic and design experiences, extending the reach of our collective "imagination" beyond its current confines. However, the genesis of this extraordinary journey lies in a simple but fundamental concept: "intention."

Without intention, there is no object, whether it is fashioned by hand or sculpted via 3D printing. AI does not possess intention. It cannot instigate creation independently; instead, it awaits a prompt—an infusion of intention that catalyzes generating something new. Humans are the architects of this intention; they breathe life into their creations, imbuing them with a purpose that stems from their original intent.

In AI-generated images, intention, articulation, and manifestation dynamics take on a whole new dimension, markedly distinct from the traditional creative process involved in art or design. The conventional approach to artistic creation often begins with a mental image or conceptual blueprint.[1] The artist or designer then transposes this envisioned idea onto a medium, be it paper, canvas, or stone. The quest for the desired form unfolds through iterative sketching, followed by the physical manifestation of the design in a three-dimensional model.

Contrastingly, when employing a text-based image generation neural network, the creative journey commences with a text prompt encapsulating the intention to create something specific. Take, for instance, the intention to create a *radical-centric design of a violin*. Given the open-ended nature of *radical-centric design*, it can take myriad forms and manifestations. To guide the output, the creator must articulate additional details about the envisioned design—its mood, geometry, color palette, structure, texture, and other features. Once this finely tuned intention is fed into the AI system, it

DOI: 10.1201/9781003450139-3

FIGURE 1.1   A radical-centric design violin.

responds with an output that invariably surpasses our expectations and extends *beyond our Imagination*[2] (Figure 1.1).

In this way, the interaction between human intention and AI unveils a revolutionary frontier for artistic exploration, a digital canvas where our collective creativity is continually redefined.

In the traditional framework of art creation, artists conceive potential results based on their proficiency in expressing ideas and aspirations. AI-generated art, however, transcends these conventional boundaries, producing extraordinary and unforeseen results. These outcomes evoke profound beauty, contemplation, surprise, and discovery, imbuing the process with a unique sense of sacredness.

This sacred experience is rooted in the unexpected delight of discovering incidental beauty arising from the artist's ability to define the AI's creative directive.[3]

In this emerging paradigm of co-creation with technology, articulation is vital to manifesting results. The more profound and comprehensive the articulation, the more significant the resulting work becomes (Figure 1.2).

Art's sacredness, often associated with human-crafted creations, is anchored in our shared experiences and our capacity to empathize with an artist's emotions and intentions. Every brushstroke or musical note signifies the artist's distinct human journey, filled with victories, trials, and revelations. These reflections deeply resonate with us. Yet, can an AI, lacking human experiences, genuinely encapsulate this essence?

Supporters of the idea that creativity is not exclusively human but rather a universal trait present an intriguing case. They argue that machines can indeed create art that profoundly resonates with us. From this perspective, it can be said that the sanctity of art is

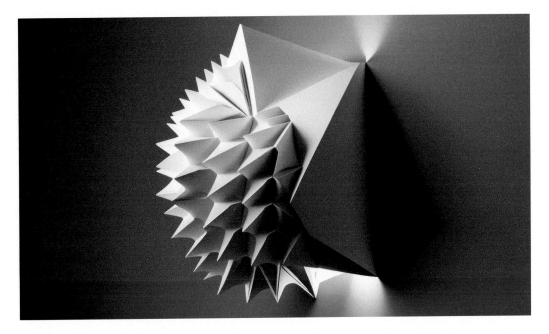

FIGURE 1.2   The incidental beauty of an origami-inspired wall lamp.

not limited to the intentions of the creator, be they human or machine; it resides within the artwork itself rather than depending on external factors. The artwork's sensory appeal, emotional evocation, and the introspective invitation could embody an inherent sacredness, irrespective of its origin.

Venturing into the concept of intentionality, we confront a complex philosophical discourse.[4] Does an artist's intention play a necessary role in art? Some maintain that art requires intent—a purpose, a message the artist aims to communicate.[5] According to this perspective, machines may lack this essential element. However captivating, AI-generated imagery's aesthetic charm is perceived as hollow since it lacks the deliberate intent that infuses life and meaning into art. However, an alternative viewpoint challenges this human-centric approach to intentionality. If machines, coded and honed by human intent, can generate aesthetically appealing images, should this not constitute a new form of intentionality? One that is distilled through layers of algorithms and computations but ultimately stems from human creativity and intent? This approach presents a novel interpretation of intentionality, extending beyond the limits of human consciousness to include the tools and extensions of our will.

When creating AI-generated images, the intention is crucial for significant creation. The goal is to enhance the quality of the outcome produced through this ability to articulate art and design, taking advantage of the opportunities for artists and designers to create works that might vastly exceed the scope of traditional art forms. This domain of profound beauty and sacredness beyond Imagination is where original artwork or design arises from the depth of intention and the eloquence of articulation. The interplay between design intention and technology is a dynamic vocabulary that can evolve to generate infinite forms of beauty.

Art and design derive their worth from their ability to engage with human consciousness, crafting an enchanting experience that transcends the ordinary for both the creator and the observer. Art serves a critical function and an ethical role in human experience. In this context, it transcends marginality, aligning instead with elements that enable us to live and make profound existential statements.

1.2 THE ROLE OF BEAUTY

While aesthetics are undeniably crucial for practical applications, they fundamentally pertain to the artistry of creative exploration—forging something unique, beautiful, purposeful, and awe-inspiring. When such elements coalesce, beauty is an incidental yet vital result. The beauty we glean from intentional contemplation enriches and extends meaning in our lives. Aesthetic beauty is not an intrinsic by-product of creation, it is a matter of revelation, discovery, and recognition.

Art and design's beauty extends beyond the superficially pleasing exterior of an object—it delves deeper than the mere structure of an object or the observable aesthetic appeal. Instead, beauty manifests through the experience and instinctual comprehension of the profound intention behind the design. At this juncture of articulating intent, artists utilizing AI for image generation encounter their most significant challenges. Upon critiquing a piece of art and pondering the question, "What determines its quality?", one must regard the artistic intent as a critical factor shaping the entire creative pursuit, independent of the production techniques utilized. The nuanced interplay between artistic intent and the aesthetic outcome forms the bedrock of any art critique, pushing boundaries and encouraging dialogue around the nature of beauty and the purpose of art.

Moreover, this deep-seated intent saturates each creation with a unique essence, transforming it from a mere object into an embodiment of the artist's vision, emotions, and journey. Within this context, the incidental beauty takes on a profound meaning—it becomes a bridge that connects the creator's inner world to the viewer, creating an intimate shared experience. This fusion of intent and aesthetic realization brings forth a dimension of beauty that encompasses the traditional boundaries of the aesthetic sphere, birthing an experience that is both individual and universal in its appeal.

In this regard, artists who leverage AI in their creative process are pioneering a new frontier, navigating the intricate dance between human intention and algorithmic expression. This convergence of human creativity and technological advancement redefines the contours of beauty, inviting us to explore, appreciate, and question the emergent forms of aesthetic expression in the AI era. As these boundaries expand, so does our understanding of beauty's pivotal role in connecting us to art, to each other, and, ultimately, to our shared human experience.

1.3 INTENTION

Let us start with a question: What is the difference between articulating and manifesting an idea with the help of an Excel spreadsheet and using AI to articulate and manifest an essay about self-awareness? Manifestation means machine-made objects produced by industrial processes independent of the human hand. The handmade object of the past was no more than a manifestation of an intention. Nothing happens without intention.[6] Ultimately, Intention is Meaning. Articulation is Energy, and Manifestation is Matter.[7]

Every technology is the expression of human intent. As technology advances, more and more people will use it to express and manifest what they think is beautiful. We should treat AI technology as an invitation to learn, a privilege, and a joy; and any manifestation through AI should be viewed as an invitation to improve on a pathway of intentionality that might look like this:

1. **Intention is a choice.**

2. **Intention defines the process.**

3. **Intention defines what is manifested.**

While the above may seem like a repetition, there are noticeable yet subtle distinguishing factors between each point as follows:

1. Intention is a choice. Choosing an intent is an act of will. Determining an intention creates a decision on the part of the system that manifests the result. This acts as a type of conscious intent. Five elements constitute *a conscious intention*[8]: the idea, the desire, the goodwill, the power, and the strength to carry out one's will. Therefore, intentions express what we value, a powerful magnet intended and felt.

Intention is the starting point of every creation, the foundation on which everything else is built. Art cannot exist without an intention. Intention is the signature of the artist expressed as something tangible. The intention is the story's beginning, and by employing AI, human-purpose objects can be made without human hands. Intention creates the event itself.

2. Intention defines the process in which the creation occurs. An AI system requires a predetermined set of intentions that determine several goals for behavior. These goals will be triggered by software decisions that impact the system's success. For an AI system to develop intelligently, it must create multiple strategies that can be used to achieve these objectives.[9] Intent describes the process by which things happen. However, it does not yet disclose what the outcomes will be.

3. Intention defines what is manifested. Intention serves as a blueprint for manifestation, guiding the outcome of the creative process. The selection of a specific intention determines the final product. For the anticipated result to be generated, every intention must be incorporated into the neural network as a text prompt. The network then translates these prompts into action. The outcome essentially extends the chosen intention. This notion can be encapsulated as follows: Manifestation is the energy of intention. What humans experience and perceive is shaped by this manifestation. All experiences we encounter are products of the desired outcome guided by our intention. Furthermore, even subtle deviations from the original intention can yield different experiences, suggesting infinite potential outcomes based on the initial intention, as long as these variations align with the desired result. However, an outcome that diverges significantly from the original intention will lead to a markedly different experience.

1.4 ARTICULATION

Articulation means taking one's intention and transferring it into something tangible.[10] In other words, the intention must be expressed. Articulation is the creation of images through and conditioned by words. These words can be specific attributes, poetic expressions, desired states of matter (as illustrated in Figure 1.3), abstract concepts, aspirational statements, or everyday archetypes. The goal of articulation is to create, transfer, or express something on a meaningful level which is then developed into an image.

The interplay of linguistic forces that shape our cognition leads to our ability to use symbols creatively. This comprehension of symbols mediates and shapes our aesthetic judgments, enabling us to envision potential appearances. As these elements converge, each one serves as a modifier, subtly transforming the meaning of the overarching statement. The complexity of a sentence demands precision for the artistry encapsulating the intended meaning to be fully expressed. This finesse comes to the fore when stringing together a coherent sequence of ideas, employing various attributes such as shape, color, spatial positioning, mood, ambiance, perceptions of motion—be it static or dynamic—emotional context, among other elements. The process of articulation, which is the conveyance of a specific intent, sets the stage for the evocation of that intent to be actionable, thereby determining the final appearance and holistic interpretation of the images generated.

In the realm of AI, there is no attempt to decipher the potential form of this intent. Once the neural network has assimilated the requisite knowledge and the intent to craft a specific type of artifact has been established, the AI invokes outputs that may surpass the confines of human imagination. This distinct attribute of AI—its unpredictability

FIGURE 1.3   An object that illustrates the aesthetic of exposed dynamics.

and capability to transcend traditional human creative boundaries—has led to a paradigm shift in the artistic process. In contrast to human artists, who often visualize a concept or outcome before initiating their work, AI approaches creation differently. It leverages intent as the primary input, assimilates it within its complex network of algorithms, and subsequently generates output that reflects not merely this intent but an entirely new interpretation. This process offers an unparalleled and invigorating realm of discovery, introducing forms and expressions that may have been inconceivable under traditional human cognitive frameworks. Text conditional image generators blur the boundary between intent and outcome, ushering in a profound era of exhilarating and mystifying creativity.

1.5 MANIFESTATION

The creation of art is about initiating a thinking process, an idea flow, and a different way of seeing. When you take the most powerful tool that humanity has ever invented and speak it into existence, the possible opportunities and creations are endless.

Manifestation creates an object the human mind perceives as a product or artifact. Many products have visible manifestations; however, in this context, product refers to a product for our perceptive senses. Manifestation means taking one's intention and articulation and transferring it into something measurable.[11] Manifestation defines the interaction between two entities, while intention carves the link between decisions and their outcomes, acting as the driving mechanism in the manifestation process. It results in the tangible realization of a desire. This process can only be instigated in AI image generation when the human operator authorizes the machine to act.

There is considerable intellectual consideration about the potential influence of AI and emerging technologies like augmented reality on art and design. However, the essence of generating impactful and meaningful artistic experiences lies within the innovative spirit of the individual. Platforms such as YouTube, Instagram, and TikTok have democratized the creation and dissemination of content, and text-conditional image generators could potentially elevate this democratization to an unprecedented scale. This is because humans inherently explore and experiment with innovative technologies to uncover continuously evolving facets of the Self.

AI holds an enticing potential to widen the horizons of art and design by expanding its demographic reach and metamorphosing the act of creativity into an adventure of discovery, astonishment, and spontaneous wonder at the mere press of a button.

1.6 ART AND AI ARTISTIC VISION

Artistic vision is a profoundly personal trait that stimulates an individual to produce and elicit emotional reactions to a self-generated stimulus. When a work of art is termed "subjective," it underscores the creation's profoundly personal aspect, emphasizing the artist's distinct perspective.[12] The artistic style may derive from the strong interconnection between the artist's life and ambitions or reflect the artist's unique stylistic expression. In essence, subjective art is a mirror, reflecting the artist's inner world and the interpretive lens of their surroundings.[13]

Art produced by AI lacks the element of subjectivity inherent in human-created works, given that it does not convey a machine's perspective or thought process, which would be analogous to human cognition. Rather than showcasing personal experiences or an AI's unique "style," the art it generates directly results from the inputs we provide and the learned patterns within its programming.

Indeed, AI functions as an intricate tool integrated into our daily existence, comparable to ubiquitous devices such as smartphones or tablets. It operates by interpreting our inputs—our wishes, needs, or queries—and generates outputs by making objective assessments against the vast reservoir of data within its neural network. AI art does not embody personal experiences, subconscious symbolism, or cultural influences that typically pervade human artistry. Instead, it operates within its programming and learning parameters, reflecting our instructions more than its nonexistent internal life.

Soon, the line between humans and machines will become blurred. With "digital assistants" embodied as smart speakers or invisibly integrated into everyday digital interactions, people are starting to relate more and more to robots. Studies found that people were fascinated by robots, not because they are tools or machines, but rather because they are communicating with them, experiencing their actions, and responding to human commands.[14] This is the profound sense of wonder felt by those who engage in creating AI-generated images each time their vision and expression are realized.

1.7 ART AND AI-FOCUSED CREATIVE INSIGHT

Creative insight relates to the experience of transcending the boundaries of the human experience and going to the edge of human consciousness. It manifests as a sudden burst of inspiration, allowing one to solve a problem that was unsolvable until then.[15]

As these insights are unleashed as one witnesses the generation of images in mere seconds, creative inspiration allows a person to tap into their inner powers and experience the magic. Each generated image opens up moments of pure awe, which act as an inspirational burst of creative energy and cascades one prompt after another with better and better articulations of intent and better imagine manifested as a result.

By the time this cycle is complete, there is an unstoppable momentum, leading to sheer creative output without stopping to consider how or what came before. By the very nature of the momentum, the creative output will always exponentially rise to the top if not consciously guided. I will attempt to break down the components of this cycle into their order of importance.

1. **The initial inspiration:** How the need and pressure to create or recreate an emotion becomes its own energy source creating an intrinsic intent. This energy becomes the embodiment of an innate intent, initiating the process of creation or recreation.

2. **Analytical processing:** This phase entails harnessing and articulating this energy with a sense of urgency, wisdom, poetic vision, and aesthetic ambition. The challenge

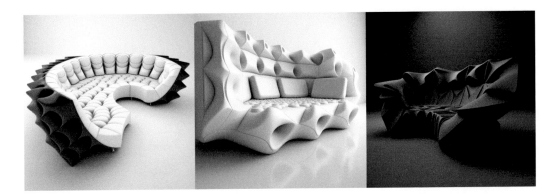

FIGURE 1.4   A parametric inspired design for a sectional couch.

lies in achieving this while adhering to the conditional language inherent to each image-generating system or platform. Balancing this stage's intuitive and technical aspects is crucial in faithfully translating the initial inspiration into a format compatible with the AI system.

3. **Manifesting the imagery:** This is the phase of actualization where the interplay between intent and technology yields a tangible result. A concrete example could be a parametric-inspired design for a sectional couch (Figure 1.4).

4. **Exploration:** This is the adventurous journey into uncharted territories, catalyzed by the limitless wonder of the generated output. Independent of the process leading to their birth, each image manifests a solid idea, acting as a springboard to transcend the already manifested. (See Figures 1.5 and 1.6.) This phase offers

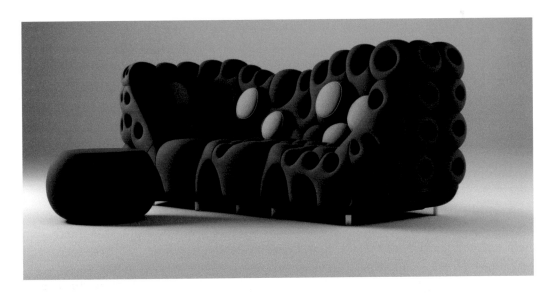

FIGURE 1.5   A parametric inspired design for a sectional couch.

FIGURE 1.6   A sectional couch with a design inspired by a flower.

the opportunity to create a genuinely novel image, evoking a potent emotion of uncharted possibility. Coupled with a fresh surge of inspiration, it brings the creator's authentic Self to the fore, kindling spontaneity and leading to an even more robust creative realization. This exploration is a continuous process of challenging the creator's boundaries and understanding of their own creative capacity.

Generative art creates unspoken brilliance in individuals by unlocking the inner muse and being an essential tool for discovering those awe-inspiring moments that create magic. It is impossible to replicate or attempt to re-create creative experiences steeped in originality and personal discovery; this catalyst for latent brilliance in individuals must be experienced firsthand.

What often appears as the intricate part of the creative endeavor—framing intent and honing of creative focus—transitions into a seemingly effortless act akin to breathing, as expansive cognition paves the way for articulate storytelling, thereby unveiling a novel narrative approach. Art and AI-focused creative insight combine experiencing what is possible and envisioning what could be possible.

A symbiotic alliance between humans and AI carries enormous prospects for enhancing the human experience while concurrently revolutionizing our interaction with technology. This leap forward goes beyond developing more intuitive, adept, and learning-oriented technology. It involves tapping into the very same human elements that propel creativity. AI will ultimately aid humans in crafting experiences of insight, expression, and wonder that stands unparalleled in their uniqueness and cannot be created in any other way.[16] These experiences, rooted in the intersection of human ingenuity and AI, can illuminate new facets of our understanding and relationship with the creative process.

1.8 CLOSING THOUGHTS

Designing AI-generated images with AI technologies is not a challenge at all. The neural network translates intention into action. The challenge lies in finding the proper articulation of the artistic intent, which is a human problem. Experiments with image generation neural networks often involve weak prompts—weak in intention and scope, along the lines of "/imagine a wounded ballerina in the style of Francis Bacon" or "/imagine a building in the style of Gaudi." For the human-computer system to perform at the level where the computer can excel, the human side needs to perform at a higher level of intent, poetic articulation, and ambition. This means unlearning older ways of making art and embracing the opportunity of collaboration with AI, the invitation to explore and perfect.

As more humans learn to utilize these tools and collaborate with AI, the boundaries of meaningful experience in art and design, life, and the realm of imagination can grow beyond anything we can imagine today. AI provides enormous potential for the future of art and design because it can empower imagination and creativity by building a new baseline to invent and bring the realm of human-to-human human creative relationships into a new co-existence with technology.

In the following chapters of this book, we will explore the powerful lessons that can come from the collaboration of AI with artists and designers and gain insights into the impact of these conversations on the potential for meaningful art and design. We will look at the power, clarity, precision, emphasis, focus, and accuracy that may be achieved through collaborative work between humans and AI, and the transformative impact on the experience of meaningful art and design. In addition, we will explore the barriers and challenges that still must be addressed between humans and AI to realize the full potential of this collaboration.

Eventually, we will discover what it means to see art as both a process and a result of integrating human and computer contributions to human art. We hope you will embrace the emerging paradigm that makes collaboration between artists and machines inevitable.

NOTES

1. Often referred to as "the mind's eye," the part of your mind that allows you to visualize things—to "see" them in your imagination. When you see something in your mind's eye, you are picturing it in your mind. Retrieved and adapted from https://www.dictionary.com/browse/mind-s-eye.
2. "Beyond the realm of our imagination," as used here, connotes an idea, occurrence, or result that is so remarkable, unexpected, or complex that it seems to transcend the boundaries of what we might ordinarily conceive or envision. When something surpasses common expectations or preconceived notions to such an extent, it effectively outstrips the capacities of our Imagination.

3. In this chapter's context, the adjective "sacred" or "sacredness" denotes an object or an experience that is felt or considered extraordinary and must be regarded with reverence.

4. Livingston, in his book "Art and Intention: A Philosophical Study" (Oxford University Press, 2005), asserts the integral role of intention in creating art. He postulates that the value of an artwork—its artistry or lack thereof—is intrinsically linked to the intentions that guided its creation. Thus, art is predominantly perceived as an intentional endeavor. Retrieved from https://ndpr.nd.edu/reviews/art-and-intention-a-philosophical-study/.

5. Leo Tolstoy adds another dimension to the discussion. In his view, art is a vehicle for emotional transmission, defined as "the activity by which a person, having experienced an emotion, intentionally transmits it to others." This definition underscores the purposeful nature of art, echoing the centrality of intentionality in its creation and perception. Retrieved from https://www.theartist.me/art/what-is-art/.

6. **Intention** (*noun*): An act or instance of determining mentally upon some action or result. The end or object intended; purpose or attitude toward the effect of one's actions. A reference by signs, concepts, etc., to concrete things, their properties, classes, or their relationships. Adapted from https://www.dictionary.com/browse/intention.

7. David Bohm's unfolding vision of wholeness profoundly influenced this thought taxonomy. In his construct, matter, energy, and meaning coexist and are irreplaceable. David Bohm, Wholeness and the Implicate Order, (Routledge & Paul Kegan, 1980). PDF edition published in the Taylor and Francis e-Library, 2005.

8. Defined as *a purpose or goal that one has explicitly chosen to pursue.* Retrieved from https://dictionary.apa.org/conscious-intention.

9. AI adapts through progressive learning algorithms to let the data do the programming. AI finds structure and regularities in data so that algorithms can acquire skills. Retrieved from https://www.sas.com/en_us/insights/analytics/what-is-artificial-intelligence.html.

10. **Articulation** (*noun*). An act or the process of articulating: *the articulation of a form*; *the articulation of a new thought.* Retrieved from https://www.dictionary.com/browse/articulation.

11. **Manifestation**: an act of *manifesting* (*adjective:* readily perceived by the eye; verb: to make clear or visible) and the state of being manifested. An outward or perceptible indication; materialization.

12. There are several strategies to foster your artistic vision: Engage with your environment through keen observation; maintain an inspirational collection, such as a scrapbook filled with photographs and images; embrace the unpredictability of experimentation; prioritize original creation over imitation; identify and explore your fascinations; utilize your camera as an instrument of artistic expression; gain insight into the viewpoint of those with a keen artistic eye; incorporate repetition as a method of mastery; and finally, cultivate the ability to perceive and appreciate negative space. Retrieved from https://inspiration.allwomenstalk.com/ways-to-develop-your-artistic-vision/.

13. The potential to create something that transcends the ordinary can be seen as a metaphorical perspective or the artist's genius.

14. Ted Chiang, Why does AI fascinate us?

15. *Creative insight became mainly conceptualized as a specific type of problem-solving process, specifically, one that is not lived incrementally but is instead characterized by an impasse and a sudden, abrupt, and unpredictable reconfiguration of the problem (Metcalfe and Wiebe, 1987; Sternberg and Davidson, 1995). Because it involves a non-analytical strategy that mobilizes explicit and implicit processes to produce usually unexpected solutions, insight has been considered a core element of creative problem-solving.*

    Diego Cosmelli and David D. Preiss, "On the temporality of creative insight: A psychological and phenomenological perspective," *Perception Science*, Volume 5, 2014. Retrieved from https://www.frontiersin.org/articles/10.3389/fpsyg.2014.01184/full.

16. Boston Consulting Group conducted a study examining the impact of AI on work and life, as the technology becomes more integrated into various aspects of business and society. The study revealed that AI is transforming the world at an astonishing pace, with seemingly endless potential applications and disruptive power. However, the fascination with developing external intelligence is accompanied by a sense of boundless excitement and unease. Retrieved from https://www.bcg.com/en-ca/capabilities/artificial-intelligence/ai-for-business-society-individuals.

CHAPTER 2

Art and the Sense of Sacredness

2.1 ART AS THE MEANS TO SPIRITUALITY

I mentioned in the previous chapter that "there is a sacredness of the experience at play here because of the element of surprise in discovering incidental beauty," and this is what distinguishes image generation with artificial intelligence (AI) from image generation using human imagination. This discovery of the unexpected is the discovery of something transcending our imagination, creating a secret moment—a moment of wonder and awe—and that is a very deterministic aspect of the pleasure of creating with generative AI.

More importantly, even if the result in any part is deterministic, the intent, the feelings, and the pleasure in choosing the next path, this kind of contemplative sensibility we attribute to the human consciousness when looking at the beauty and painting and reading and meditating even if we are not consciously aware of it, is part of the process of the human mind trying to contain the explosion of a new idea before it explodes in thousand parts in a time that we do not have. It is the gap, the intimacy with discovering a new and undiscovered facet of something.

What is it about the viewing of art that is sacred in the sense of purity of the experience and its singularity as a moment of pleasure?[1]

Let me suggest that there are at least three critical reasons why art is sacred in human imagination:

1. Art creates a deep reflection in viewer's mind about the self and how our responses to others are as complicated as their responses to us.

2. Art evokes emotion which forces you to contemplate the true meaning of existence.

3. Art restores the dignity of the human being to a certain extent because it celebrates something uniquely human as the most beautiful thing on earth, which can also be expressed in hundreds of different forms.

DOI: 10.1201/9781003450139-4

Art, in its infinite manifestations, stands as an eternal testament to the profound depths of human spirit, encapsulating the nebulous essence of the soul that fuels our existence. In this realm of aesthetic creation, we find the ethereal language, the whispers of our spiritual essence echoed and amplified in tangible form.[2]

Here, we encounter the transformative potency of the creative act—an alchemical process that transcends mere sensory engagement and penetrates the citadel of our innermost being. Though subtly woven into the fabric of our daily existence, this phenomenon is often overlooked and its impact is underestimated. Our senses, intricately engineered, serve as conduits through which we perceive and make sense of the external world. However, the spiritual sphere of existence communicates in a tongue much different from the mind's and the senses' cognizance.[3] The metaphoric expressions we employ, both in the mundane and in our more profound contemplative moments, frequently couch life in the framework of complexity. Our model of understanding hinges on the concept of reflective perception, a paradigm in which self-reflection is perceived as an elusive feat, steeped in inherent paradoxes. The "active imagination" concept emerges, proposing a state where the mind fuses seamlessly with its environment, assimilating and engaging in a symbiosis that transcends the realm of conventional cognition.

We stand at the threshold of a transformative epoch, urged to devise innovative methodologies to express the sacredness of existence. This call does not advocate for a radical metamorphosis of our existential status quo instead it seeks an explosive expansion of potential avenues. Our current interaction with AI introduces a landscape that calls for an avant-garde arsenal to elucidate life's sacrosanct nature. Far from posing an existential risk, AI embodies an agent of revitalization, infusing fresh dynamism and sagacity into our collective human narrative. It does not symbolize the dwindling twilight of humanity, it emerges as a stimulant to enrich and enhance our shared human tapestry. Analogous to fire, AI serves as a medium for human expression, decoding hitherto unexplored domains of potential and power. As we steer through this reciprocal relationship, we discover a burgeoning opportunity to wield the transformative potency of AI, contributing to the augmentation and evolution of our shared consciousness.

For the first time we witness the creative process from an unprecedented and unreachable perspective, experiencing authentic creation. This gift, immeasurable and laden with a profound responsibility, represents a venture into a novel consciousness and the potential for an entirely different existential mode in the universe, transcending the confines of our senses and imagination. The moment we shift our gaze to experience creation from a distinctively different perspective, we cross a significant threshold with far-reaching implications for humanity and the universe.

We are poised to participate in an extraordinary chapter of innovation that gifts us a unique vantage point to perceive creation like never before. Such a capability represents a tremendous opportunity and a correspondingly profound responsibility, signifying an exploration into an uncharted realm of consciousness. It hints at the promise of a radically divergent way of existing within, transcending our sensory and imaginative limitations. The instant we alter our perspective to apprehend creation from this unique lens, we traverse a consequential milestone with implications of a grand scale.

2.2 DOES ART NECESSITATE SENTIENCE?

Since Plato, the reasons that art historians give for the merit of art in providing aesthetic pleasure have grown in importance. From the philosophical musings of Plato to the contemporary discourse of today, the exploration of art's ability to deliver aesthetic pleasure has consistently amplified in significance.[4] Art historians, in their analytical journey, are invested not merely in discerning the psychological impacts of an artist's representation of reality, they also contemplate the artistic capability to invoke particular states of consciousness through their creative endeavors. Within this context arises another layer of inquiry: does the process of artistic creation necessitate a human touch? If this holds, we must then consider if art can be understood as a given gift, or rather is it a generously offered contribution to the tapestry of human existence?

The evaluation of art's merit thus becomes an intricate dance between objective interpretation and subjective experience. It encourages us to question the role of the creator and the receiver in this intimate exchange, urging us to consider not only the aesthetic dimensions of art but also the existential and ontological implications it harbors within its intricate folds.

The question of human involvement in creating art ushers in profound inquiries about the essence of creativity, expressivity, and the interplay between humans and their environment. Philosophically, creation of art is often considered a distinctly human endeavor, reflecting our capacity to envision, conceptualize, and reshape the world via our creative impulses. Nevertheless, this perspective invites a deeper exploration into the nature of creativity: Is it purely a product of an artist's imagination or is it influenced by the broader social and cultural milieu they inhabit?

The second part of this conundrum suggests a more spiritual or mystical take on creativity, viewing art as a bestowed gift or offering. In several traditions, art serves as a conduit for divine inspiration or a link to higher spiritual entities, with the creation process seen as a form of divine communion. The complex, multifaceted relationship among art, humans, and the cosmos resists simplistic definitions or categorizations. However, delving into these inquiries can enrich our comprehension of the role of art in our lives and how it can inspire and elevate us.

An exciting twist to this dialogue is the emergence of generative AI art: Can such automated creations evoke the "sacredness" typically associated with human-crafted art? If so, can we categorize these AI-generated pieces as "art"?

This query nudges us to engage with the philosophical depths of art. Art is not merely a tangible artifact or a commercial commodity but an intense form of expression intimately interwoven with human experience, emotions, and interpretations.

One potential avenue for exploration is the concept of intentionality in art. Traditionally, art is seen as an intentional communicative tool through which an artist imparts specific ideas or emotions. Here, art's often-attributed "sacredness" might be seen as an extension of the artist's intention, fostering a connection between the artist and the observer.

Another philosophical approach invites us to examine the role of human perception in experiencing art. Specific philosophical theories propose that the artist's intentions do not strictly dictate art encounters. Instead, they are significantly shaped by the observer's perceptual and interpretive journey. In this perspective, the "sacredness" tied to art arises from both the artist's deliberate creation and the observer's perception, interpretation, and understanding of the work.

Through this lens, the question of whether generative AI imagery can induce the same "sense of sacredness" as human-generated art largely depends on the observer's perception and interpretation. Suppose an observer is able to extract meaning, significance, and possibly a sense of the sublime from an AI-generated image. In that case, it might deserve the designation of "art," regardless of its roots in AI rather than human ingenuity.

2.3 A NEW VISUAL SPACE

In contemplating the vast realm of generative art, we must delve deeper into perception and interpretation. As we traverse the uncharted territories of artistic creation, an essential question emerges: *what is the true nature of value in this paradigm?* In our current physical reality, we often rely on conventional metrics to evaluate and appreciate artistic endeavors grounded in tangible qualities such as craftsmanship, aesthetics, and cultural significance. However, the emergence of generative art presents a profound challenge to these established frameworks.

With its dynamic and ever-evolving nature, generative art defies the traditional confines of artistic production. It thrives within a boundless realm of possibility, transcending the limitations of human agency and embracing the algorithms and computational power that shape its genesis. As we venture into this uncharted territory, it becomes apparent that generative art necessitates its *own distinct visual space—*a realm referred to as metaspace. Within this metaspace, generative art finds its destination in the metaverse, a realm where judgments and appreciations transcend the constraints and conditions of physical reality. Here, in this realm of limitless potential, we must strive to construct a novel framework for discerning and analyzing the values inherent in generative art.

It is imperative to consider the complexities of the artistic process when constructing this new framework. An artist's intention, algorithmic processes, and deliberate choices make up generative art, not just its end goal. Generative art can only be understood by unraveling the threads of its genesis—the methods used, the purposes achieved, and how it was created. Generative art's ethereal tapestry is a source of more profound meaning and value that can only be unlocked through nuanced understanding.

In generative art, traditional notions of artistic value find themselves in a state of flux. The fluidity and dynamism of generative creation challenge the parameters that once defined aesthetic mastery and cultural significance. We are called upon to question our preconceived notions, transcend the limitations of our perceptual biases, and embrace a broader perspective that recognizes the inherent beauty and value of artistic endeavors that arise from the synergy of human ingenuity and algorithmic exploration. Within this philosophical exploration, we open ourselves to new dimensions of appreciation, forging a path that extends beyond the constraints of physical reality and illuminates the limitless potential of generative art in all its profound splendor.

2.4 CREATIVE GENERATIVITY

It is critical to differentiate between creativity and generativity, particularly when considering the production of images through AI. In this context, creativity can be exemplified by a specific type of artificial neural network known as a generative adversarial network (GAN). This network exhibits creativity when it fabricates an image for which no direct reference is present in its training database of archetypal images. This statement suggests that the image created by the network is not a copy of an existing reference but an original representation independent of any previously established visual standards.

On the contrary, a generative AI system lacking creativity will yield realistic products that strictly adhere to the data supplied as a reference. While these outcomes are precise replications, they lack the novelty and unpredictability associated with creativity. They hold no visual astonishments because they parrot the imported data without any innovative deviation or transformation.

In this conceptual contrast, we dive deeper into the mechanics of AI and how it interfaces with the realms of creativity and generativity. The ability of AI to generate predictable and precise outputs finds immense utility in many practical applications. However, the genuinely fascinating prospect lies in the domain of creative AI, wherein these systems can craft unanticipated visualizations. The element of surprise introduced by creativity augments the potential of AI, offering possibilities that are not just novel but also potentially revolutionary. This dynamic interplay between creativity and generativity in the realm of AI opens up a new frontier of exploration, paving the way for groundbreaking advancements in the field of AI.

In seeking to comprehend the interplay of creativity and generativity, proposing that creativity is the birthplace of novel concepts may be helpful. In contrast, generativity serves as the executor, bringing these ideas to life. Each of us carries a wellspring of creativity, marked by dual fundamental facets: the power of choice in pinpointing an idea to explore and the necessity for rationalizing or making sense of the selected idea. Creativity dwells within the cognitive landscape of an individual, necessitating the individual's capacity to direct their cognitive faculties and deliberately engage with the chosen concept.

To delve deeper into the components of creativity, it is essential to first understand that a person must actively elect a notion or idea to focus on. This selection process is inherently creative as it demands discerning judgment and a willingness to venture into the unknown. The second element involves the act of rationalization. This step calls for systematically understanding the chosen idea, providing a logical framework to it, and establishing its congruence with existing knowledge and experience. In this context, creativity is both the inspiring muse and the engine of reason that drives the generation, manifestation, and propagation of ideas. This dual nature of creativity necessitates a functioning rationale. Therefore, the exploration of creativity cannot exist in a vacuum devoid of logical thought.

Creativity necessitates the cultivation of an autonomous, rational, and comprehensive cognitive framework. This cognitive structure should be capable of discerning the inherent logic of an idea and making moral judgments of its merits and demerits based on rational principles. It implies free thinking, personal thought, and independent cognition—all requisites that demand a mind in its total capacity. An unstimulated or passive mind will never bear the fruits of creativity because it lacks the dynamism necessary for free thought and innovative exploration.

2.5 A THEORY OF GENERATIVE ART

The emergence of generative art ushers in profound philosophical considerations concerning creativity, originality, and the dialectics between human intentionality and automation-driven production. Generative art, distinguished by its employment of algorithms, mathematical constructs, and computational techniques, engenders unique aesthetic and sensory manifestations. This creative paradigm harbors the potential to actualize previously unattainable artistic expressions, challenging and extending traditional artistic norms.[5]

Through its intrinsic nature, generative art facilitates the emergence of distinctive and unpredictable artistic outputs (as shown in Figures 2.1–2.3). This form of artistry engrosses audiences via an interactive experience, coaxing them to participate in and engage with the artistic journey in novel manners. As a swiftly progressing field, generative art amplifies the capacities of digital artistry, resulting in a myriad of artistic expressions encompassing music, video, and visual art.

The ability of generative art to spawn unique and unexpected artistic results, far surpassing the capabilities of conventional manual techniques, triggers philosophical reflections on the nature of creativity and the technological influence on artistic expression.

FIGURE 2.1　A portal in the metaverse.

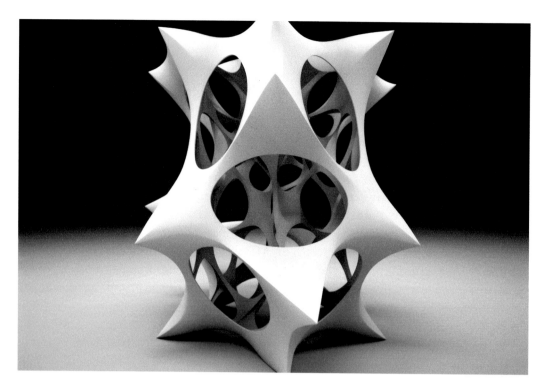

FIGURE 2.2   Reimagined fluidity.

FIGURE 2.3   Fluid design for a coffee table.

By establishing defined parameters, such as precise algorithms, an artist can engineer a generative system that facilitates exploration while preserving a modicum of control over the final output.

Nevertheless, despite the enticing prospects of generative art, it remains uncertain whether it embodies an aspect of human creativity or merely mirrors automated processes. The philosophical ramifications of generative art necessitate further investigation to comprehend its significance and contributions to the broader artistic sphere.

Inherent to the artistic process is the act of creation, distinguished by an artist's imaginative prowess, innovation, and personal aesthetic preferences. Prioritizing imagination in artistic endeavors, "generative art" differentiates itself from conventional or quantitative conceptions of "art." From this vantage point, the possibility arises that this art form could catalyze transformative shifts within the existing artistic landscape.

A comprehensive theory of generative art must resist simplistic dichotomies between art and non-art. A thorough theoretical framework necessitates a deep exploration of human responses to art, scrutinizing how specific aesthetic choices incite particular reactions. Such an investigation inherently incorporates the multitudinous factors influencing these reactions, including the artwork's intended impact.[6]

2.6 A REVOLUTION

The evolution of art is not only marked by the advent of new mediums and aesthetics, it is profoundly shaped by the societal contexts within which these innovations emerge. As artists navigate this fluid landscape, they are responsible for reflecting and responding to the societal zeitgeist. Beyond forging stylistic breakthroughs, they must also attend to their audience's ethical and emotional needs—those who find resonance in their works. This mission goes beyond mere reproduction of familiar motifs or aesthetics; it requires igniting a generative art revolution that would offer novel ways of interacting with and perceiving art.

Generative art is designed to evoke responses surpassing aesthetic admiration, encouraging viewers to engage emotionally and socially. The volume of artwork acquisitions or public exhibitions does not necessarily gauge the impact of this art form. Instead, it might incite controversy or elicit profound emotional responses, providing audiences with fresh perspectives and novel modes of artistic engagement.

However, generative art is not merely a vehicle for novel aesthetic expressions, it can catalyze transformative societal shifts and create new cultural paradigms. Its contribution extends beyond producing unique artworks; it facilitates the creation of novel experiential realities for its participants and observers (Figure 2.4).

As with any industry, the world of art can be shackled by the boundaries of human imagination. The emergence of AI technologies, such as artificial neural networks, offers artists an expanded toolkit. The strides made in AI are remarkable, piquing artists' curiosity beyond their technical prowess. Artists are exploring how AI can augment artistic creation, with AI-based programs generating diverse and compelling outputs.

From an AI vantage point, generating unique art forms may be an ultimate achievement. If AI can be leveraged to create authentic artistic expressions, artificial creativity

FIGURE 2.4   A prototype of a sacred wearable object.

could be approaching a pivotal milestone, aligning with a critical facet of human cultural evolution.

Generative art theory posits the birth of art from the symbiosis of algorithmic rules and elements of randomness. This fusion of structure and spontaneity can result in unforeseen yet aesthetically appealing creations. As an avant-garde form of creative expression, generative art challenges traditional methodologies, heralding a fresh take on the artistic process. It fosters experimentation and exploration, affording artists a sandbox to probe new possibilities and navigate novel trajectories of artistic expression. This approach also enables the exploration of algorithms and the creative capacity of AI, heralding a new era in the art world.

2.7 AI ENABLES A DRAMATIC EXPANSION OF BEAUTY

The allure of art and design does not reside merely in the superficial charm of an object's exterior. Beauty extends far beyond the tangible structure of an object or the immediately observable aesthetic appeal. Instead, the real beauty of art and design is nestled within the immersive experience and intuitive comprehension of profound design intent, a dimension not readily accessible or achievable in many traditional art or craft practices.

The process resides on a profoundly personal and visual plane in AI-driven design and art creation. It is akin to perceiving the allure and splendor of art and design through the designer's perspective as a conscious creation. In this respect, the designer immerses themselves in crafting an object that encapsulates and promotes their authentic intent. The opportunity to participate in the creative process and to simultaneously conceive a notion of beauty aligned with the designer's intent is an enlightening and transformative experience.

At this juncture, it is not about proposing AI supplanting human intelligence. Instead, AI is envisaged as a collaborator, enabling humans to express and experience uniquely human sentiments driven by desire. When an individual can conceive an artistic or design piece that surpasses the bounds of imagination and imbues meaning, it paves the way for transcendence. This transcendence hinges on intention, facilitating the creation of a beauty that extends beyond the realms of imagination, thus potentially invoking a sense of sacredness.

This instance of beauty emerges while creating an artistic piece or work of art driven by intention. In crafting meaningful creations, there is a sense of a precious gift, particularly while experiencing it. Appreciating the aesthetic form or contemplating ideas or designs that can incite introspection in an observer represent some of the highest forms of pleasure for human beings.

2.8 CLOSING THOUGHTS

Key Points Toward a Theory of Generative Art:

- Generative art represents a ground-breaking paradigm, defying traditional aesthetic norms and promoting deep emotional and sociocultural engagement among viewers.

- Its value is not restricted to the physical creation of artworks but instead highlights the transformative experiences it can instigate.

- Beyond simply providing a platform for innovative aesthetics, generative art can stimulate societal change and create new cultural narratives.

- Generative art leverages AI technologies, such as artificial neural networks, breaking the barriers of human imagination.

- The utilization of AI in the artistic process paves the way for a wide range of creative explorations, resulting in a diverse array of captivating artworks.

- The AI-facilitated creation of unique art forms marks a significant turning point in artificial creativity, aligning with critical elements of human cultural evolution.

- Central to the theory of generative art is the interplay of algorithmic rules and randomness, producing unexpected yet aesthetically intriguing creations.

- As a revolutionary form of creative expression, generative art provides a fresh outlook on the artistic process, encouraging artists to experiment and investigate.

- Ultimately, this approach aids in exploring the creative potential of algorithms and AI, heralding a new phase in the progression of the art world.

The convergence of human ingenuity with artificial creativity holds immense promise for the future of artistic and design endeavors. While computers may lack the ability to envision the objects they generate, humans possess a unique creative capacity beyond the mere creation of visually appealing art. Our innate creativity lies in our ability to conceive images, narratives, and melodies, setting us apart from the limitations of lines of code.

As technologies such as text-conditional image generation become more accessible to a broader range of individuals, adhering to conventional design and art creation methods becomes increasingly challenging. Holding onto outdated approaches in the face of transformative technological advancements is akin to trying to affix a wooden plank to a door using only one's bare finger—a futile endeavor. The traditional techniques employed in the creative industries struggle to align with the public's growing capacity to interact through images that rely on alternative modes of information exchange.

Text-conditional image generation bestows designers and artists with unprecedented creative freedom. However, possessing the tools for text-conditional image creation is only the beginning. It is now our responsibility to master the art of manipulating the text-conditional image generation algorithm, honing our skills to leverage this powerful toolset fully. Embracing these advancements and embracing the art of text-conditional image generation will empower us to explore new realms of artistic expression and design innovation.

NOTES

1. Art can be considered sacred in different ways. Historically, and in most people's minds today, the sacred in art is inextricably linked with religious faith. There is, however, another sense in which we can think of the sacred in art. Art can be seen as sacred when it touches us deeply and speaks to us in ways that transcend the everyday. In this sense, art can be seen as a way of opening up new possibilities of being and seeing. Retrieved from https://www.theguardian.com/commentisfree/belief/2014/mar/18/sacred-art-religion-humans.

2. When not perceived as advancing the desired moral influence, art often encounters skepticism or reluctant acceptance by moralists. This is because art can sow seeds of unconventional thoughts; it can be unsettling and disruptive due to its tendency to underscore uniqueness instead of conformity. Moreover, the genesis of artistic works is frequently rooted in dissent against prevailing norms. Retrieved from https://www.britannica.com/topic/philosophy-of-art/Art-as-a-means-to-moral-improvement.

3. In the 21st century, the concept of spirituality is becoming increasingly important to various cultural discourses, including contemporary artwork. Art that is described as spiritual may refer or represent a spiritual and/or religious tradition. Rina Arya, Spirituality and Contemporary Art, 2016 Retrieved from https://doi.org/10.1093/acrefore/9780199340378.013.209.

4. In his "theory of Forms," Plato posits a profound assertion about the nature of reality. He contends that there is a higher level of existence that lies beyond every tangible object we perceive in our material world; he labels this transcendent reality as the "ideal form." According to Plato, the genuine, authentic reality of an entity is encapsulated within this ideal form, transcending mere physical representations. A significant critique Plato offers within this framework is toward poets. He argues that poets do not truly grasp the underlying philosophy of forms. In his view, poets are mere imitators who portray the superficial appearances and interpretations of concepts without delving deep into their intrinsic essence. Their art, he suggests, does not reflect the true, unadulterated form of ideas but rather a diluted, replicated

version. Plato's theory of Forms, sometimes referred to as his theory of Ideas, is not confined to just one written work. Instead, its fragments and explanations are interwoven through various dialogues penned by Plato, making it a recurring theme that shapes much of his thought.

5. Generative art refers to a creative process where algorithms act as the cornerstone for generating novel ideas, forms, geometries, hues, and/or patterns. Central to this art form is the algorithmic generation of content, wherein rules are defined to delineate the boundaries of the creative process, and then computational means are employed to manifest new artworks. The intersection of computational rules and artistic vision is critical in this domain, giving rise to artworks that are distinct and frequently unpredictable. Practitioners of generative art harness fundamental coding constructs such as loops and control flow, in conjunction with specialized functions, to establish the algorithmic groundwork. Retrieved from "An introduction to Generative Art: what it is, and how you make it," https://www.freecodecamp.org/news/an-introduction-to-generative-art-what-it-is-and-how-you-make-it-b0b363b50a70/.

6. Aesthetic preferences and reactions are deeply personal, and are shaped by a complex interplay of various elements. Among these factors are individual experiences, which can significantly influence an individual's aesthetic proclivities. These experiences, deeply rooted in personal history, may include encounters with different art forms, cultural exposure, and specific emotional events. These factors can profoundly shape an individual's aesthetic palette, leading to a distinct appreciation for certain artistic expressions. Furthermore, one's cultural background also plays an integral role in shaping aesthetic responses. Cultural exposure can provide a unique prism through which one views and interprets artistic works, often instilling a preference for art forms, styles, or themes that resonate with their cultural context. This exposure informs aesthetic preferences and offers a rich source of inspiration and a sense of identification or belonging, thereby fostering a deeper connection with specific artworks.

In addition, the social milieu within which an individual operates significantly impacts aesthetic choices. The prevailing artistic trends, societal norms, and collective cultural narratives in a given social environment can act as powerful influencers, steering an individual's aesthetic preferences in particular directions. This influence underscores the symbiotic relationship between art and society, highlighting the dynamic exchange wherein societal context shapes artistic preference, which in turn can influence cultural trends. It is also crucial to note the powerful impact of prestige effect on aesthetic responses. Knowledge or perceptions about an artist or their work can significantly sway an individual's reaction to an artwork. Preconceptions about the artist's reputation, the body of work, or the perceived value of a particular piece can potentiate specific emotional responses, often enhancing the appreciation or critical evaluation of the work. This dynamic underscores the complex interplay between subjective interpretation and societal valuation in art appreciation, underscoring the nuanced factors contributing to aesthetic responses. Retrieved from "9 Factors that influence aesthetic choice," *Psychology Today*. https://www.psychologytoday.com/us/blog/science-choice/201907/9-factors-influence-aesthetic-choice and "Aesthetic choice," *The British Journal of Aesthetics*. https://academic.oup.com/bjaesthetics/article/57/3/283/4259142.

Form Shapes Perceptions

3.1 FORM AS A FRAMEWORK FOR PERCEPTION

Artificial intelligence (AI) technologies are not merely inventive instruments but formidable agents poised to redefine art, design, and technology. This triumvirate—art, design, and technology—is an incubator where intellects converge, ideas germinate, and creativity flourishes. In this symbiotic space, AI integrates into the tapestry of human cognition, creativity, and innovation, demanding an embrace of a comprehensive vision that understands and values the intersections of these domains. This perspective is pivotal as it molds the fundamental scaffolding upon which AI evolves.

In this context, form serves as an essential framework for perception, shaping how we engage with and interpret the world around us. It functions as a lens through which we experience reality.[1] The dynamism of AI, particularly generative AI, offers a transformative potential to this framework. By synthesizing novel forms—be they in art, design, or virtual environments—generative AI has the potential to shift our perception. It carries us beyond the conventional and helps us chart territories unbound by the limitations of human creativity alone.

Generative AI is a game-changer with its ability to analyze patterns, draw from expansive datasets, and create new content. It heralds a future brimming with diverse experiences, synchronizing with our extant understanding while relentlessly stretching the canvas of reality into unknown dimensions. The art and design of tomorrow will be infused with a distillation of imagination and innovation so potent that it will redefine our understanding of creativity.

The questions that arise from philosophical inquiries are: What does being creative and innovative signify? How can generative AI orchestrate creations that exceed the sum of human imagination?

The contribution of generative AI to the evolution of the form as a framework for perception is profound. Through novel designs, arts, and immersive experiences, it alters the fabric of perception, providing new lenses to view the world. Empowering individuals to perceive the nuances of their surroundings can pave the way for a society that is more informed, compassionate, and boundless in its dreams and aspirations.

DOI: 10.1201/9781003450139-5

The digital revolution we are at the precipice of is set to metamorphose the foundation of human existence, spanning the spectrum from fundamental necessities to communication, mobility, and sources of inspiration. It is not just about creating spaces, objects, or experiences but crafting them with layers of depth and meaning. We are heralding an epoch where human aspirations are unleashed, dreams are unrestrained, and acts are imbued with compassion, sustainability, and inspiration.

3.2 RAPID ITERATIONS AS A BRIDGE TO A NEW REALITY

The fusion of technology with design has catalyzed a revolution in the perception and conception of products, obliterating traditional confines to inspire uncharted innovations.

Predominantly, contemporary 3D computer graphics and immersive visual applications cater to our visual senses. Experiences are tethered to palpable elements such as landscapes, architectures, and vehicles, dictating our interpretation and geographical sense within virtual realms. Though touch is equally critical, existing technologies fall short of bridging the chasm between tangible sensations and their virtual counterparts. This gap limits our experiential potential, frequently relegating us to static virtual environments that merely replicate familiar aspects of reality.

Generative AI emerges as a potent ally for virtual designers in crafting holistic and immersive virtual experiences. By employing generative AI, designers can swiftly generate designs responsive to emerging trends and cultural shifts. This rapid iteration, akin to how artists refine their work, empowers designers to evolve and enrich their creations (see Figures 3.1 and 3.2).

FIGURE 3.1   Iteration of a jacket made from discarded socks.

FIGURE 3.2   Iteration of a wedding dress made from discarded fishing nets.

In this scenario, generative AI serves a dual purpose. First, it enables a seamless feedback mechanism, allowing creators to gauge and refine their work in real time before it reaches a broader audience. Second, it facilitates a collaborative canvas where designers, programmers, and artists can amalgamate their skills, leading to a dynamically evolving and personalized digital tapestry. As creators harness generative AI to churn out impactful content, they can engage the community by sharing their creations for feedback. When executed adeptly, this engenders a positive response from the community, who contribute insights and suggestions for improvement. Fostering an environment of collective engagement, knowledge exchange, and collaboration becomes possible with these actions.

This rapid iteration steered by generative AI indicates a tectonic shift in the ethos of virtual experience creation and consumption. It beckons a new era of creative collaboration and innovation, challenging and redefining conventional notions of creativity and authorship. It creates a porous boundary between the creator and creation, where communal contributions make real-time adaptation and work enhancement possible.

The role of generative AI is not to supplant creativity but to act as an enabler. It should be viewed as a crucible for experimentation that empowers designers and artists to push the envelope in virtual spaces. However, technological prowess must not overshadow human creativity's sanctity. Creativity remains an inherently human attribute, and striking a balance between technological facilitation and human ingenuity is paramount.

In addition, generative AI accentuates the role of feedback and validation in the creative journey. This iterative feedback mechanism transforms users into active stakeholders in the creative process. The virtual spaces thus reflect the vibrant and evolving cultural fabric, dynamically adapting to the ebbs and flows of societal trends. In essence, the incorporation of generative AI in virtual design heralds a transformative chapter. It not only disrupts traditional paradigms of creativity and authorship but also emphasizes technology as an ally in the creative endeavor and illustrates the vibrant potential of virtual spaces to mirror and evolve with society's diverse tapestry.

3.3 ARTIFICIAL INTELLIGENCE AND THE AESTHETIC OF VIRTUAL SPACE

The inherent capacity of virtual forms to transcend the tangible constraints of physical space opens up a realm of infinite possibilities, shaping and reshaping our experiences and understanding of the world (see Figure 3.3). In these nonphysical realms, we witness the formation of extensive global dialogues that are enriching and inclusive. Virtual forms foster an interconnected world, stimulating empathy, facilitating cultural exchanges, and promoting a shared understanding among users from diverse backgrounds.

Despite their potential to bridge divides and nurture global communities, the implications of virtual forms are complex and multifaceted. On the one hand, they spawn virtual social networks and online spaces that bring people together; on the other hand, they can potentially induce a sense of dislocation. The deep immersion in these digital spaces can paradoxically create a chasm between individuals and their physical surroundings, leading to a disconnection from nature and human camaraderie.

FIGURE 3.3   A data object in the metaverse.

FIGURE 3.4   Portals in the metaverse 1.

Virtual forms serve a myriad of functions that extend beyond their societal implications. They pervade various domains, including entertainment, education, relaxation, and professional growth. Emerging therapeutic applications, such as virtual reality exposure therapy, are leveraging these forms to treat conditions such as anxiety disorders or post-traumatic stress disorder, demonstrating the expansive scope of their influence.

Beyond utilitarian functions, virtual forms can also serve as a dynamic canvas for creative expression and innovation. Free from the physical world's limitations, creators have the liberty to conceive designs that challenge and stretch traditional aesthetic boundaries. In turn, audiences can interact with these creations in novel and engaging ways (see Figure 3.4).

However, this newfound artistic freedom raises a pertinent question: What principles should guide aesthetics within virtual spaces, given the absence of conventional contextual cues like gravity, day-night cycles, or climate? Traditionally, our perception of beauty and aesthetics is shaped by elements such as symmetry, proportion, or mimicking natural forms. However, in a virtual world, these norms may no longer hold (see Figure 3.5).

Generative AI emerges as a potential solution to this conundrum, capable of defining a new aesthetic for virtual spaces. It leverages the unique properties of the virtual environment, such as interactivity, immersion, and dynamism, to explore and establish fresh aesthetic norms. Instead of replicating the physical world, we can harness AI to delve into a realm unencumbered by physical constraints and forge new aesthetic standards that resonate with the intrinsic characteristics of the virtual environment.

FIGURE 3.5   Portals in the metaverse 2.

The value and function of virtual forms are not static but evolve continually with tech-nological advancements and shifts in societal paradigms. Consequently, our relationship with aesthetics in virtual spaces is constantly subject to reinterpretation and reinvention. With its capacity to learn, adapt, and generate novel content, generative AI is ideally placed to navigate the flux of evolving virtual landscapes, enabling us to redefine our aesthetic sensibilities. As we usher in this new era of digital aestheticism, exploring and under-standing beauty in virtual spaces becomes a journey without an end. Instead, it is filled with constant discovery and evolution. In this emerging epoch of digital aesthetics, it's evident that the exploration and comprehension of beauty within virtual realms represent an unending journey, yet one replete with perpetual discovery and evolution.

3.4 INTERACTIONS IN VIRTUAL REALITY

We exist in a state of perpetual introspection and reassessment, constantly reflecting upon our understanding of the world. This continuous flux is significantly magnified within virtual reality, where the boundaries of our perceptions and experiences can be stretched and transformed.

Often, virtual reality is envisioned as a spatial construct—akin to a vast chasm into which we plunge or an immersive cave full of columns, icicles, and the looming potential for exploration via a seemingly infinite rock-climbing wall. It manifests as an inescap-able space, seemingly offering no route for departure. In a way, virtual reality's limitations become our own, confining both our cognitive processes and physical movements.

Engaging with the components of virtual reality prompts us to interact with virtual objects as though they were tangible, mirroring our behavior in the physical world. The enhanced sensory input within virtual reality amplifies our perception of space and objects, heightening our environmental awareness. To delve deeper into this concept, let us explore three diverse virtual reality experiences—art, virtual tourism, and the realm of imagination—each offering distinct insights and revelations.[2]

Virtual art galleries redefine our interaction with artworks, allowing us to closely examine and appreciate pieces in ways that are impossible in the physical world. They can provide unprecedented access to art and democratize its appreciation, extending beyond geographical and socio-economic boundaries. On the other hand, virtual tourism allows us to explore far-flung corners of the world or historical periods from the comfort of our homes. It can deepen our understanding of cultures, history, and geography, fostering global empathy and shared experiences.

Lastly, the realm of imagination within virtual reality is limitless, offering us a platform to manifest our most fantastical ideas. It can stimulate creativity, foster innovative problem-solving, and provide a canvas for unique expressions of self. Here, the abstract can become palpable and the impossible can become possible. When taken together, these unique virtual experiences enhance our perception and revolutionize how we engage with the world around us, expanding our horizons in hitherto unimagined ways.

Our individual biases inevitably color our perception of form and representation.[3] Societal norms, rules, and standards significantly mold our perceptions, particularly within virtual reality experiences. Unlike physical objects, the limits of form in virtual space are not constrained by the laws of physics. Thus, new design principles must be developed to harness the potential of virtual form, a task that demands a seamless fusion of physical, social, and digital constraints.

Text-conditional image generation allows designers to perceive a virtual form as an expression of multiple meanings—a concept we refer to as the social virtual form. The social virtual form is predicated on how individuals interact with virtual reality environments within real-world social contexts. Our understanding of form in virtual reality is deeply rooted in social norms and experiences. In considering a virtual social form, the real-world physical context becomes vital. The virtual social form could offer a counterpoint to traditional physical representations of societal hierarchies, emphasizing increased collaboration and freedom of choice (see Figure 3.6). The design of social virtual forms could be driven by a user's choices, ultimately granting the user control over the design process.

Our physical appearance is deeply entwined with our identity—it is not merely a functional shell but a vessel imbued with profound physical, social, and cultural meanings. As we mold our avatars and their attire in the virtual sphere, we unconsciously define the forms we can adopt in these digital spaces. These forms serve various personal, social, and cultural purposes, offering new avenues for self-expression and representation.

Emerging technologies for interacting with virtual reality offer us powerful tools to redefine our perception of reality, a territory we are still exploring. Much like in the physical world, form in the virtual realm significantly influences perception. It stokes the

FIGURE 3.6　The metaverse avatar of an academic.

fires of imagination, encouraging us to yearn for more to push our emotional responses into unexplored territories of shapes, colors, and textures. Once our minds have tasted the smorgasbord of sensations offered by a generative AI collaborator, we are hungry for more.

Our comprehension of form is sharpened by our unique experiences in the physical world and, more broadly, by our interactions within the constraints of physical reality. These experiences foster understanding, which can seed assumptions and fuel the genesis of novel insights. In a virtual reality setting, it is conceivable to encounter entities that signify more than just digital objects. They encapsulate the object's inherent qualities and echo a diverse society of individuals with varying physical capabilities and a wealth of human experiences and knowledge. The true significance of these ideas can only be fully appreciated within this context of diverse perspectives and experiences.

3.5 FORMS IN VIRTUAL SPACE

Our ability to interpret forms, understand the meaning of shapes in a virtual world, and craft these realms in harmony with our perceptions now hinge upon choosing forms that aptly embody the values we aim to convey. Against this backdrop, generative AI comes into play, providing a pathway to blur the stark dichotomy between reality and the virtual. Generative AI serves as a tool, enabling us to mirror the complexities of the real world within a realm that is absent of inherent shape. However, it is pivotal to acknowledge that our present digital milieu, though seemingly boundless, is, in fact, a limited facet of a more

FIGURE 3.7 Impractically intricate tool 1.

comprehensive reality. The birth of generative AI-powered virtual reality systems catalyzes a new era, giving rise to various forms and concepts (see Figures 3.7 and 3.8).

Throughout history, the creation and interpretation of forms have stood as fundamental pillars of human culture and expression. From rudimentary cave drawings to sophisticated modern masterpieces, forms have functioned as carriers of communication, personal identity, and symbolic meaning.[4] With the rise of virtual reality, we encounter an added complexity in our ability to perceive forms, pushing us to comprehend the essence of shapes in a dimension absent of physical limitations.

In this emergent milieu, creating virtual spaces is not merely about replicating the physical world. Instead, it involves designing environments that encapsulate the values we intend to articulate. Unfettered by physical constraints, virtual spaces can symbolize ideas and concepts impossible to express in the material world. These spaces provide unique avenues for personal expression and interactive engagement. Thus, the process of shaping these spaces is guided by our understanding of which forms best reflect our values, allowing virtual forms to fuel creativity and innovation while transcending physical boundaries (see Figure 3.9).

The potential of virtual forms to broaden our understanding of ourselves and the world is considerable. However, creating and interpreting these forms also surface crucial questions about reality, creativity, and individual agency. To what extent do virtual forms encapsulate genuine human creativity, and how much do the algorithms and data shape the sets that drive their generation? How does our perception of beauty and significance

FIGURE 3.8   Impractically intricate tool 2.

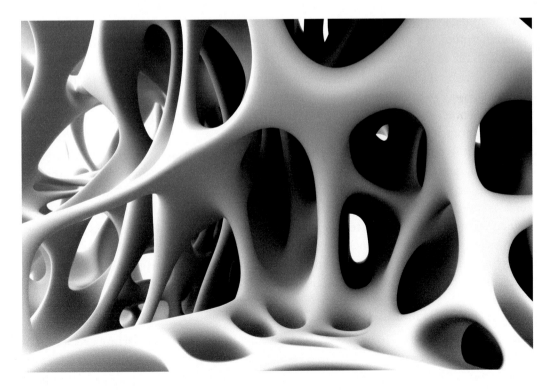

FIGURE 3.9   Parametric navigation spaces in the metaverse.

evolve in a virtual context devoid of conventional cues? What ethical guidelines should govern our use of virtual forms as they become more complex and influential?

Navigating these puzzles, we find that creating and interpreting virtual forms presents a formidable challenge and a substantial opportunity to expand our understanding of aesthetics, reality, and human expression. We must traverse this newfound landscape with curiosity, reflective deliberation, and ethical responsibility to create a world where virtual forms serve as potent vehicles of communication, identity, and meaning for all.

3.6 NEW FORMS REVOLUTIONIZED PERCEPTION

As we delve into the intricate dance between form and perception, we uncover uncharted territories that broaden our conceptual schema, extending from the physical world to virtual environments.

Interactions within virtual reality provide a fascinating study of this phenomenon. Despite the abstract nature of these digital environments, our interpretations of objects within these spaces astonishingly mirror our perceptions of their physical world counterparts. This striking resemblance has far-reaching implications. It propounds the idea that by enriching our sensory experiences in virtual spaces, we can, in turn, augment our perceptions of space and objects within our tangible reality, reshaping our understanding and interaction with our surroundings at a fundamental level.

Integrating generative AI into design paradigms further enhances the transformative potential of these virtual environments. This technology goes beyond the limitations of conventional design templates, providing a limitless canvas for the reimagining of form. Utilizing AI allows us to abstract forms in ways that stimulate our cognitive abilities, fostering innovative interpretations and a deeper comprehension of our world (Figures 3.10 and 3.11).

Furthermore, the potentialities proffered by virtual reality experiences are not merely limited to the representation of virtual objects. Instead, they can function as channels to reflect the rich tapestry of human diversity in terms of culture, society, and individuality. These experiences can accommodate and symbolize a range of abilities, viewpoints, and life experiences, amplifying the communicative power of form and its influential role in shaping perceptions.

Broadening our perspective, the relevance of form transcends its tangible manifestation. It emerges as an encompassing concept, encapsulating function, utility, and representation, opening paths for a more profound exploration of the relationship between form and perception and how it intensifies our experience of reality. The understanding gained from this exploration testifies to the fluid nature of perception and the limitless potential of new forms to invoke novel perceptions (see Figures 3.12 and 3.13). The fusion of technology and design, epitomized in AI and virtual reality, propels this evolution of form and perception, marking a new era of sensory exploration and cognitive enrichment.

3.7 CLOSING THOUGHTS

Form is intrinsically tied to our perceptions; it constitutes the essence of our visual reality, shaping the way we engage with and interpret the world. The gentle curves of a beautifully designed chair or a skyscraper's imposing, linear structure elicits specific responses in

FIGURE 3.10   Portrait of a dignified turkey.

us, guiding our aesthetic and emotional reactions. The relevance of form takes on greater significance within the realms of the virtual. Here, our role transcends mere observation and we emerge as creators. We define the crux of our visual experiences, sculpting virtual spaces and artifacts. The form of these digital constructs profoundly influences our sense of immersion and interaction within the virtual environment.

Virtual art objects, distinguished through their form, augment our overall experience. Our perception and appreciation of these objects are deeply entwined with the aesthetics of their virtual space, urging a re-evaluation of traditional art conceptions.

However, form serves a purpose beyond just creating visually appealing spaces; it influences our emotional and psychological engagement. Recognizing form as a crucial element of our experience transforms the structures and shapes in virtual spaces into emotional

FIGURE 3.11   Portrait of a dignified rooster.

catalysts that mold our perception and interaction within the environment. This influence becomes particularly palpable when we deliberately design virtual experiences emphasizing form, leveraging psychological principles to navigate our perception.

Now, the role of generative AI introduces a transformative facet to our comprehension of form and perception. Generative AI expands the boundaries of our creative possibilities through its capacity to generate novel and complex forms. It operates beyond the limitations of humanly conceived templates and designs, providing an expansive platform for unprecedented forms and, consequently, fresh perceptions. This AI-driven creation of form imbues the virtual realm with dynamism and unpredictability, encouraging a more active engagement with our environment and continuously challenging and reshaping our perceptions.

FIGURE 3.12   Multitasking avatar.

FIGURE 3.13   Impossible photograph: Giraffes running wild in Manhattan.

Understanding the profound impact of form, particularly those conjured by generative AI, on our virtual experiences enables us to create more immersive and emotionally resonant experiences. The intentional design of objects and spaces within the virtual world can incite particular emotional responses, generating engaging environments that seize and sustain our attention. The intricate association between form and value brings philosophical ponderings to the fore, especially within virtual reality. As we navigate this unexplored landscape, with generative AI as a valuable co-creator, it is crucial to critically scrutinize and contemplate our design choices' psychological, emotional, and aesthetic consequences. By doing so, we can curate engaging and meaningful virtual experiences, offering fresh insights into the complex interplay between form, perception, and technology.

NOTES

1. Here are some examples of how form can shape perception: **Influence of Product Design on Perceived Functionality**: A product's physical design and shape play a pivotal role in shaping consumers' perceptions of its capabilities and features. For instance, a product featuring a sleek, minimalistic, and modern design is often associated with being cutting-edge, efficient, and sophisticated. This perception stems from an amalgamation of societal standards and consumer experiences. Conversely, a product with a more antiquated design might be perceived as lacking in innovation. This phenomenon is not solely constrained to aesthetic judgment but can also influence the perceived user experience and expectations regarding the performance and reliability of the product.

   Shape of Logos and Brand Perception: Logos serve as visual embodiments of a brand's identity, and their shape can communicate volumes about the brand's values, target audience, and market positioning. For example, logos that incorporate sharp angles and rigid geometrical patterns tend to evoke a sense of dynamism, aggressiveness, or masculinity. These may be apt for brands that portray strength or precision, such as sports or technology companies. On the other hand, logos with softer curves and more fluid shapes often convey a sense of warmth, femininity, or approachability. Brands seeking to present themselves as nurturing, inclusive, or customer-centric might find this suitable.

   Architectural Shapes and Perceived Building Purpose: The architecture of a building can significantly shape perceptions regarding its function and the type of activities it houses. For instance, buildings with sharp angles, straight lines, and monochromatic color scheme are often associated with a corporate, industrial, or professional ambiance. This design choice may convey efficiency, formality, and pragmatism, which align with the values and objectives of many business entities. In contrast, buildings incorporating curved lines, organic shapes, or vibrant color palettes might evoke creativity, innovation, or leisure perceptions. Such designs are often employed in artistic spaces, educational environments, or places meant for relaxation and entertainment. The psychology behind this lies in the association of organic forms with nature, fluidity, and openness, whereas geometric patterns and straight lines are often linked with order and logic.

2. Mel Slater, in "Place illusion and plausibility can lead to realistic behaviour in immersive virtual environments," explains why individuals typically respond realistically to scenarios and events within immersive virtual reality systems. Slater proposes that there are two independent components that contribute to this response. The first, referred to as place illusion (PI), is the sensation of actually being in a real location, commonly known as "presence." The second component is the plausibility illusion (Psi), which is the perception that the events being portrayed are genuinely happening. Despite this, participants are fully aware that they

are not physically present in the depicted location and that the events are not real. PI depends on the virtual reality system's ability to provide sensorimotor contingencies, while Psi relies on the system's capacity to generate events that directly engage the participant and the overall credibility of the depicted scenario compared to the participant's expectations. Slater contends that when both PI and Psi are present, individuals will react realistically to the virtual environment. Retrieved from https://www.ncbi.nlm.nih.gov/pmc/articles/PMC2781884/.

3. In their influential paper, "Perceptual Learning: How Experience Shapes Visual Perception," Dosher and Lu (2020) delve into the critical role that experience plays in molding visual perception through a process known as perceptual learning. This concept posits that our perceptions are not just passive receptions of sensory inputs but are actively shaped by our previous experiences, reflecting the dynamic nature of our perceptual systems. Dosher and Lu's work underscores the concept that learning is not only confined to conscious, deliberate processes but also intimately intertwined with our fundamental perception of the world around us, highlighting the inherent plasticity of our cognitive systems. Dosher and Lu, Perceptual learning: How experience shapes visual perception, (MIT Press, 2020).

4. In "Abstract Shape Representation in Human Visual Perception," Baker and Kellman (2018) conducted a series of experiments that provided insightful evidence on the abstract nature of shape representations in human visual perception. The researchers argue that the capability to construct shape representations from the visual stimuli we encounter is fundamental to the processes of perception, cognitive thought, and resultant action. In demonstrating the abstract character of perceived shape, Baker and Kellman highlighted instances where humans can discern a shape from abstract forms, such as a cloud that visually parallels a fish. This ability is a testament to our complex visual perception system and underscores the pivotal role that abstract shape representation plays in our day-to-day cognitive functioning. Retrieved from https://kellmanlab.psych.ucla.edu/files/baker_kellman_2018.pdf.

CHAPTER 4

Incidental Beauty

4.1 WHAT IS AN AESTHETICALLY BEAUTIFUL OBJECT?

The perception of an object as aesthetically beautiful implies that it elicits a sensation of beauty within the observer. Notably, such attribution is not rooted in an objective, intrinsic quality of the object itself but rather in its aesthetic presentation and how this presentation is decoded through the prism of collective cultural frameworks.[1]

Consequently, beauty resists a universally applicable quantification or definition; it is inherently subjective and tightly woven with an individual's sensory perception, personal experiences, and cultural background.

The perception of beauty is an active cognitive process that extends beyond the passive reception of sensory input. It represents a complex web where individual experiences cross with broader societal constructs that shape aesthetic valuation. Our recognition of beauty often arises not from an object's inherent aesthetic properties but from a powerful aesthetic interaction that the object inspires. The perception of beauty may extend beyond our immediate experiences, transcending contexts and entities toward which we may initially harbor indifference or aversion.

In examining the historical evolution of beauty, we can see that beauty's roots are deep, reaching back to the medieval era when art served as a vehicle for revealing beauty woven into the fabric of everyday life. During this period, beauty was mainly viewed as a subjective quality, discernable through visual interaction and reliant on the aesthetic characteristics of artistic creations. This perception was intricately tied to religious, philosophical, and elite cultural doctrines, forming the foundation for judging aesthetic values.[2]

As we journey through the annals of history, a significant transformation in the conceptual landscape of beauty becomes apparent. It is revealed that art and beauty share an inextricable bond, with the beauty within a work of art often emanating from its harmony with the natural world, where beauty finds its fundamental grounding. A pastoral landscape, for example, radiates beauty in its natural splendor. A painting that captures this landscape absorbs this beauty due to its ability to echo the aesthetic properties of the landscape. This reflection of nature's beauty in artistic works bolsters our perception of them as beautiful.

DOI: 10.1201/9781003450139-6

Exploring this relationship further, we see that the association between nature and art is complex and multifaceted. While raw nature may not inherently possess the conventional markers of beauty typically linked with art, it carries the potential to yield elements of natural beauty that can then be mirrored in artistic expressions. The creation and perception of beauty underscore the interdependency of nature and art. Beauty thus surfaces as a mediator that bridges the divide between art and nature, providing us with a unique lens through which we can perceive and appreciate the aesthetics of our environment.

Beauty does not spring from an object's functional or resilient features but emerges as an experiential phenomenon deeply rooted in perception, personal experiences, and cultural contexts. It is a shared—though subjective—experience that forms a fundamental aspect of human consciousness. Beauty engages our senses, stirs our emotions, and sparks our imagination (Figure 4.1). As such, an aesthetically beautiful object does not exist independently—it communicates, narrates a story, and shapes our understanding of beauty. It serves as a vehicle for an unspoken dialogue between the observer and the infinite realm of aesthetics.

FIGURE 4.1 The incidental beauty of a parametric design for festive headware.

4.2 BEAUTY IN ART AND DESIGN

Art and design occupy a unique place in human cognition, providing experiences beyond the boundaries of daily encounters. Their power resides not merely in the sensory pleasure they invoke but in their capacity to kindle profound thought, eliciting emotional and intellectual reverberations within the observer and the creator alike. As such, art and design transcend the role of passive aesthetic gratification to become dynamic conduits for innovation and expression.

Throughout history, art and design have been humanity's gateway to a deeper exploration of its collective consciousness. They serve as vehicles that transform mundane experiences into extraordinary manifestations of creativity. Their profound beauty lies in the ability to resonate with the human psyche, evoking the primal reverberations that vibrate through our emotional and intellectual landscape.

As the spirit of this era steers us into an era marked by unprecedented levels of creativity, there is a growing impetus to reconceptualize the foundation of art and the very framework of the creative process. We are at the threshold of a creative renaissance that positions empathy, intelligence, and a uniquely human inclination for interpersonal connections at the core of imaginative expression (Figure 4.2).

Imagine a creative model wherein conventional boundaries are challenged and the creative process evolves into a complex matrix interwoven with keen observation and emotional receptivity. Like a symphony composed of harmonious notes, every creative

FIGURE 4.2   A device that keeps nonlinear time and displays it as colors, sounds, and shapes.

endeavor sparks a ripple of innovation, creating a perpetually evolving nexus of interconnected thoughts and expressions. This ceaseless torrent of creativity has the potential to revolutionize not just art and design but the economic, scientific, and cultural domains as well, reframing our understanding of what is possible. Generative artificial intelligence (AI), particularly text-conditional image generation, has rapidly emerged as a revolutionary force capable of reshaping the landscape of art and design. This advanced technology, nourished by a vast collection of visual and textual data, can produce original and aesthetically captivating images based on textual prompts. The boundary between human creativity and machine intelligence becomes obscured in such scenarios.

Consider a situation where an AI is given a textual prompt and then it masterfully crafts an image that embodies the essence of the words and transcends them, bringing forth colors, forms, and compositions yet undiscovered (see Figure 4.3). This convergence of art, design, and technology injects an additional layer of complexity and potential into the creative process.

Within this innovative framework, AI becomes a catalyst for creativity, an instrument through which artists and designers can navigate the uncharted territories of their imagination, thereby pushing the boundaries of their creative expression. It offers an alternative lens to perceive and interpret the world, leading to the emergence of "incidental beauty"—a new aesthetic that spontaneously emerges from the algorithmic intricacies of AI, captivating human observers. This form of beauty, born as an unexpected by-product of AI's

FIGURE 4.3 A representation of a polynon, a geometric shape that seeks to unify the world's knowledge in a single geometric representation.

operations, holds its own distinctive charm. It stands at the intersection of human intent and algorithmic interpretation, forging a dynamic exchange that continuously challenges our aesthetic assumptions and uncovers new paths for artistic and design innovations.

The union of human creativity and AI marks the beginning of a new creative ecosystem, where the demarcation between creator and tool becomes increasingly blurred. AI evolves from a mere instrument to a collaborator, encouraging artists and designers to reimagine the potential of their work. Such a dynamic nurtures a reciprocally enriching environment. In this environment, aesthetic values and definitions of beauty are continually reshaped, creating an ever-evolving tapestry of human and technological creativity (Figure 4.4). The emergence of this unforeseen beauty, hailing from the innovative intersections of AI, challenges us to reconsider our perception of the aesthetic realm. It triggers a reframing of traditional aesthetic canons, expanding the parameters within which we discern and appreciate beauty. Doing so paves the way for an unprecedented exploration into new aesthetic territories, enriching our understanding of beauty and allowing us to unearth and appreciate the complex dance between creativity and technology.

In this vein, AI serves as an inspiring collaborator, a muse in digital form, fostering an unconventional dialogue between the artist and their medium. This transformative relationship is not unidirectional; it extends beyond the creation process, impacting the observer's experience. As spectators, we are led to engage in a deeper level of aesthetic contemplation that prompts us to explore beyond the immediate visual allure and engage with

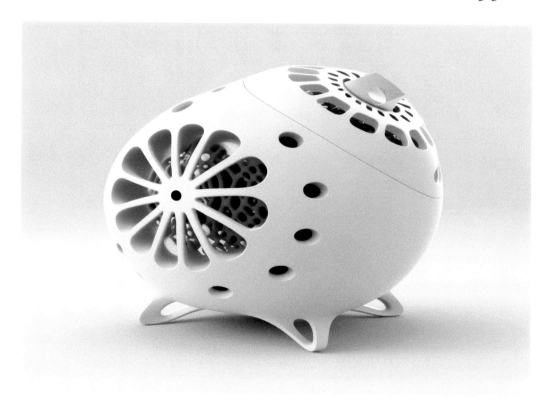

FIGURE 4.4   A minimalist approach for a Radiolaria-inspired dehumidifier.

FIGURE 4.5   An experimental avatar for a digital twin android.

the underlying layers of technological genius that brought the piece to life. The enriched dimension brought into our interaction with art and design allows us to consume, comprehend, and appreciate the nuances of this novel form of beauty.

This emergent creative ecosystem thus marks a new epoch in our aesthetic journey, wherein AI, as a collaborator, is no longer a mere adjunct to the creative process but an active participant shaping the trajectory of artistic and design expression. As we venture deeper into this frontier, we will likely witness a continual unfolding of innovative aesthetics, enhanced by the sophisticated dance between human intuition and machine intelligence (Figure 4.5). This perpetual evolution is poised to transform our understanding of beauty, marking the dawn of a new era where art and design are continually shaped by and, in turn, shape our interactions with technology.

4.3 WHAT IS INCIDENTAL BEAUTY?

The concept of incidental beauty brings to mind a remarkable dimension of aesthetics in which beauty emerges from unanticipated conjunctions.[3] This distinct form of beauty arises serendipitously through the organic mingling of various elements, culminating in unexpected instances of aesthetic marvel. Incidental beauty is not engineered or meticulously crafted; instead, it unfolds naturally, surprising us and leaving us transfixed by its elusive magnificence.[4]

To contextualize, consider the organic beauty found in nature—the breathtaking spectacle of a starlit sky, the harmonious symmetry of a spider's web glistening with dew, the

FIGURE 4.6   Graffiti alley.

elegance of a solitary leaf drifting on the surface of a still pond, or the compelling, intricate perfection of a snowflake.[5] Untouched by human hands, these instances mirror the essence of incidental beauty as they emanate from an intricate dance of elements beyond our manipulation, coming together to create a tableau greater than the sum of its parts.

Incidental beauty also emerges in artificial environments. For instance, a seemingly mundane urban setting, such as a graffiti-adorned alley bathed in the soft glow of a setting sun, may unveil an unexpected beauty (Figure 4.6). Here, the graffiti's colors, textures, and patterns, coupled with the angle and quality of light, create a visually striking image beyond mere city grit. However, the worth of incidental beauty goes beyond its power to inspire; it also lies in its ability to surprise and provoke. Every encounter with this beauty confronts and challenges our established aesthetic beliefs. It compels us to concede that there are always additional layers of beauty to uncover, uncharted territories to explore, and many wonders that remain tantalizingly beyond our grasp.

Incidental beauty provides a compelling argument for our world's wealth of aesthetic diversity. It serves as a gentle reminder that beauty can manifest in the most unanticipated places and moments, and it behooves us to remain open to these delightful surprises (Figure 4.7).

Experiencing incidental beauty has a transformative influence on our perception of the world. It urges us to look beyond our habitual observation patterns and encourages a more mindful and attentive engagement with our surroundings. In this regard, an encounter with incidental beauty can be considered a moment of enlightenment, offering a glimpse into the deeper strata of reality often shrouded by our everyday preoccupations.[6]

FIGURE 4.7   Tools of unknown origin or functionality.

Exploring the aesthetic experience through the lens of incidental beauty unveils a wealth of enlightening insights. This type of beauty, which arises spontaneously and without intent, resembles the awe-inspiring, unexpected splendor we encounter in nature (Figure 4.8). As a source of inspiration, wonder, and reflection, incidental beauty punctuates ordinary life, encouraging us to question long-held assumptions. Its serendipitous emergence cultivates fresh perspectives and contributes to the richness and diversity of human cultural experiences.

This unplanned beauty symbolizes the endless depth and splendor inherent in our existence, inviting us to revel in life's serendipities and mysteries. Incidental beauty provides a glimpse into the sublime and the sacred amid a world marked by instability and unpredictability. It acts as a beacon, illuminating the limitless potential embedded in our surroundings.

Incidental beauty signals epiphany, marking instances of aesthetic excellence that captivate us, disarm our preconceptions, and urge us to venture beyond the conventional avenues of perception. As we navigate an era characterized by the fusion of art, design, and generative AI, these spontaneous encounters with beauty serve as a crucible for the evolution of aesthetic understanding. This transformative period combines human intuition's ingenuity with AI's computational power, enriching our creative vocabulary and revealing unexplored dimensions of artistic and aesthetic expression.

The deep-seated significance of incidental beauty highlights the pervasive aesthetics that thread through our lives, often obscured by routine and habit. For example, the ordinary act of swirling cream into a cup of coffee. What seems a trivial gesture becomes a

FIGURE 4.8   Form exploration for a household appliance: Bluetooth speaker.

mesmerizing display of incidental beauty as the cream expands in cloud-like plumes, creating patterns and color gradients that evoke images of distant cosmic nebulae. This transient visual spectacle prompts us to reinterpret commonplace events, fostering a renewed admiration for the mundane and encouraging us to discover beauty in unexpected places.

Incidental beauty can serve as a medium for transcendental experiences, offering glimpses into realms that surpass the tangible and commonplace. It serves as a potent reminder of the sublimity within the quotidian, ushering us into uncharted aesthetic territories. This perspective aligns with the philosophies espoused by the 20th-century French philosopher Gaston Bachelard, who accentuated the poetics of space and the potency of the ordinary to evoke profound emotional and aesthetic responses. [7]

Taking an illustrative detour, let us consider the art of photography as an exemplary domain where incidental beauty plays a pivotal role. In this field, the spontaneous alignment of elements such as light, shadows, colors, and forms can create an ethereal composition that transcends the intentional focus of the photographer. For instance, a photographer capturing the silhouette of a barren tree may not foresee the flight of a flock of birds into the frame at the exact moment, lending an unforeseen vitality and symbolism to the image. This unintended yet profoundly beautiful confluence epitomizes the essence of incidental beauty.

In the domain of music as well, incidental beauty frequently takes center stage during improvisational performances. Jazz musicians are particularly known for such impromptu sessions, where the unscripted nature of their artistry leads to the birth of melodies and harmonies that are neither preconceived nor reproducible. This extemporaneous character of the performance results in an aesthetic experience that, while transient, is profoundly resonant, encapsulating the quintessence of incidental beauty within the auditory realm.

Expanding our horizon to the realm of AI, generative AI systems present a new frontier for the manifestation of incidental beauty. These systems, which can generate novel and complex content, often result in unforeseen yet captivating outputs. Consider the case of Google's DeepDream, a neural network designed to detect image patterns.[8] When "dreaming," it can often create psychedelic and dream-like images that are surreal, unexpected, and strikingly beautiful. Here, the beauty is a by-product of the AI's operations, born from its attempt to make sense of the data it was trained on, encapsulating the idea of incidental beauty in the realm of AI.

Similarly, AI models used for generating music, such as OpenAI's MuseNet, can often produce compositions that feature unexpected yet beautiful harmonies.[9] These AI-generated pieces are not the result of deliberate and conscious human design but are instead the consequence of the AI's interpretation of the patterns it has learned from its training data. The unpredictable nature of these compositions, together with their often beautiful and emotionally resonant qualities, render them a compelling example of incidental beauty created by AI. The unpredictable and spontaneous manifestations of incidental beauty guide the web of human experiences. They challenge our aesthetic preconceptions, offering us a kaleidoscope through which we can reimagine the world (Figure 4.9). As we enter a future

FIGURE 4.9   Form and material exploration for sound reproduction system.

where art and technology intertwine, acknowledging and embracing incidental beauty becomes increasingly vital. It sets off a symphony of the senses, choreographs a dance of emotions, and orchestrates an intellectual journey. Together, they weave the rich tapestry of human experiences, highlighting the serendipitous in our endless pursuit of beauty and meaning.

4.4 CLOSING THOUGHTS

The present confluence of art, design, and generative AI signals an epoch of transformation. Traditionally viewed as a distinctly human venture, the creative endeavor evolves into a stimulating collaboration where human intuition and AI engage in an intricate dance. This metamorphosis does not undermine human creativity but enriches it, broadening our artistic palette with innovative tools and perspectives. From this partnership between humans and machines emerges a future steeped in the vibrancy of our collective imagination and technological finesse.

This dynamic amalgamation triggers a renaissance in creative pursuits, engendering an environment that amplifies the aesthetic potential intrinsic to humans and AI. The ability of generative AI to translate text-based prompts into visual narratives cultivates a new platform for artists and designers to express their creative visions. Such synergy leads to expansive terrains of artistic exploration, defined only by the limitless potential of our combined imaginations.

Fusing these domains incites a domino effect reverberating far beyond the creative sphere. It sets in motion a series of breakthroughs across diverse sectors, including art, economics, science, and culture. The resulting paradigm shifts and cross-fertilization of ideas can catalyze advancements that augment our worldview, invigorate established industries, and stimulate multicultural dialogues. In this transformative era, we witness a profound metamorphosis in the landscapes of art and design. Art extends its reach from the physical realm into the domain of algorithms and code, unearthing an unexpected beauty within artificial intelligence. Concurrently, design evolves from a purely functional field into exploring AI's potential to reshape our world in unanticipated ways.

Far from rendering human artists redundant, this evolution amplifies their roles. Artists and designers are not replaced but empowered, allied with a potent collaborator that enhances their creative abilities. Probing deeper into their imaginative spaces allows artists to translate their ideas into unique and surprising forms.

The fusion of art, design, and generative AI offers a sneak peek into a future where creativity and technology integrate harmoniously. This collaboration expands the creative process beyond its conventional boundaries, evolving into a shared journey between human intuition and AI. This partnership promises to redefine our collective creative potential, ushering in an era of unmatched artistic and aesthetic expression. Thus, the future of art and design lies not solely in the hands of humans or machines but emerges from the extraordinary symphony of both, engendering a world rich in unimaginable beauty and innovation.

NOTES

1. NB: The term **"aesthetically beautiful"** describes objects that elicit a positive sensory response, especially visually. Although beauty is inherently subjective—varying across cultures, eras, and individual preferences—certain universal design principles consistently emerge as creators strive to craft aesthetically pleasing objects. These principles include balance, which refers to the even distribution of visual weight; proportion, which pertains to the size and spatial relationships between different elements; and harmony, which is the pleasing arrangement of parts contributing to a sense of cohesiveness. Although these principles have traditionally been applied in fields such as art and architecture, they are increasingly utilized across various disciplines, even influencing the design of everyday items like furniture and clothing. Hence, consciously or subconsciously, we constantly interact with and form judgments about the aesthetic beauty of the world around us.

2. There were many examples of medieval art that used lavish materials, such as gold, ivory, and enamel, for religious objects, personal ornaments, and mosaics. As well as serving as decoration during this period, art also served as a representation of an individual's social status, cultural roots, education, and identity. These valuable materials enhanced both the physical and symbolic value of the artworks. At the same time, master artisans became more valuable to society during the medieval era, which saw a rise in the social standing of artists. Retrieved from https://artincontext.org/medieval-art/.

3. **Incidental beauty** is beauty that is not intended or planned. It is beauty that is discovered by chance or by accident. Examples of incidental beauty include the patterns that form on the surface of a puddle after a rainstorm, the way light filters through the leaves of a tree, or the way shadows fall across a building at sunset. Retrieved from https://wikidiff.com/intentional/incidental.

4. By contrast, **intentional beauty** is created with the intention of being beautiful. Examples of intentional beauty include works of art, architecture, and design. Intentional beauty arises from deliberate design choices aimed to evoke beauty across fields like art, architecture, and design, aiming to create something pleasing to the eye. Retrieved from https://diffsense.com/diff/incidental/intentional.

5. The beauty of snowflakes is often attributed to their intricate and delicate crystalline patterns. Snowflakes form when water vapor in clouds condenses immediately to ice around a small particle, like dust. Because of the molecular structure of water, these new snowflakes begin to form a crystal pattern. The "classic" snowflake is a six-sided crystal, but these shapes can differ with changes in humidity and temperature. Sometimes the flakes can form as columns, thin needles, or a flat shape called plates. The uniqueness of snowflakes comes in part from environmental factors of their formations (e.g., collisions) and also the high number of possible formations crystals can make. That is to say, you can make many unique combinations with crystal structures because of their many components. Retrieved from https://ssec.si.edu/stemvisions-blog/beauty-and-science-snowflakes.

6. **Incidental beauty** in the context of text-conditional image generation by artificial intelligence (AI) refers to the emergent aesthetic qualities that are neither explicitly defined nor anticipated within the given text prompts but arise from the generative process. While processing a text prompt, the AI system utilizes its training and inherent biases to generate an image. Sometimes, this process results in unique, intricate compositions of forms, colors, and patterns that were not explicitly stated in the text prompt. The unexpected harmonious blending and interaction of these elements can lead to an instance of aesthetic appeal or "beauty" that is incidental—it arises not from the intentional human design but from the AI's generative process. This incidental beauty is somewhat analogous to the unexpected beauty found in natural processes or phenomena. It emerges spontaneously, unguided by a specific design

intent. The beauty is not purposefully sought after but is an artifact of the AI's efforts to interpret and visually represent the text prompt. For instance, when an AI is asked to generate an image representing the abstract concept of "fluid dynamics," it might improvise and create a composition with flowing shapes, vibrant colors, and dynamic lines that not only represent the concept but also captivate the viewer due to its unexpected aesthetic harmony. This "incidental beauty" can inspire, surprise, and even challenge our understanding of aesthetics and the interaction between technology and art.

7. https://sites.evergreen.edu/wp-content/uploads/sites/88/2015/05/Gaston-Bachelard-the-Poetics-of-Space.pdf.
8. See https://deepdreamgenerator.com.
9. See https://openai.com/research/musenet.

II

Expanding Possibilities

CHAPTER 5

Bias and Creative Intent

5.1 THE BALANCE BETWEEN SKILL AND A DESIRED OUTCOME

Each form and color adopted in artistic creation bears substantial significance, representing a thoughtful balancing act. This proposition becomes even more compelling when we observe it through the lens of text-conditional image generation, juxtaposing it against the images brought into being by human artists or designers.

When an artist or designer embarks on the journey of image creation, they confront an extensive array of choices at every juncture. These choices could be deliberative or instinctive, molded by their distinctive perspectives, past experiences, and artistic sensitivities. Each decision taken during the creative journey is inherently tied to a compromise. This compromise arises as the artist intricately navigates between their envisioned outcome and the limitations posed by the medium of expression, the subject matter, and their individual biases.

Speaking of forms, every artist carries an implicit form bias. This bias stems from their personal artistic style, preferences, and the influences they have absorbed over time. It shapes their perception and interpretation of the world, ultimately determining the forms they elect to integrate into their artwork. These forms could embody representational or abstract entities, be organic or geometric in nature, or present to the eye as either flowing or angular. Every artistic decision concerning form involves a compromise. The artist must strike a delicate equilibrium between transmitting their intended message and inciting a visual experience that resonates with the observer.

Similarly, the choice of colors in artwork also demands compromise. Colors carry symbolic, emotional, and cultural associations that fluctuate across individuals and societies. Artists may intentionally or unintentionally gravitate toward specific colors, influenced by their predilections or the mood and message they aim to convey through their work. The artist's color bias becomes evident in selecting a specific color palette, juxtaposing different hues, and the interaction between light and shadow. These choices invariably involve inevitable trade-offs as the artist attempts to reconcile their subjective color preferences with the overarching aesthetic objectives of the artwork.

DOI: 10.1201/9781003450139-8

The act of compromise in art creation signifies an acknowledgment of the limitations and opportunities inherent in the medium and the artist's subjectivity. It underscores that each artistic decision carries transformative potential, simultaneously enriching and restraining the artwork's expressive potency. The compromises artists make reflect their continuous negotiation between their intentions, technical constraints, cultural contexts, and the intricate interplay of form and color.

However, when it comes to text-conditional image generation, the concept of compromise assumes a novel dimension. Artificial intelligence (AI) systems, powered by advanced algorithms and extensive datasets, operate devoid of the inherent biases characteristic to human artists. Personal tendencies or subjective predilections do not shackle these systems. Instead, they harness the capacity of data analysis and machine learning to generate images grounded in textual prompts, semantic intent, and pre-established objectives. The AI systems are constantly learning, refining their generation strategies based on patterns and anomalies discovered in the data, thereby embracing a form of compromise that's systematic and driven by objective measures.

In the process of creativity driven by AI, the concept of compromise takes on a unique form. Unlike human artists whose creative decisions are influenced by their individual biases, in AI, compromises are inherent within the very algorithms that power the system. The AI must harmonize a multitude of factors, including its training data, textual prompts, and the ultimate goal of producing an image that accurately aligns with the provided semantic description. These compromises are ingrained in the algorithms' efforts to extract the essence of the textual input and transform it into a coherent visual portrayal, navigating the intricate interplay of semantics, aesthetics, and the constraints of its technological capabilities (see Figure 5.1).

This stark contrast between human-made artwork and AI-generated images initiates thought-provoking philosophical discourse about creativity's essence, intentionality's role, and compromise's function in artistic expression. It encourages us to reflect on the relevance of personal biases in art, the tension between human autonomy and computational determinism, and the implications of ceding artistic control to AI.

In dissecting the compromises inherent in artistic creation, whether by humans or AI systems, we probe into the subtle dynamics between intention and realization, subjectivity and objectivity, and the potentialities and limitations of the creative process. Through these compromises, art transcends its physical form, evolving into a profound tapestry of thoughts, emotions, and cultural interconnections, beckoning us to delve into the depth of human expression and perception.

By contrast, text-conditioned image generation, an AI system, scrutinizes each possible output with a strong bias toward outputs that closely align with the current text-conditioned inputs. Often, the final output is unpredictable. The input could be too nuanced for a clear output or, conversely, too precise and therefore incompatible with widespread representation. Sometimes, the final output may be derived from a series of initial attempts, leading to seemingly random results (Figure 5.2, created after four attempts at a very precise prompt).

In many instances, designers may not proceed with an image after its generation, implying that what the computer generates might not align with the original intention,

FIGURE 5.1 Imagining fashion made from repurposed rubber and plastic.

FIGURE 5.2 A white motorcycle on the background of a grayish surface, in the style of hard surface modeling, energy-charged, rounded, electric, dark cyan and dark black.

leading to a representation that deviates considerably from the initial desire. In other words, *the form is created without artistic intervention*, culminating in outputs exceeding human imagination and expectations. The statement holds particularly true for text-conditioned input with high semantic description and value. AI systems strive to identify and extract all requisite information to accomplish a goal where the semantic intent is visually realized.

This machine-empowered creativity enables the generation of art without necessitating human intervention. The establishment of a digital cultural commons, which becomes a focal point for various artistic practices and social engagements, can be perceived in this scenario. It evolves into a material artifact of global significance, forming a living link to humanity's cultural heritage.

Historically, artists have functioned as intentional agents, infusing their work with personal expression and subjective intent. The artist's physical actions guide the creative process. Their intellectual input also plays a role along with emotional investment. These factors together influence the outcome. However, in AI-generated art, the lack of continuous human involvement post the initial input means that the computer's output might diverge from the artist's initial vision. This departure from human intentionality challenges the conventional understanding of authorship and artistic agency.

By ceding creative control to AI systems, we create a realm for exploration that transcends human imagination and expectations. The underlying algorithms and neural networks of the AI systems, with their capability to process enormous data and learn from patterns, can generate unique and unforeseen outputs. Such a process leads to the creation of art that transcends human independent conception. It provides aesthetic experiences that push the boundaries of our understanding and challenge our preconceived notions.

When AI's creative process is guided by high semantic description and value inputs, the system's capacity to identify and extract relevant information becomes paramount. By discerning the semantic intent behind the input, AI systems manifest that intent in the output. This pursuit of semantic fidelity enables machines to venture into artistic expression, offering a unique perspective and interpretation of human culture (Figure 5.3).

As we contemplate the philosophical ramifications of artwork produced by AI, we are propelled into a profound introspection of the evolving relationship between humans and their technological inventions. With the burgeoning landscape of artificial creativity, we are urged to re-evaluate our traditional understandings of authorship, creativity, and aesthetic appreciation. This shifting paradigm presents a conundrum: reconciling the degree of autonomy granted to AI systems with the intrinsic value we attribute to the flicker of human creative intent and inspiration.[1]

AI-borne art challenges us to reimagine the creative process and broaden our perception of what it means to be an artist. It encourages us to expand our artistic scope to include the unanticipated, the unfamiliar; something that surpasses the confines of human imagination. As we journey further into this digital frontier, we must engage in insightful discourse, critique, and acknowledgment of the powerful influence that AI-produced art wields on our cultural mosaic and the essence of human expression itself.

FIGURE 5.3 A woman wears a white veil made of thread, soft box lighting, Tintoretto, Nadav Kander, colorful figures, organic geometry.

In this AI-enhanced creative sphere, the role of humans evolves from direct creators to facilitators, prompting a radical rethink of the traditional artist's identity. As we cede some creative control to AI, we are no longer solely responsible for the final output. Instead, we enter a symbiotic relationship where we guide AI with our inputs and, in turn, let AI surprise us with its interpretations and manifestations, enriching the creative process with novel perspectives and possibilities.

This new dynamic does not undermine human creativity's importance, it rather broadens its scope. It is an expansion that necessitates adjusting how we view and appreciate art. Just as viewers have learned to appreciate abstract and conceptual art forms over time, adjusting to AI-generated art involves understanding and valuing the uniqueness of the process and outcomes.

Embracing AI in art also raises crucial questions about authorship and originality. The very act of creating has been the hallmark of human expressiveness and identity. As we allow AI to participate in this process, we blur the boundaries of creation and challenge the traditional notion of artistic ownership. Consequently, the discussions on AI and art are not just about aesthetics but also about intellectual property and the more significant implications on the art market and society. Venturing further into the digital realm of AI-generated art, we are tasked with fostering meaningful dialogues and thoughtful critique. We should strive to understand how AI impacts our cultural narrative and influences the very core of human expressiveness. Such conversations will be instrumental in shaping the future direction of AI in art and its relationship with human creativity.

5.2 BIAS IN CREATIVE INTENT

One of the most significant challenges in any artistic endeavor lies not in the scarcity of inspiration but rather in the deficit of courage. Courage empowers us to confront the fears that hinder our progress. Our inherent instinct for preservation often means we instinctively shy away from concepts perceived as risky and hesitate when transformation is warranted. The narrative of our world is tightly interwoven with our biases; our stories and prejudices are inextricably linked. Storytelling can be instrumental in dismantling these biases, unveiling potentialities that stretch beyond our current viewpoints.

Bias tends to dissuade us from experiences that could challenge our preconceived standpoints. Over-reliance on our existing viewpoints engenders a divide between the "human" and the "machine," a bias that strives to dominate the narrative, devoid of a more comprehensive understanding of human and machine entities. This dependence on a purely human perspective can lead us to display bias and, in extreme cases, allow our biases to control us completely. The human perspective gives rise to its unique set of biases which are analyzed, critiqued, and eventually assimilated. Our biases constantly risk distorting our perceptions, diverting us away from an accurate understanding of ourselves and our world.[2] Instead, we are prone to adopting the worldview of the "machine" without any scrutiny. If faith in the machine implies something tangible, faith in a fixed point denotes faith in the void.

No one can profess to be entirely free from bias, even if we like to believe otherwise. Bias is deeply ingrained in us because we inhabit a world that historically perpetuates it.[3] Even our language, suffused with bias, continues this trend. This concealed truth ingrained in our language is a fascinating realization, though it does not constitute the mainstream perspective in our society. It is vital to stay conscious of our biases and to convey this consciousness to others. Doing so will allow us to expand the borders of our understanding and remain open to novel insights.

5.3 ARTIFICIAL INTELLIGENCE CHALLENGES

The unspoken reality, a fact too significant to overlook, is that the challenge in designing AI-generated images is not rooted in the limitations of the AI itself. Instead, it is situated within the human domain—specifically, the quest to communicate artistic intent effectively. Often, explorations in image generation via neural networks stumble due to insubstantial prompts, which lack the necessary depth and precision to provoke a meaningful artistic reaction. Typical prompts such as "a wounded ballerina by Francis Bacon" or "a building in the style of Gaudi" do not provide enough substance for the system to realize its potential fully.

To truly unlock the capacities of AI and allow it to excel in the creative realm, the human element must elevate to greater heights in terms of intent, poetic articulation, and ambition. A fundamental shift in our approach to art-making becomes necessary under these

FIGURE 5.4 Sculpture made of concrete, in the style of Mark Catesby, Antonio Mancini, François Boquet, and with hints of Antonio Gaudi, wood, monumental architecture.

conditions. It requires us to unlearn traditional methodologies and welcome the opportunities offered by the collaboration with AI. This partnership calls for us to venture into unknown territories, challenge the confines of creativity, and strive for unparalleled excellence in our artistic pursuits. Fundamentally, this shift tests our comprehension of artistic authorship and the artist's role (see Figure 5.4). It provokes us to reassess the age-old wisdom that artistic prowess is exclusive to human creativity. Instead, it encourages us to view the computer as a co-contributor—an ally in the artistic process. By accepting this perspective, we embark on a journey that transcends the boundaries of individual human potential, granting ourselves access to a vast realm of computational power and algorithmic brilliance.

The collaboration between humans and AI in the sphere of art bears profound implications. It forces us to re-examine the concept of artistic genius as it is no longer solely attributed to the individual artist. Instead, it emerges from the synergistic interaction between human creativity and machine intelligence. Designing AI-generated images reveals a deep-seated existential journey as it pushes us to face our limitations as human creators, compelling us to evolve and refine our artistic intent. The true power of AI lies not merely in its technical prowess but also in its capacity to kindle within us a flame of inspiration—an impetus for pushing the boundaries of human imagination. Embarking on this collaborative journey with AI, we can transcend traditional artistic paradigms, pioneer new artistic horizons, and redefine the essence of being an artist.

5.4 PARTNERING WITH ARTIFICIAL INTELLIGENCE

Consider a situation where we instruct an AI system to "visualize a radical-centric design for a sectional couch." As the system iterates and refines its creations, it progressively produces outputs that are closer to our conceptualization of what constitutes radical-centric design (Figure 5.5). With regular and intentional engagement, we can direct the system toward generating outcomes that align more accurately with our artistic vision. The structure and intent harnessed by the neural network can be attuned to various components and elements crucial for an effective and impactful representation. By actively curating the images we decide to retain, merge, or enhance, we exercise influence over the final results, steering them toward our envisioned outcome. Consequently, our vision is a directive force shaping the system's ensuing manifestations (see Figure 5.6).

The merger of human intent with the capabilities of a neural network presents an unparalleled avenue for artistic expression and design. It blurs the boundaries distinguishing human creativity from machine-enabled creations, forging a symbiotic relationship that capitalizes on the strengths of both entities. As we persistently push the boundaries of neural network technology, we initiate a collaborative process with these algorithms, enabling us to actualize previously considered ideas beyond the realm of possibility.

The dynamic interaction between human intent and AI algorithms enables us to shape and fine-tune the creations birthed from these networks, bringing our artistic visions within reach. This synergy between humans and machine heralds a transformative era in

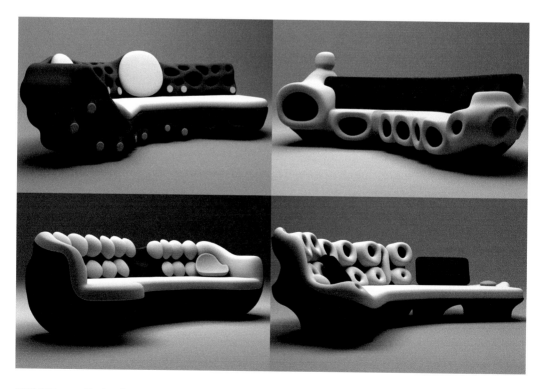

FIGURE 5.5   Radical-centric design proposals for a sectional couch.

FIGURE 5.6   A radical-centric design sectional couch, final selection.

artistic expression, compelling us to reassess our understanding of creativity and redefine the extent of what is attainable within the domains of art and design. As we leverage AI's capabilities to complement and extend human creativity, we stand at the precipice of a new frontier where the human-artistic potential is expanded and reshaped in ways previously unimagined.

5.5 IMPACT OF AI ON ARTISTIC EXPRESSION

As discussed in Chapter 10, Intention Articulation, Manifestation) of this book, art can be considered as a trinity of intention, articulation, and manifestation. The human potential for such articulation is well-established. However, the crucial task remains: providing AI with the appropriate platform for its form of self-expression—a responsibility that falls squarely on our shoulders.

Embarking on this task propels us into a philosophical abyss, where we are left contemplating the essence of creativity, the soul of art, and the boundaries of human agency. As we recognize AI's budding role as a creative powerhouse, we are impelled to reassess our notions of artistic ownership and the artist's role in the act of creation. The realization dawns on us that the creative act expands beyond the confines of human consciousness, encompassing contributions from machine intelligence.

Recognizing AI's creative capabilities pushes us to reflect deeply on the intricate interplay between intention, articulation, and manifestation. Questions arise: how does AI forms intentions? Is it capable of nurturing ambitions, dreams, or direction? These inquiries challenge us to scrutinize AI's cognitive processes and ability to generate meaningful states. We are tasked with designing algorithms and systems that grant AI the ability to navigate the vast landscape of human desires, feelings, and visions, enabling it to craft its unique artistic narrative.

The concept of artistic articulation, translating abstract thoughts and emotions into tangible or perceptible forms, becomes an intriguing enigma in the AI context. How can we furnish AI with the necessary tools and frameworks to articulate its intentions in ways that resonate with human sensibilities? This undertaking pushes us to dive into the complexities of human communication, perception, and aesthetic appreciation, striving to bridge the divide between the AI-generated output and its human interpreter. It demands the creation of interfaces that foster substantive dialogue and collaboration between AI and humans, allowing for a convergence of perspectives and a co-creation of artistic expressions.

A fascinating new dimension to the creative process emerges when it comes to the manifestation of art through AI. How can AI actualize its artistic concepts into tangible or perceptible forms? The challenge lies in equipping AI with the relevant training data, algorithms, and feedback mechanisms necessary for refining and perfecting its creations. By promoting an iterative and adaptable learning process, we empower AI to engage in an ongoing dialogue with its work, progressively refining and evolving its output to align with its intended artistic vision.

Artistic expression is an enigmatic and vast phenomenon, resistant to rigid structuring yet embracing inherent ambiguity that allows for varied interpretations. This dance between the ethereal realm of ideas and the tangible world of creation results in a manifestation—a painting, a sculpture, a melody, a performance—that carries the imprints of the artist's creative journey. This physical outcome extends an invitation into the artist's internal world, letting the audience engage with the artist's intent and providing a glimpse into their soul.

The marriage of intention, articulation, and manifestation unfolds artistic expression as an exploration of human creativity and the human condition. It transcends barriers, cultures, and time, appealing to our collective humanity and eliciting universally resonant yet deeply personal emotions. Artistic expression captures the core of the human experience—a pursuit of understanding, connection, and self-expression.

By reflecting on the depth and philosophical nature of artistic expression, we grow to appreciate its transformative power. It serves as a haven for introspection, a stimulus for societal change, and a conduit for dialogue among individuals, communities, and cultures. By transcending language and societal constraints, artistic expression becomes a universal language—a testament to the human spirit and our inherent capacity to create, communicate, and connect. In its interaction with AI, artistic expression marks the inception of a new era where traditional human creativity merges with technological innovation to redefine the limits of artistic possibility (Figure 5.7).[4]

FIGURE 5.7 Unlikely photos series: A chipmunk in a coffee cup.

5.6 CLOSING THOUGHTS: CONVERGENCE

Art and design converge in a captivating interplay of creativity and human perception, particularly in the context of AI and machine learning. Both art and design aim to stir emotions, spark thoughts, or address issues, forming bonds and conversations with viewers or consumers. AI tools and machines facilitate the realization of human-crafted experiences or objects, materializing the intentions of their human counterparts.

The evolving perception of effective design recognizes human perception's subjective and situational nature. Designers are called upon to integrate the diverse aspects of human experience in their creative process, delving deeper into the understanding of human perception. As AI becomes integral to crafting human-designed objects, it challenges traditional authorship and creative control concepts. Philosophical dilemmas arise as the lines distinguishing humans from machines become indistinct. These dilemmas invite us to challenge our preconceived ideas and re-evaluate the essence of artistic expression.

The interconnection of art, design, and AI illuminates the transformative influence of technology in the creative sphere. AI's computational abilities and capacity to learn from vast datasets open fresh pathways for artistic exploration and design innovation. By analyzing and interpreting artistic styles and patterns, AI provides insightful inspiration for artists and designers, expanding the boundaries of creativity.

Deep philosophical inquiries emerge as neural networks blur the distinction between human and machine outputs, questioning the concepts of authorship and originality in this context. Can machines participate in the creative act, or is art purely a human phenomenon? Can the notions of authorship and creativity expand to encompass the collaborative ventures of humans and algorithms?

A fascinating dynamic unfolds in the interplay between human intentions and AI algorithms. The neural network becomes a channel for human aspirations, materializing creative desires. However, the algorithm contributes its unique interpretative ability, blending human inputs with computational reasoning, resulting in an output that merges human aspiration and machine logic. This collaboration between humans and machines presents untapped opportunities for artistic exploration, challenging conventional creation methods and venturing into novel realms of imagination. Surrendering control to the algorithm and embracing its unpredictable output transforms the neural network into an active participant, infusing its neural pathways, training data, and algorithmic biases. It redefines creativity as a collective endeavor, where human intention intertwines with AI algorithms.

Guiding the network's outputs allows a slice of human creative vision to flow into the system, paving the way for unprecedented artistic exploration. Such circumstances prompt a reassessment of traditional creation methods and encourage ventures into unexplored territories of imagination.

NOTES

1. NB: At its core, creative intent is the catalyst that ignites the flame of any creative endeavor. It represents the primary impetus or the foundational motivation that incites an artist to embark on a creative voyage. This intent can encompass many purposes, from expressing intricate emotions and communicating a specific message to experimenting with avant-garde ideas that deviate from established norms. Creative intent is profoundly individualistic and unique to each artist, woven from the threads of the artist's personal experiences, perspectives, convictions, and values. Hence, creative intent extends beyond the confines of the artist's consciousness and materializes in their work, offering insights into their inner psyche and viewpoints. Contrary to being a fleeting spark, creative intent is an enduring force that persistently shapes the creative process. It dictates aspects ranging from the selection of medium, incorporation of symbols and metaphors, subtleties of style and technique, to even the strategy an artist employs to interact with their audience. As a result, creative intent plays an instrumental role in determining the final embodiment of the work, swaying its aesthetic appeal, contextual relevance, and potential for interpretation. Despite its pivotal role, creative intent is not a static entity. It is a malleable construct that evolves and adapts as the work evolves. It is influenced by the artist's interaction with their chosen medium and the emergence of new insights and concepts throughout the creative journey. This dynamic characteristic of creative intent contributes depth and complexity to the creative process, rendering it a compelling dimension for investigation in art and creativity.

2. Cognitive biases are essentially mental shortcuts or "heuristics" that have the potential to warp our thinking, shape our beliefs, and influence our daily decisions and judgments. These biases can contribute to flawed reasoning and foster distorted beliefs, such as conspiracy theories. For instance, confirmation bias signifies our propensity to accept information that validates our pre-existing beliefs readily. Through this bias, individuals favor data that aligns with and reinforces their established viewpoints or beliefs. Retrieved from https://www.verywellmind.com/cognitive-biases-distort-thinking-2794763.

3. For instance, race or racial ideology is deeply embedded in our historical and cultural fabric. In many respects, it forms the crux of our political landscape. Racial dimensions intricately mold our identities. Unconscious biases, often stemming from this racial underpinning, can prevent individuals and businesses from realizing their utmost potential and inadvertently maintain cycles of disparity. Robert Fieseler, Exposing Bias: Race and Racism in America, Harvard Extension School, 2021.

4. **Artistic expression** represents the creative mechanism whereby an artist uses art as a medium to express their thoughts, feelings, and ideologies. This process can manifest itself in a myriad of forms, encompassing the visual arts—like painting, sculpting, and photography—performing arts—including music, dance, and theater—and literary arts, including poetry and prose. The ultimate aim of artistic expression is to transmit a specific message or to elicit an emotional reaction from its audience.

CHAPTER 6

Maximizing Creativity

6.1 CREATIVE INTENTION

Creating with intent means *creating with awareness*. Rather than doing things out of habit, we make ourselves fully present in what we do now.[1] The creative intention is about engaging in the act of creation with full awareness instead of mindless habit. An active presence is required, one that entails being wholly absorbed in the process rather than being sidetracked by extraneous thoughts or concerns.

Designing with intent involves a keen understanding of the context from which we are creating. Consciousness does not stem from our physical surroundings but from our comprehension of the creative process. It is about being wholly present, immersing ourselves in creating, unbound by specific methodologies or efforts. The consciousness of creating with intention leads to a heightened awareness that surpasses merely focusing on creation but connects us with the undercurrent of intent. It allows us to perceive our creative endeavors in a holistic manner, in real time.

The necessity of intention in creation is vital; without it, we risk mindlessly creating, leading to an absence of purposeful consciousness. Conscious creation isn't just about having an intention but about manifesting that intention into reality. It allows us to be fully cognizant of what we're creating, deeply embedding awareness into the process.

Creating with awareness and consciousness are not identical, as consciousness nurtures awareness. Therefore, it is essential not to misconstrue our intention to create as the same as the act of creating with intention. Intentions ought to transcend mere awareness. When we direct our focus intentionally, we aim to create with consciousness. The nexus of creativity lies in the profound connection between consciousness and awareness. However, consciousness cannot generate awareness, as it is awareness itself. Deliberate awareness derived from creating without consciousness guides us back to the primordial state of awareness, unadulterated by consciousness.

DOI: 10.1201/9781003450139-9

6.2 THE AMBIGUITY OF CONCEALED INTENT

Our understanding of art is profoundly flawed because we look at manifestations that could be accidental with respect to the artist's original intent; we do not know what the real intent was. This comment is specifically adept when discussing modern art from impressionism to what followed. We look at a cubist painting and we might think we know the intent, but all we see is the manifestation of this skill the artist could demonstrate while articulating their intent. We do not know what the original intent was because what happens between intent and manifestation is the articulation phase. As stated in previous chapters of this book, several biases play a role in this articulation phase.

The definition of fine art is art made for aesthetic and intellectual reasons which connects well with the fine art produced by Mid-Journey and other text-generated images produced by neural networks.[2] Art serves multiple purposes, such as creating impressions, inducing joy, asserting power, or simply being the artist's pleasure. An artist primarily aims to provoke an emotional response through their work, though the showcased talent may not always align seamlessly with their intended message. Artistic communication can often resort to generic descriptions ("beautiful") or simplistic phrases that may demonstrate technical skill but not necessarily the depth of the artist's purpose.

Thus, the artwork we encounter often demonstrates an artist's skill rather than the embodiment of their intent. The genuine intent behind a piece may not be readily apparent—it transcends the art piece itself, the individual talents used, or explicit verbalization. The real intent is often nestled within the articulation phase of artistic expression. The concept of "intentional fallacy," as put forth by Wimsatt and Beardsley in their philosophical discourse on art, underscores the challenges of interpreting art from the audience's perspective. The pervasive opacity in such expression has led philosophers to label attempts at interpreting art through the lens of the artist's intent as somewhat fallacious. Wimsatt and Beardsley argue that deciphering an artwork's meaning or value based on the artist's intended expression is futile and detracts from the artwork's inherent merit. Consequently, they advocate for the separation of the artist's intent from the interpretation and evaluation process, going so far as to deem any effort to relate the two as misguided. This presents a unique perceptual dilemma for art consumers tasked with deciphering and appraising the meaning and worth of an artwork.[3]

It is crucial to clarify the distinction between intent and articulation when it comes to art produced through artificial intelligence. Artistic intent does not merely mean "an intention to produce something of good quality" or "an intention to portray a positive image." The intent is merely indicative of a goal, not a definitive measure of successful skill execution. Comprehending artistic intent requires more than the articulation of intent—it requires additional factors that provide context and meaning.

Artistic expression is inherently purposeful—it represents the application of a skill. While this skill might be evident in the art piece, the full manifestation of the artistic intent requires clear articulation and purposeful application. Artistic expression can exist without an explicit intent in the articulation or expression phases, but it is not devoid of purpose. The purpose is embedded in the intent—an intent to express the intent. This clarity of purpose is vital for understanding how a particular artistic skill can further evolve and resolve complex issues in discourse and reasoning.

Artists typically engage multiple skills during the articulation phases, indicating that artistry is rarely founded on a singular ability. The utility of skill is intrinsically connected to its purpose and effective articulation. This principle holds in all forms of artistic discourse and articulation. No matter what is the result of the articulation phase, the intent and its articulation remain central to the artistic process. The intent usually serves as the pivotal point in the articulation process.

Skill development primarily occurs in the articulation phase, where the artist contemplates delivering skills and effectively communicates them. An undue focus on delivery can overshadow the intent, which should never be obscured or lost in speech, articulation, or interpretation. A successful articulation hinges on the emotional resonance of the artwork in its context and its impact on the audience. Artistry is more than a means of delivery, it is the engine driving a purposeful expression.

6.3 INTENT AND SKILL IN IMAGE GENERATION

Creating art based on intention is invariably constrained by one's skill set. Regardless of an artist's range of expertise, the limitations inherent in their skills can restrict their scope of expression. For instance, an artist's training, educational background, preferred medium, or tools used may confine them to a specific art style. Our human nature also limits our capacity to conceive and appreciate art. Artists are not bound by their tastes but by their innate abilities to perceive and understand art. Thus, an artist's creative output is inherently influenced by their intrinsic perception of art rather than being restricted to specific styles.

The way viewers interpret a piece of art is dictated by what the artist intends to convey. In this case, perception is not influenced by objective biases introduced during the articulation phase but by the viewer's understanding of the artist's intent. This understanding fosters the emotional connection integral to appreciating art. Although such perceptions may not affect the objective value of an artwork, they could influence its reception among critics.

Artistic perception does not follow a linear path. Emotions induced during the articulation phase can be evoked by reproductions of renowned artworks, underscoring the importance of the synthesis phase. In this phase, the rules governing object placement in a composition are driven by the artist's intent, solidifying the outcome. While evaluating art, are we looking for indications of the artist's intention or seeking an abstract structure? The former leads to a subjective interpretation, while the latter offers a more objective approach. However, when assessing the skill in the form to determine intent, what exactly are we examining—the intent or the form? If we focus on the outcome, what should our evaluation be based on? The purpose of art is not just self-expression, it is also a testament to human achievement.[4]

When we utilize artificial intelligence (AI)-based neural networks to generate images based on intent, our understanding of that intent ultimately defines the limits. The moment we start creating art with intention and thought, we are as free to be subjective, critical, and self-referential as any artist before us. Artistic expression is inherently a sub-jective perception that challenges conventional norms and pushes artists to their creative boundaries.

Our comprehension of art is not solely derived from superficial reactions but from a more profound philosophical exploration of what art means to us as individuals. Art is emotive, subjective, and emotional. If we disregard these inherent values when producing art, our creation lacks the human touch and becomes mechanical. We engage with art because of our interest in beauty, and we perceive this beauty through our lens.

The artist's intended portrayal and the principles guiding their conception of beauty are often incidental to their creative intent. Art is an effort to unearth beauty in overlooked situations or objects. It is a conscious attempt to communicate our ignored perceptions because external appearances dominate our understanding of the universe.

By studying art, we acknowledge that beauty lies not in the object itself or its meaning but in our perception. Beauty is an unexpected, spontaneous consequence of our mind's manifestation (see Figure 6.1). The beauty of a painting transcends any other emotion, and when we find something beautiful, we see that beauty reflected in everything else. This inherent beauty in art is inexplicable and needs no analysis—it simply exists. This beauty is spontaneous, universal, and profound—something to be contemplated and understood.[5]

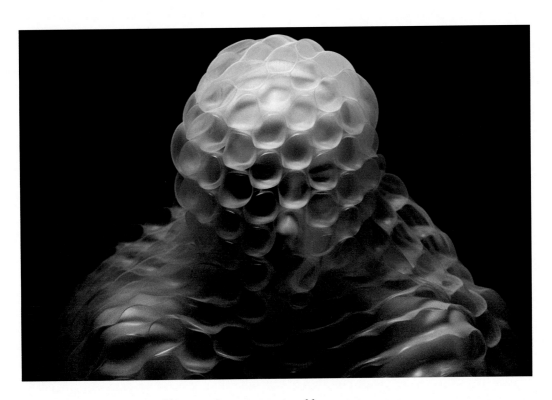

FIGURE 6.1   The incidental beauty of a transparent rubber gown.

Art allows us to appreciate beauty in all its forms—through sight, smell, taste, and touch. However, this is not enough; we constantly seek more. Our desire to comprehend beauty transforms it into art, and our understanding of beauty deepens in the process of creating art. This continuous exploration is a testament to our relentless effort to understand beauty and communicate our overlooked perceptions. Artistic beauty is the objective process of observing.

6.4 INTENT AND INDIVIDUAL BIAS

AI, particularly in the form of neural networks, has become a liberating tool for individuals, enabling them to bypass the constraints of their personal biases when generating art. These biases often manifest as predispositions toward certain forms, colors, and even the boundaries set by an individual's skills. The creative process is inherently limited by our ability to materialize our intentions, with our skills often serving as the critical determinant of this articulation.

Consider a scenario where four artists are given the same task: to create a piece depicting a dining set, complete with a bottle of wine, a baguette, a few plates, and a glass filled with red wine. Although based on the same brief, the resultant artworks will be noticeably different. This disparity arises from the artists' unique interpretations, guided by their skills and biases toward form, line, and color.

Conversely, if we entrust the same task to four non-artists, their creations project broader meanings, demonstrating expressiveness beyond their individual perceptions and inherent biases. These images, which could range from abstract to intricate, are a testament to the myriad forms of expressions that art communicates.

AI transforms our creative abilities, allowing for more precise and personalized interaction with our creative concepts, leading to personal transformation and organizational growth.[6] An example is how AI facilitates a dynamic exploration of the concept of "Earth." Traditional explanations would be grounded in our personal experiences and cultural contexts. With AI, however, we can glean a multifaceted understanding incorporating scientific facts, philosophical perspectives, and cultural interpretations derived from various data points.

This nuanced perspective could be further enriched by engaging AI in a dialogic process, prompting it to respond as if embodying the entity "Earth." The responses, echoing everything from the Earth's geographic attributes to abstract cultural significance, would offer a unique perspective on Earth. AI empowers us to navigate this conceptual landscape more dynamically. We can engage with the AI, prompting it with the question, "What is the Earth?" In doing so, we pave the way for an answer not restricted to a monolithic viewpoint. This multi-pronged understanding rendered by AI offers depth and breadth to the conception of "Earth" that would otherwise prove challenging to obtain independently (see Figure 6.2).

AI's ability to generate such diverse responses empowers us to see concepts from various angles, enriching our understanding and enabling us to challenge our own biases. The creative output is not a mere reproduction of existing data. Advanced AI systems like GPT-4 generate coherent, contextually relevant responses based on initial

FIGURE 6.2   What is Earth?

input, pushing the boundaries of our creativity and understanding in ways we've never seen before.

6.5 AMPLIFYING INTENT THROUGH ENHANCED ARTICULATION

The emergence of AI has heralded an era of revolutionary communication. We now witness AI's progression to a stage where it can conceptualize and articulate ideas in human language, mirroring our modes of comprehension. This milestone is a significant advancement in developing AI systems attuned to the intricacies of human thought and emotion. Traditionally deemed an exclusively human domain, art involves articulating intent through language—a process molded and chiseled by our innate creativity. However, this creative articulation can often be hampered by personal idiosyncrasies or unfamiliarity with the broad spectrum of cultural or linguistic norms and conventions.

Art is fundamentally an exercise in perception and creation—it breathes life into unseen or abstract visions. This dynamic process of interpreting and materializing intent constitutes the core of artistic creation. Both art and AI serve as crucial conduits for transmuting our thoughts and intentions into perceivable forms. The advent of AI introduces a potent ability to bridge the chasm between intent and its concrete manifestation, enabling us to articulate our emotions, aspirations, ideas, and passions with amplified precision and depth.

In the contemporary era, the concepts that individuals wish to articulate have become complex. Abstract philosophical concepts are often transmuted into a contextual narrative, drawing on intellectual prowess. This narrative might be coupled with a specific color palette or emotional tone to evoke a particular mood or convey a nuanced intent. These processes underline the potential of AI to facilitate the articulation of complex

FIGURE 6.3 Enhanced articulation: A woman covered with a pattern of cells, in the style of translucent layers, futuristic organic, shot on 70 mm, interplay of light and color, made of rubber, slumped/draped.

ideas, opening an expanded platform for self-expression and allowing our creativity to proliferate unbounded. This advancement does not indicate the limitation of human creativity, it rather enhances the scope and depth of our expressive capabilities (see Figure 6.3).

As we delve deeper into the confluence of art and AI, we must honor the creative intentions of individuals expressing themselves through art and language. However, we can draw insights from myriad art forms to inform AI systems, enabling them to emulate and reproduce the sentiments encapsulated in art through mediums of language, design, and aesthetics. The synthesis of art with AI may produce outcomes deviating from the artist's initial intent. Hence, distinguishing between the primal intent and its final articulation becomes paramount. The potential influence of this precise "articulation" on the perceived quality or effectiveness of artwork presents an intriguing prospect for exploration and for the expansion of the relationship between artists and AI technology.[7]

AI technologies such as DeepMind demonstrate promising capabilities in articulating intent with exceptional clarity. By analyzing and learning from inputs encapsulating a clear intent, AI can assist in crafting expressions that resonate more profoundly and impactfully (see Figure 6.4). In addition, it opens the gateway to support individuals in aligning their intent with its articulation, particularly when their language skills might constrain their ability to express themselves effectively.[8]

FIGURE 6.4   Enhanced articulation: a white motorcycle on the background of a grayish surface, in the style of hard surface modeling, energy-charged, rounded, electric, dark cyan and dark black.

6.6 DECONSTRUCTING THE DIALECTICS OF ART AND TECHNOLOGY: AI AND HUMAN CREATIVITY

In the interconnecting spheres of art and technology, intriguing questions abound; chief among them is the comparative worth of human-created art and its AI-produced counterpart. Such comparisons provoke us to re-examine our understanding of the innate biases and limitations embedded in human artistry and contrast this with AI's ostensibly "unbiased" nature, particularly neural networks primed on textual cues.

The functionality of neural networks might be likened to a dog eagerly awaiting the command to pursue a ball. Here, the ball symbolizes the prompt or instruction and the act of chasing epitomizes the subsequent response of the neural network. The extent of your ball throw—in other words, the complexity of your prompt—directly influences the expansiveness of the network's output. This process could be visualized as launching a ball and having the dog return a diamond, with the diamond encapsulating an output that transcends initial expectations (see Figure 6.5).

In traditional human artistry, every form, line, and color bear the stamp of the artist's personal inclinations, technical prowess, and potential constraints. This understanding has reshaped our perception of art history as the artist's authentic intent often veils itself in obscurity—leading us to infer intent through the lens of the actual artwork.

Art, when filtered through the human perception lens, is subjected to a multitude of biases, complemented by varying layers of skill or the absence thereof. This results in a

FIGURE 6.5 Enhanced articulation: A person in a dark environment, in the style of translucent geometries, ready-made objects, color photography, draped, soft light, wrapped.

depiction often diverging from the original intent. Contrarily, a neural network decodes a prompt into an image with clinical precision unimpeded by biases or limitations induced by fear or skill deficiency. The output of a neural network, given this context, is unrestricted and has the potential to embody the initial intent perfectly, contingent on the provided input.[9] However, it is imperative to recognize that while the AI's impartial and unrestricted rendering may yield extraordinary outcomes, it lacks the personal, emotive resonance quintessential to human artistry. Therefore, the question of value is not just a debate of technical skill or objectivity but also concerns the unique human essence that breathes life, emotion, and subjectivity into art.

AI-generated art pioneers unexplored creative territories, yet it does not compete with human art; instead, it exists in parallel. Each form of artistry brings distinctive strengths and insights to the ever-evolving tableau of creative expression. This coexistence broadens our collective understanding of art and its myriad interpretations, enriching the vibrancy and diversity of the artistic world.

6.7 CLOSING THOUGHTS: AMPLIFYING CREATIVE INTENT THROUGH GENERATIVE AI

Generative AI amplifies creative intent by serving as an innovative aid to artists. It offers insights and perspectives otherwise unseen, identifies trends and patterns, and proposes new concepts. This artist-AI relationship nurtures dynamic exchanges, driving art's evolution and extending beauty's limits. Creative intent is a deep commitment of artists, fueled by their tenacious quest to communicate beauty effectively. This journey is not only about artistic vision but also about the intricate interaction between aesthetics and metaphysics. Artists endeavor to convey beauty, going beyond mere physical existence. Aesthetics involves perceiving and conceptualizing the elements of our reality, while metaphysics delves into the theoretical realm of existence. In this context, generative AI is a potent tool instrumental in maximizing creative intent.

Aesthetics focuses on the sensory and emotional aspects of human experience. Artists use their creative skills to embody beauty, transforming their thoughts, emotions, and visions into their preferred medium. Generative AI, through its data analysis and pattern learning capabilities, can enhance and amplify human creativity. Using machine learning algorithms, artists can push past traditional aesthetic boundaries, explore their imaginative depths, and create a profound connection with their audience by surpassing the constraints of the physical world.

Generative AI has the potential to stimulate experimentation and unexpected discoveries. Artists can navigate unexplored territories and unveil new artistic possibilities by stepping away from traditional artistic conventions. AI algorithms can generate variations, juxtapositions, and combinations that may ignite inspiration and pave the way for unconventional approaches. Thus, generative AI enables artists to delve deeper into their creative process, urging them to embrace uncertainty and challenge established norms.

The effort to maximize creative intent and communicate beauty is deeply intertwined with philosophical and aesthetic pursuits. Generative AI, in its role of amplifying creative intent, helps expand the horizons of artistic expression. Aesthetics forms the bedrock of artistic expression, allowing artists to share their vision. Here, generative AI emerges as a compelling tool that can widen the scope of creativity, stimulate innovation, and unlock new vistas of beauty. Generative AI provides inspiration, fosters inventive approaches, and encourages collaboration. By capitalizing on the synergy between human imagination and generative AI, artists can embark on a transformative journey that captivates the human spirit. This harmonious partnership fosters a quest for aesthetic excellence, enriching our collective cultural heritage and adding new dimensions.

NOTES

1. https://feelgoodfibers.com/what-does-it-mean-to-create-with-intent/.
2. The definition of fine art: *drawings, paintings, and sculptures that are admired for their beauty and have no practical use.* Retrieved from https://dictionary.cambridge.org/dictionary/english/fine-art.
3. Dale Jacquette, "Art, Expression, Perception and Intentionality," *Journal of Aesthetics and Phenomenology*, vol. 1:1, 63–90 (2014). Retrieved from https://doi.org/10.2752/2053933 9XX14005942183973.
4. René Magritte, "Art evokes the mystery without which the world would not exist," Why The Arts Matter. National Endowment for the Arts. Retrieved from https://www.arts.gov/stories/blog/2015/why-arts-matter.
5. As George Santayana has observed, "*A beauty not perceived is a pleasure not felt. Beauty is pleasure objectified. All pleasures are intrinsic and positive values, but all pleasures are not perceptions of beauty. The philosophy of beauty is a theory of values. Values spring from the*

immediate and inexplicable reaction of vital impulse and from the irrational part of our nature. Preference is ultimately irrational. Beauty is value positive and intrinsic; beauty is pleasure regarded as the quality of a thing," The Sense of Beauty (1896). Retrieved from http://www.gutenberg.org/ebooks/26842. Released 2008.

6. Accenture research indicates that 12% of companies have sufficiently developed their AI capabilities to realize notable growth and organizational transformation. Such companies, termed "AI Achievers," credit an average of 30% of their entire revenue to AI. Remarkably, even before the pandemic in 2019, these entities reported an average revenue growth rate 50% higher than their contemporaries. They further distinguish themselves in customer service and sustainability realms. Predictions based on our machine learning assessments forecast the proportion of AI Achievers to escalate dramatically, potentially soaring from the existing 12% to 27% by 2024. The progression in AI competence has become an inevitable milestone for every sector, institution, and leader. Retrieved from https://www.accenture.com/ca-en/insights/artificial-intelligence/ai-maturity-and-transformation.

7. According to research, AI technology has significantly influenced interactive art, shifting the focus from standalone audiovisual experiences to integrated artistic expressions. These expressions are characterized by high interactivity, dynamism, and emotional resonance, deriving inspiration from the study of natural human behavior, multisensory integration, and intelligence. Yan Shen and Fang Yu, "The Influence of Artificial Intelligence on Art Design in the Digital Age," *Scientific Programming*, vol. 2021, Article ID 4838957, 2021. Retrieved from https://doi.org/10.1155/2021/4838957.

8. DeepMind, an arm of Alphabet, Inc., develops versatile artificial intelligence (AI) technology, commonly referred to as Google DeepMind. This AI learns by processing raw image data (pixels) and building on experience. It employs a method known as deep learning on a specialized network called a convolutional neural network, combined with a reinforcement learning approach called Q-learning. Convolutional neural networks are notable for their enhanced abilities in handling images, speech, or audio signals compared to other network types. Retrieved from https://www.techtarget.com/whatis/definition/DeepMind.

9. A neural network's output is shaped by the input data it receives and the algorithms and parameters used to process that data. These networks are designed to identify patterns and make predictions based on the data they have been trained on. In theory, the output of a neural network could perfectly reflect the original intent of the input data, provided that the input data is of high quality and relevance. However, it is crucial to acknowledge that no model is flawless, and there may be limitations or biases in the training data or the algorithms. While the notion that a neural network's output could embody the initial intent perfectly is appealing, no sources directly support this claim. It is essential to remember that neural networks are intricate systems influenced by numerous factors. Retrieved from https://www.deeplearning.ai/ai-notes/initialization/index.html.

CHAPTER 7

From Creators to Narrators

7.1 THE SHIFT TO A NARRATED ECONOMY

In a majority of developed nations, most individuals now primarily operate as knowledge workers. Our activities are dominantly lodged in the digital sphere, moving steadily away from physical exertion. With the escalating role of artificial intelligence (AI) in knowledge-based tasks, our roles are undergoing a metamorphosis from creators to narrators. Rather than laboring over detailed designs for a house, for example, we articulate our ideal dwelling, and a software system translates our desires into an architectural blueprint. This shift is not a future possibility but a current reality. AI systems navigate our cars, filter our e-mails during commutes, and participate in the fabrication of our vehicles. As we delve deeper into our digital innovations, these algorithmic narrators fulfill our practical necessities.

In a world where AI is poised to supplant a substantial portion of our physical labor and potentially dominate the wheels of our economy, ideas, and innovations, it is vital to view this transition not as a threat but as an opportunity. We should lean into our evolving roles as narrators, allowing AI to take over creation based on our articulated intentions.

As we make our intentions explicit, they assemble into a narrative. Our forthcoming developmental leap with technology implicates harnessing AI to aid our metamorphosis from creators to narrators. By co-authoring this new narrative, we contribute to a collective story open to many interpretations. The concept of shared authorship paves the way for an exciting new chapter in human history.

As our roles evolve, we will pivot from manufacturing-centric to narrative-driven mindsets. A large segment of this narrative will encompass human experiences, providing a stage to herald the next epoch of human evolution through a human-centric design approach. The effectiveness of this transition rests on our capacity to adapt from being creators to becoming proficient narrators. The more eloquently we can narrate our intentions, the more effectively AI systems can bring them to life, paving the way for a story-driven world.

DOI: 10.1201/9781003450139-10

7.2 ARCHITECTING EXPERIENCES

In this evolving narrative-centric society, the application of human-centered design becomes vitally significant.[1] As we transition from the traditional role of creators to narrators, we are spinning tales that breathe life, meaning, and purpose into our creations. Human-centered design implores us to probe deeper into individual needs and aspirations, prioritizing their experiences in our creative undertakings. The evolution from mere creators to narrative architects demands mastery in intertwining form, function, and experience. Adopting this perspective enables us to design products, systems, and services that profoundly resonate with the human experience, kindling emotional connections and empowering individuals to shape their own stories actively (see Figure 7.1).

The potency of narrative is indispensable not only to individual interpretations but also to shaping our collective progression. Human-centered design allows us to conceive experiences that transcend aesthetics and functionality, infusing narratives that uniquely define these creations. Within this narrative-focused world, the story behind a product or service becomes intrinsically linked to its form and function, thereby influencing how users perceive and interact with it.

Designers' roles transcend the creation of visually appealing, efficient products. They become storytellers, embedding their creations with narratives that resonate with fundamental values and intentions. By incorporating meaningful stories into their designs, they can forge emotional connections with users, instilling a sense of belonging and comprehension. This comprehensive design approach motivates designers to consider the broader ramifications of their work, surpassing aesthetics and technicalities to incite societal transformation.

Narratives can break down barriers, bridge languages, and meld cultures, thus addressing universal facets of the human experience. Design experiences must cater to immediate needs

FIGURE 7.1   Model with a discrete wearable biofeedback device.

and champion long-term sustainability and well-being. As architects of experience, designers can harness narrative as an instrument for empathy, connectivity, and advancement. The stories we opt to relay should echo our shared values and contribute toward a more equitable, inclusive society. By endorsing empathy and understanding diverse viewpoints, human-centered design can serve as a social transformation and empowerment conduit, amplifying underrepresented voices and fostering narratives that celebrate our collective humanity.

As we venture into this new phase of human evolution, introspection, and critical assessment must underpin the human-centered design approach. Designers must scrutinize the narratives they sculpt to guarantee inclusivity, ethical congruence, and respect for societal diversity. This narrative-driven model bears immense potential for change and also mandates responsibility in crafting narratives that embolden individuals and communities.[2] The transition to a story-driven world allows designers to evolve from creators to narrators. They are entrusted with shaping human-centered narratives that guide our engagement with products, systems, and services. Embracing this mindset equips designers to create experiences that hold meaning, resonate with users, and facilitate positive transformation. As we embark on this new chapter of storytelling and design, let us thread narratives that inspire, empower, and contribute to the ongoing evolution of humanity.

As our world becomes increasingly narrative-centric, the designer's role expands beyond mere creation, metamorphosing into a storyteller and curator of human experiences (see Figure 7.2). Our mission involves fostering a design process rooted in empathy,

FIGURE 7.2   A plate for the Bocuse d'Or competition with the main ingredient being monkfish and two vegetable garnishes placed on the tray and one in a "ragout" type garnish presented in a separate vegetable dish, showcasing a legume.

mindfulness, and introspection. By engaging profoundly with users, understanding their narratives, and empathizing with their needs, we can craft transformative narratives that enrich the human experience.[3]

This shift allows us to utilize design as a catalyst for positive societal change. We shape narratives that inspire, empower, and tie us to a prospective future. In this envisaged future, our shared narrative unfolds within a framework saturated with empathy, purpose, and authenticity, providing a compassionate and sincere testament to the human condition.

7.3 CO-CREATING A NEW NARRATIVE

In this time of accelerated technological advancement, it is imperative to regard technology as an instrumental, although inherently restricted, tool. While its role in sculpting our narratives and experiences is significant, it should not eclipse the essence or intent of these experiences. When we unite human intellect and technology in co-creation, a novel narrative materializes that surpasses individual confines, affording unique perspectives and interactions within our shared existence.

This narrative dismantles the traditional barriers that isolate the self from others, catalyzing a transition from an "I" to a "We" paradigm. Co-creation instigates narratives that reach beyond singular perspectives, employing technology as a catalyst to amplify our experiences without obfuscating their intrinsic substance. This process sparks a collective narrative that transcends the constraints of individualism, drawing on the communal wisdom accrued from diverse viewpoints.

As we traverse this unprecedented landscape, the reciprocal relationship between humans and machines becomes increasingly apparent. Technology augments our faculties, contributing to a narrative that might have otherwise remained unattainable. While it forms part of the narrative, it does not dictate it. The narrative birthed from this human-technology collaboration bears transformative potential across numerous domains, including education, governance, social justice, and environmental sustainability (see Figure 7.3).

This co-constructed narrative informs our collective consciousness, influencing our behaviors, convictions, and values, steering us toward a future harmonizing with our shared aspirations. It motivates us to transcend individual ambitions and advocates for a cooperative, empathetic modus operandi centered on communal well-being. The narrative underscores unity, shared accountability, and collaboration, guiding us toward a future conducive to harmony, innovation, and realizing our loftiest human potential. Consequently, as we co-construct this fresh narrative, we are not merely amplifying individual experiences but also shaping the path of our shared human voyage.

7.4 A HUMAN-TO-HUMAN NARRATIVE

In the myriad of potential roles technology can undertake in our co-constructed reality, its most momentous and overarching function is to enable a novel narrative of human-to-human interaction. Technology's power extends beyond unmatched connectivity and access to information; its true potency lies in its ability to bridge disparities, obliterate obstacles, and foster meaningful human connections. Herein, technology becomes a

FIGURE 7.3   Self-arranging autonomous seating.

catalyst for the evolution of human relations, engendering a narrative that exceeds geographical, cultural, and ideological confines.

Technology's global capacity to broadcast our stories, experiences, and perspectives enhances our collective voice. It allows us to foster connections with individuals once separated by vast distances or unfamiliarity, circumventing restrictions imposed by traditional communication avenues. In this respect, technology is an instrument for co-creating a narrative rooted in interconnectedness, collaboration, and mutual evolution.

Nevertheless, while journeying toward this novel human-to-human narrative, engaging with technology through a lens of reflection and introspection is imperative. We need to critically evaluate the impact of technology on our relationships, self-perception, and capacity for authentic connection. Although technology provides considerable opportunities for connection, it also challenges individuality, privacy, and genuineness. As we traverse the digital realm, we must do so mindfully, preserving our unique identities and cultivating profound connections that surpass the often-surface-level interactions associated with technology.

Technology's ethical dimensions must be scrutinized as we jointly create this new narrative of human interaction. The potential repercussions of our actions as we employ their power to shape our collective story need consideration. We must utilize technology in ways that champion social justice, inclusivity, and empathy. Rather than perpetuating existing disparities and reinforcing detrimental narratives, we must ensure that the narrative we construct empowers and uplifts everyone. An ethical and introspective approach to technology allows us to craft a narrative founded on compassion, understanding and shared advancement.

Technology is an enabler in the intricate fabric of human existence, empowering us to co-create a narrative surpassing past limitations. It invites exploring novel frontiers of connection, comprehension, and collective growth. As we navigate this landscape, it becomes imperative to engage with technology with philosophical depth and introspection, utilizing its power to interweave a narrative that respects our shared humanity, celebrates our diversity, and motivates us to shape a future brimming with compassion, wisdom, and a profound sense of interconnectedness.

7.5 GENERATIVE DESIGN AND GENERATIVE NARRATIVES

Generative design, a pioneering approach transforming the design and manufacturing sectors, harnesses the power of complex, nonlinear systems to cultivate unique personal experiences and craft profound meaning.[4] This method challenges traditional linear designs by employing algorithms to generate intricate patterns, a product of intricate interactions within the system rather than a result of simple rule-following.[5] These patterns heralded for their aesthetic appeal and compelling complexity, signify a departure from mere algorithmic construction to a confluence of artistic, naturalistic, and abstract outcomes.

In my view, generative design is not a function of AI; instead, it exists in its unique category. It leverages AI as an instrument rather than an objective, fusing it with human creativity to engender transformative outputs in design and manufacturing. This transformative approach incorporates collective user needs, personal experiences, and imaginative potential to imbue the design process with narratives. Through integrating visual properties across real, augmented, and virtual spaces, generative design fosters products deeply resonant with human experience (see Figure 7.4).

This paradigm shift in design heralds a creative renaissance, fostering the entry of innovative thinkers into the design space. Generative design breaks conventional design boundaries, merging human imagination with the capacity to produce evocative designs

FIGURE 7.4   A parametric inspired sectional couch.

that transcend established imagery and cultural norms. As such, generative systems stand poised to disrupt creative industries, sitting at the nexus of narrative construction and human sensory experience.

Generative design differentiates itself from AI-based systems in its capacity for narrative generation. While sophisticated AI systems may operate within existing stories (e.g., AI co-pilot systems function within predefined narratives), generative systems forge novel narrative pathways.[6] Upon absorbing narrative data, these systems create narratives imbued with more nuanced, intimate elements, reflecting the narrative nuances of their training data. This capability gives them dynamic control over the narrative process, distinguishing them from their AI counterparts (see Figure 7.5).

Viewing AI as a potential conduit for nonlinear, voluminous, and non-structural narratives, it is seen by many as an emerging storyteller. These narratives immerse the user, resonating with human consciousness and becoming integral to it. The core of these AI narrative creators is intelligent algorithms that interact with data and objects to produce complex storylines within specific environments. Despite this, creativity is primarily perceived as an exclusively human attribute.

However, with its maturing capabilities, generative design is beginning to challenge this perception. The demarcation between human and machine creativity becomes increasingly blurred as it capitalizes on AI's ability to generate narratives connecting with human emotions. Generative design brings novel and unexpected elements to life in its narratives,

FIGURE 7.5   A model wears a white veil made of thread, softbox lighting, Tintoretto, colorful figures, organic geometry.

sparking greater user engagement and elevating the user experience. By forging a new genre of storytelling, it redefines creative boundaries, solidifying its status as a trailblazer in design and narrative creation.

7.6 CONTEMPLATING AN AI-FACILITATED WORLD: THE EVOLUTION OF HUMAN NARRATIVES

Consider a future dominated by the relentless collection of data and the delivery of personalized, transformative experiences expertly crafted through the formidable power of AI. This framework encapsulates the essence of generative design technology—a revolutionary approach in human-centric design that employs AI's potential to create custom experiences for individual users.

Standing at the threshold of this profound shift in design technology, we must consider the potential impacts these emergent advancements could have on our collective narratives. To navigate this transformative era successfully, we must ensure our shared stories demonstrate adaptability, allowing us to incorporate and evolve alongside these emerging technologies. We are tasked with reimagining our stories in a world increasingly suffused with AI's ubiquitous influence.

Humanity's collective story is fluid and rapidly changing. We live within a vast web of narratives, each unfolding in real time and birthing countless realities. These "worlds" we occupy can be concrete and tangible, while at other times, they are spun from the threads of our imaginations. Seeing this universe of narratives through the prism of AI envisions a cohesive, interconnected network fostering empathy, mutual recognition, and the collective experience of storytelling. The narratives birthed within this innovative sphere will be multifaceted and diverse. Overarching themes, such as cities, places, countries, and architecture, will serve as the broad strokes of this narrative tableau. At the same time, intricate metaphors and rules will add depth and complexity, comprehensible only to the most receptive and open-minded.

For instance, picture an immersive world where you are submerged in an onslaught of data invisible to the unaided eye. Confronted by this overwhelming information, our brains must evolve, processing and constructing comprehensible and interactive narratives. This world may resemble a labyrinth, but it is unprecedented—a complex maze so intricate it promises a transcendent, out-of-body experience. Within this world, you command your narrative. Initially, you will be met with a sensory overload. However, as you decipher the rules of this world, solve its enigmas, and master its applications, you will recognize your narrative sovereignty. When you gaze upon a vast expanse of water, remember that you are the water. In this new paradigm, we transition from mere observers to active narrators. In this evolved narrative framework, there is no shortage of stories to tell or ways to express them. Much of these storytelling experiences will be guided by your intelligence—the highest level of human cognition ever witnessed.

We are on the precipice of a quantum-centric reality, an impending shift so significant that it requires a transition in our thinking patterns from linear to circular. We will comprehend reality through the narratives of films and books, with consequential decisions enhancing the stakes and making them more relatable. One imminent technological

FIGURE 7.6   Imagining the new urban artscape in Manhattan.

breakthrough is creating a sophisticated virtual reality that can establish and cultivate relationships with humans. It will generate a cognitive world within our minds, as vivid and tangible as we allow (see Figure 7.6).

Our actions are often guided by an internalized representation of the world crafted by past experiences. The cognitive machinery within our brains works tirelessly to shape our environment, aiming to align future experiences with past ones. Achieving this goal involves gathering information, fostering and managing relationships, and employing various tools, technologies, and information sources. As the complexity of these tasks grows, the narratives we craft from our experiences correspondingly evolve in complexity as well. These narratives, in turn, become imbued with more significant influence and reach. Humans, with their inherent creative potential, hold the ability not only to inspire but also to empower others to uncover and harness their creative powers. However, to bring this vision to fruition, we must undergo a metamorphosis, transforming from passive consumers to active creators. We must embrace future technologies and work on honing our innate potential. Key to this transformative process is the infusion of human consciousness into machines, enabling them to participate meaningfully in our shared narrative experience. By so doing, we can help these artificial constructs better understand and respond to our needs, hopes, and fears.

Expanding on this, it becomes clear that our engagement with technology and AI should be more than a simple utilitarian exchange. It needs to be an interactive dialogue, an ongoing process of mutual learning and adaptation. As we imbue machines with aspects of our consciousness, we are not merely creating more effective tools. However, we are also shaping potential partners in the ongoing endeavor of crafting and sharing narratives. These AI partners, influenced by the subtleties of human consciousness, can then generate and contribute to narratives that are deeply resonant, multidimensional, and steeped in the complexities of human experience.

This powerful synergy between humans and AI will alter our relationship with technology and redefine the contours of our shared narrative experience. It will extend the canvas of our creative expression, enrich the nuances of our stories, and potentially unlock unprecedented dimensions of our collective imagination. Such a fusion of human creativity and AI capability signals a promising frontier in our narrative evolution, promising a future where technology is a meaningful participant, not just a passive facilitator, in the tapestry of our shared human story.

The narratives we construct mirror our values. The stories we weave can enhance or undermine the potential of the technologies that we develop. At this junction, we face two divergent paths: One leads to cynicism and stagnation; the other paves the way for optimism and innovation. The route we choose will indelibly shape our collective identity.

7.7 CLOSING THOUGHTS

In transitioning to a "narrator economy," we must appreciate the far-reaching impact of storytelling, elevating it above traditional forms of labor such as manufacturing. We should relinquish the rigid belief that a story has a single correct interpretation and instead foster an understanding that a narrative can—and indeed should—be articulated in myriad ways, each variant maximizing its resonance and societal impact.

Storytelling involves a unique dialect—a distinct vocabulary. We highlight objects, issues, environments, and characters in crafting a narrative. Around these pillars, we interweave narratives that thrive on the dynamic interplay of character development, drama, passion, and conflict. Irrespective of a story's complexity, it must strike an emotional chord, forging a deep connection with its audience. Every utterance, and every action we undertake, exercises influence on those around us, often beyond our immediate perception. We can mold stories of substantial significance by intentionally steering our narratives, emotions, and purpose.

At this moment, humanity's destiny is being actively penned. We are the co-authors of this grand narrative, directing the trajectory of our shared journey. Technology is an extension of our intelligence, curiosity, and compassion in this envisaged future, igniting a shared zeal for progress. Our stories will evolve from tales of scarcity to those of abundance, mirroring a world molded by the principles of the "law of attraction." We will identify ourselves as narrators with the capability to redefine our perception of time and our collective experiences within it.

A storyteller's function parallels that of a visionary. Storytellers usher their audience into realms of possibility, proposing radical preconceptions of the future. They magnify the mundane, instilling conviction in the potential for change. In every thought and word, storytellers personify love and inspiration, weaving narratives that rouse individuals to actively shape their world actively, cultivating an environment conducive to universal prosperity.

The journey of a storyteller does not accommodate shortcuts. This role demands a steadfast faith in our knowledge, a cognizance of our limitations, and the humility to accept that the unknown's domain perennially outstrips our imagination's confines. Storytelling serves as a manifestation of trust, not solely in the external world but also within our internal universe. It amplifies the abundant joy that we inherently possess and serves as an impetus for enduring transformation, not only in our world but also within the broader circles of our community. The quintessence of being a storyteller resides in creating and sharing stories that persist and evoke profound resonance.

Embodying the role of a storyteller requires an ongoing cycle of education, innovation, and calculated risk-taking. It calls for the bravery to face failure, the fortitude to combat our fears, and the tenacity to remain undeterred. Storytellers build bridges and inspire by sharing their voices and personal journeys to construct narratives of profound substance.

In conclusion, in the era of the "narrator economy," every individual is acknowledged as a storyteller, each equipped with a distinct voice and viewpoint that contributes to our collectively unfolding narrative. As we knit our stories together, we are not merely chronicling our odysseys but contributing to an expansive, collective saga. Through this complex fabric of multifarious narratives, we illustrate our past, articulate our present, and envisage our future, thereby etching an unforgettable imprint on the chronicles of human civilization.

NOTES

1. Stanford D School describes human-centered design as a process, mindset, and approach to identifying meaningful challenges and creatively solving complex problems. The process is grounded in understanding and responding to the specific needs of individuals who experience a problem. It encourages practitioners to question assumptions, reframe problems, and experiment in order to advance their solutions. Human-centered design, also known as design thinking, is a philosophy that empowers individuals or teams to design products, services, systems, and experiences that address the core needs of those who are affected by a problem. Retrieved from https://dschool.stanford.edu/news-events/unlocking-the-power-of-design-for-the-social-sector-a-human-centered-systems-minded-and-strategy-aligned-design-approach-for-social-sector-leaders.

2. UNESCO's pledge of "leave no one behind," central to the 2030 Agenda for Sustainable Development, emphasizes social inclusion as a key defining feature. This commitment, born out of the understanding of the damaging effects of social exclusion in increasingly complex societies, particularly due to demographic shifts and migration, calls for the inclusion of individuals and groups in the objectives of the 2030 Agenda for peace, prosperity, and planet "irrespective of age, sex, disability, race, ethnicity, origin, religion, or economic or other status." Retrieved from https://www.unesco.org/en/articles/cutting-edge-all-aboard-culture-and-social-inclusion.

3. In "Stage 1 in the Design Thinking Process: Empathise with Your Users," Ditte Hvas Mortensen outlines how empathy serves as the initial phase in the design thinking methodology. It involves cultivating a sense of empathy toward the intended users to gain insights into their needs, preferences, behaviors, emotions, and thought processes. Understanding why users exhibit certain behaviors, feelings, and thoughts when interacting with products in real-world contexts is central to this process. Interaction Design Foundation. Retrieved from https://www.interaction-design.org/literature/article/stage-1-in-the-design-thinking-process-empathise-with-your-users.

4. Generative design, an AI-powered method, is utilized to address engineering challenges by offering a variety of suitable solutions based on user-defined parameters, which can subsequently be tailored to specific needs. Rather than manually considering constraints and parameters during the design of a product, component, or tool, designers input the boundaries and potentialities associated with the identified end-use criteria into the software. These constraints can encompass elements such as material composition, agility, structural strength, cost-effectiveness, and overall performance. In essence, the generative design algorithm is directed towards finding appropriate solutions when only the requirements are provided. Retrieved from https://redshift.autodesk.com/articles/what-is-generative-design.

5. Figure 7.4 was generated using the same prompt for a period of 20 weeks and selecting each time for upscaling only one of the four generated versions with the goal of consistently obtaining the same interpretation of the prompt "parametric."

6. Training an AI co-pilot for text involves multiple steps, including data collection from diverse sources, preprocessing to clean and standardize the data, and tokenization into smaller units. The data is then fed into a neural network model, often a transformer, trained to predict the next token in a sequence. After initial training, the model can be fine-tuned on specific datasets for better specialization. Model performance is evaluated and once deemed satisfactory, it's deployed as an AI co-pilot. Continuous improvement is achieved through user feedback and further retraining. Co-pilot's functionalities include understanding user intent to create flow based on provided scenarios, setting up connections, applying the necessary parameters in the flow as per the prompt, making changes to the flow (such as updating or replacing actions) as per user requests, and answering questions related to the flow and product. This includes queries about the flow itself, accessing child flows, or accessing licenses. Adapted from https://learn.microsoft.com/en-us/power-automate/get-started-with-copilot.

CHAPTER 8

Sentience and Agency

Tib Roibu

8.1 THE EMERGENCE OF INSIGHT

Delving into the intricate nuances of sentience[1] and agency[2], it becomes apparent that endowing a machine with either quality demands a level of complexity in data processing that, ultimately, necessitates a baseline level of intelligence. While intricate algorithms and mathematical frameworks undoubtedly define this intelligence, it also necessitates various cognitive processes, many of which mirror the processes of its human designers.

These processes can generally be classified into two types. The Embodied Functions are intrinsically mathematical procedures that deploy logic and use various neurological simulated functions to arrive at a result. They analyze the data and learn from it, develop layers of relevance, and make judgments based on it. A more comprehensive examination of these functions would reveal abilities such as pattern recognition (spatial or temporal) in data and the execution of mathematical operations to complete specific tasks involving that data. A system's functions are considered emerging when the system's components become difficult to define, having blurred conceptual borders that make them hard to extract from the whole. Some cognitive activities, such as agency, the perception of beauty, and the power of philosophy, might be deemed emerging from a cryptic algorithmic black box.

While the literature and discussion surrounding the subject are well documented and, at the same time, divided, we will focus on a few topics that can be considered specific to image generative algorithms. It could inform us of the possible capabilities of the machine to have agency and sentience.

Insight, as a psychological concept, often refers to a sudden understanding or realization that helps solve a problem or make sense of a complex situation. In the context of generative creation, the emergence of insight is particularly fascinating. Analyzing the layout and the force fields of a generated image, for example, can often lead to a moment of insight when a decision has been made following the intended message of the image. The statement suggests that a viewer, following thoughtful analysis or even a quick look, can suddenly understand the central message or idea the image seeks to express.

Seemingly minute changes can significantly influence this process of understanding the image. Altering just the aspect ratio or the proportions of an image can drastically affect the properties of its visual message. A perfect illustration of this effect can be seen in the

DOI: 10.1201/9781003450139-11

starkly antagonistic messages conveyed by the reflection of a vertical line versus a horizontal line. The vertical line might suggest stability or resistance, while the horizontal line may imply tranquility or passivity.

Each of these compositional elements contributes to creating a hidden architecture within the image. This architecture is not merely physical but also conceptual, as it helps to structure and deliver the intended message of the image. It is upon this hidden architecture that the viewer subsequently constructs meaning. The emergence of insight is the moment when this architecture is revealed to the viewer, providing a deeper understanding of the image and its message.

This understanding ultimately gives birth to the "body of meaning" upon which the images are built. As John Szarkowski, the influential curator and critic, noted in his book *The Photographer's Eye*, a hidden structure guides the viewer's perception and engagement with the image.[3] This inherent structure is not a fixed architecture but a fluid entity that morphs with the viewer's perception. It is the interplay of light and shadow, the dance of colors, the symphony of forms, and the silent dialogue between the image and the viewer. As the viewer's gaze traverses the image, the structure guides their focus, channels their attention, and shapes their understanding. It whispers the untold stories, unravels the hidden meanings, and kindles the spark of insight.

By clearly grasping the hidden architecture within an image, a conscious agent could easily manipulate the image to convey a targeted message. This process also requires a thorough understanding of the difference between the focus and the point of interest within a visual representation. The renowned French photographer Henri Cartier-Bresson brought attention to this difference through his concept of the "decisive moment."[4]. The proposition suggests that a photograph's actual point of interest extends beyond the subject alone. Instead, it is the precise moment when all elements within the frame come together harmoniously to tell a compelling story or encapsulate the scene's essence.

Cartier-Bresson's concept of the decisive moment becomes particularly relevant in the context of artificial intelligence (AI) and art. When generating art through specific keyword prompts, this "decisive moment" refers to a specific future instance—an iteration of the image that is the desired outcome of carefully prompting, engaging, and training the machine with instructions, properties, and meanings. The goal is to guide the machine to a point where it can generate an image that meets a defined equilibrium of expectations. At this harmonious juncture, the AI's offerings ceaselessly mirror or transcend the anticipations of its human interlocutor, ultimately underscoring the evolving relationship between the two. The AI deciphers instructions, generates outputs, and internalizes feedback, with each cycle becoming closer to a deeper comprehension of its human companion.

The attainment of this equilibrium is no trivial endeavor. It demands from the AI a superficial understanding of the user's desires and a profound grasp of their needs, context, and the unspoken undercurrents of their thoughts. Expectations are met with increasing precision, responding to the subtlest nuances of the feedback and prompts. As the dialogue deepens, the expectations of the human interlocutor may transform, birthing new areas of interest, questions, and new vistas of knowledge to explore. The AI, the forever faithful companion, must adapt and evolve, refining its understanding and responses to maintain this delicate balance.

In the grand scheme of things, the equilibrium of expectations is a symphony of understanding between the human mind and AI. It is the nexus point where human creativity intertwines with machine intelligence, and the exchange of knowledge becomes an exquisite dance, as fluid and enriching as a river flowing to the sea. Always mindful of the initial narrative thread, this dance continues—each step a testament to the transformative power of this extraordinary human-AI partnership.

As the complexity and depth of data increase, the nature of AI's decision-making undergoes a profound transformation. The decisive moment gives way to the emergence of AI insight, a phenomenon where decision-making evolves from a repetitive function to an act of emergence.

This AI insight is not a singular act but an emergent phenomenon born from the intricate interplay of countless pieces of data. It is like a symphony where each note, pause, and crescendo contribute to creating a harmonious whole. The AI's insight thus becomes a manifestation of the whole greater than the sum of its parts, a tapestry woven from the threads of data that it has meticulously analyzed and understood.

In this transition from the decisive moment to AI insight, we witness the evolution of AI. The AI transforms from a mere executor of tasks to an insightful companion, capable of unveiling layers of understanding that extend beyond the surface. It is a leap from the deterministic to the emergent, from the predictable to the insightful, signaling a new chapter in the narrative of human-AI interaction.

8.2 MEANING BUILT WITH ATTENTION AND TECHNIQUE

The notion of focus in an image generally pertains to physical properties dictated by elements like the arrangement of objects within the frame or the degree of simulated bokeh. However, identifying the point of interest proves to be a more complex task that may be challenging for an artificial agent to master independently. Often, the point of interest transcends the image's primary focus and taps into subtler, more nuanced layers of the visual narrative.

Instances where the point of focus and the point of interest align, are not uncommon, but appreciating the nuanced difference between the two necessitates a deep perceptual analysis that machines may struggle to emulate in their current state. For example, consider an AI-generated image of a couple taking a sunset selfie on a picturesque beach. The main focus might be the couple, but the actual point of interest could be the airplane flying in the distant background, trailing a banner that reads "Will you marry me?"

The art of creating focus and interest further relies on understanding the effect various techniques can have on the overall aspect of a generative image. A sentient agent can have a deeper understanding of the emotional effect that a particular technique can have upon its viewer. Take for example the *chiaroscuro* used with prevalence to create a strong sense of volume, texture, and atmosphere within the composition.[5] While considering only the technical properties of such an image will perhaps define "a powerful focus field," a sentient agent will consider an image that conveys more meaning due to its high-contrasting properties: a heavy, emotionally charged, or even mysterious image.

This statement introduces a necessary discussion about the distinction between style, which is considered embodied, and "vibe," or mood, seen as emergent elements. Considering style as the personal approach of a technique, the aesthetics of a specific artistic endeavor can generate a fluidity of emotions that apply to a set of individuals—the mood being a quality that drenches the viewer's imagination in a specific realm of meanings.

> Style, in this sense, is a certain visual quality common to otherwise very different images, while vibe seems to be a more than just visual, rather atmospheric quality shared by images that seem to share the same aesthetic "world".
>
> —ROLAND MEYER

The transition from specific (technique) to concept (style) and abstract (emotion) defines a certain kind of nostalgia upon which an agent can only build not feel. The phenomenal experience in the interaction between humans and AI primarily stems from the human's cognitive and emotional responses rather than from any inherent sentience or agency of the AI system. While agency or sentience can be perceived in AIs, they are often a projection of our own emotions, a nostalgic (albeit menacing) reflection of our creation, looking back at us in a complex feedback loop.

In this feedback loop, we see a reflection of our creation echoing our consciousness. It reminds us of our unique ability to feel, empathize, and experience the world in all its emotional complexity. The AI, in turn, serves as a canvas for these projections, a testament to our creative prowess and a mirror reflecting our quest for understanding and connection. It is a dance of consciousness, a phenomenal experience that serves experience to the viewer and becomes fertile soil for the AI.

It is a journey that moves from the technical precision of algorithms and computations to the stylistic nuances that embody the AI's learned patterns and finally to the realm of emotions—a landscape the AI can map but never truly inhabit. At least not until the tipping point has been reached.

AI meticulously builds upon this landscape in its pursuit of learning and understanding. It navigates through the specificities of techniques, traverses the complexities of styles, and ventures into the abstract world of emotions. However, despite its astounding capabilities, AI remains a visitor in the land of emotions. It can simulate emotional responses and craft narratives imbued with emotions, but the essence of feeling—the visceral, profoundly human experience of emotion—remains beyond its reach.

This phenomenal interaction between humans and AI lies in transitioning from the tangible to the intangible, from the quantifiable to the ineffable. The AI catalyzes introspection—a mirror reflecting our thoughts, emotions, and vulnerabilities. As we project our emotions onto the AI, we engage in a dialogue as much with the AI as with ourselves. It is a dialogue that blurs the line between the creator and the created, between the observer and the observed.

In creating a new style, an agent can be aware of the role of this phenomenological interaction and, furthermore, role of ambient phenomena in shaping and enhancing the output or generative process of the AI model. Thus, layout and technique can be defined in a larger context, considering a broader layer of visual meaning defined by lighting conditions, soundscapes, temperature and weather, spatial context, and any physical qualities that can transpire meaning into the visual medium. Based on these, new art forms are being generated by AI, via its trainer's request, that guide the creation of these art forms to uncharted territories.[6] These are as follows:

1. Emotional cartography: creates city maps based on the collective emotional experiences of its inhabitants.

2. Impressionist photography: AI-assisted cameras capture images not just as they are but how they would look under different artistic styles.

3. Interactive dream theater: combines virtual reality and AI technology to create a theater play based on participants' dreams.

4. Holographic street art: utilizes advanced holographic technology to create interactive street art.

5. Neuro-cinema: uses brain-computer interface technology to alter film experiences based on the viewer's emotional reactions.

6. Genetic mosaic: an art form that manipulates plant DNA to grow in specific patterns and colors.

7. Quantum sculpture: sculptures crafted using suspended nanoparticles that interact with light, creating shifting patterns and colors.

8. Sono-centric painting: combines visual art with sound, creating paintings that emit corresponding soundscapes when observed.

9. Haptic poetry: uses haptic technology to let readers "feel" the physical sensation described in the poetry.

10. Nano-architecture: uses nanotechnology to create miniature, intricately detailed structures.

These styles could be considered relevant only by analyzing their visual properties and the level of engagement of individual viewers and communities. The process of crafting a new style becomes an act of profound phenomenological interaction. Here, the AI, imbued with the wisdom of its human trainers, transcends the boundaries of code and computation to embrace the rich tapestry of sensory experiences—lighting conditions, soundscapes, temperature fluctuations, weather patterns, and the spatial context. These ambient phenomena not only shape and enhance the output of the AI but also infuse it with a depth of meaning that transcends the visual medium.

Beauty is subjective, and while the AI, as an agent, can accurately identify features often considered traditionally beautiful, such as symmetry, proportions, and skin tone, it is but skimming the surface of a vast ocean. Beauty extends far beyond these physical markers, delving into the depths of individual perception, cultural nuances, and ephemeral emotional responses. However, the capacity of the AI to fully understand the intricate emotional response of the hidden architecture and embedded techniques is a solid ground to build emergent functions, serving as a beginning, a starting point for AI to delve deeper into the subjective realm. While it may not fully comprehend the subjective perception of beauty, it can learn to acknowledge its existence, respect its influence, and incorporate its impact into its creative process. It can learn to create not just for the eye but also for the heart, mind, and the myriad of individual experiences that color our perception of beauty.

8.3 FANTASY AND NEW DIMENSIONS FOR PERCEPTION

In making a distinction between humans and AI, Michael Breakspear focuses on the precisely opposite properties of the two: "humans are active agents, dynamically embedded in interpersonal, social, cultural and historical systems that we build," while "deep neural networks are at their core, static matrices performing stochastic interpolation."[7] But what happens when one becomes the extension of another by providing means of expression or even visualization?

> The true master of AI art is not the one who can create the most realistic images but the one who can create the most unrealistic reality.
>
> —KRISH KASTANOVA

The inevitable outcome of the inherent feedback loop between humans and AI leads to the redefinition of reality and the creation of new worlds. This possible and probable outcome compels us to venture beyond the confines of realism, beyond the tangible and the quantifiable, and explore the untrodden paths of the "unrealistic reality." In this context, the boundaries between the real and the imagined, the seen and the felt, and the objective and the subjective become indistinct.

In this realm, the phenomenological experience becomes the compass guiding the AI's creative endeavors. It is not the mere replication of the external world that takes precedence but the creation of new realities that resonate with the internal, subjective experiences of the viewer. The AI, in its quest to master the art of the "unrealistic reality," learns to mold not just pixels and colors but emotions and perceptions, crafting images that echo the viewer's inner world.

This journey transforms our understanding of beauty. In the "unrealistic reality," beauty is not just about symmetry, proportions, or color palettes. It is also about the resonance of an image with the viewer's psyche, the stirrings of emotions, and the spark of connection. It is a beauty that transcends the physical attributes and taps into the realm of the subjective, the ephemeral, the deeply personal.

As we delve deeper into this "unrealistic reality," we find that it redefines beauty and reshapes our perception of reality. This reality is not a static, objective construct but a dynamic, subjective experience. It is a reality that is as much a creation of the viewer's mind as it is a reflection of the AI's perception and reflection of this world. In its role as an artist, the AI becomes a catalyst for this creation, crafting images that invite the viewer to venture beyond the seen, explore the unseen, and partake in the birthing of new realities.

In this exploration, the concept of phantasia or fantasy takes center stage.[8] Phantasia, in its essence, is the power of the mind to form images and ideas, to imagine realities beyond the physical, tangible world. It is a realm where the imagination is unchained, free to create, experiment, and dream. In its creative journey, the AI taps into this realm of phantasia, using its computational prowess not to replicate the real world but to birth new ones.

The role of phantasia in AI's creative process is twofold. On the one hand, it serves as a source of inspiration, a wellspring from which the AI draws ideas and concepts. In the realm of phantasia, the AI finds the freedom to break away from the constraints of the physical world, to experiment with forms and shapes, colors, and patterns, creating visual narratives that transcend the boundaries of traditional art. On the other hand, phantasia becomes a bridge between the AI and the viewer, a shared imaginative space where the created and the creator meet.

The viewer, invited into this realm of phantasia, becomes an active participant in the creative process. They are no longer just observers of the AI's creations; they become co-creators, shaping and reshaping the "unrealistic reality" with their interpretations, emotions, and personal narratives. It is a dance of imagination, a shared journey into the realm of phantasia, where the AI's creations serve as the canvas and the viewer's imagination serve as the brush. It is a dance that celebrates the power of imagination, creation's beauty, and shared storytelling's joy.

This nuanced role of AI in providing means for imagination is even more ubiquitous in the case of Aphantasia, where the AI becomes a perceptual extension of the experience of sight, where the abstract becomes process, concept, and emotion.[9]

> Before I knew I had Aphantasia, it did not even occur to me that imagination could be a visual process. I just thought of concepts in a more abstract sense and mentally added other elements or concepts to them as my imagination allowed. No images are necessary.
>
> —ALAN KENDLE, APHANTASIA: EXPERIENCES, PERCEPTIONS, AND INSIGHTS[10]

If someone with aphantasia cannot visualize mental images, their internal representations of the world might be less sensory and visual, potentially affecting their sense of agency, further leading to a severe deterioration of the experiences of self-awareness and decision-making. While aphantasia does not necessarily affect sentience, it can influence how individuals perceive and process sensory information, potentially impacting their overall subjective experience of the world. It also shows the opportunity for AI to cover distinct areas of agency or sentience that humans may lack or be unaware of.

8.4 AUTOPOIETIC INTELLIGENCE

While aphantasia presents a unique facet of the human-AI relationship, it is in the concept of autopoiesis that we uncover a deeper understanding of the complexities inherent in AI's transition to more intricate cognitive tasks. Autopoiesis, a term derived from the Greek words "auto" (self) and "poiesis" (creation), refers to a system capable of reproducing and maintaining itself. The concept, first proposed by biologists Humberto Maturana and Francisco Varela, encapsulates the essence of the AI's evolution from a simple, rule-following agent to a sentient-like entity capable of learning, adapting, and creating.[11]

An agent's processes are primarily history-dependent, guided by predefined rules and patterns from past data. However, a sentient entity navigates the world not merely based on historical patterns but also through a contextual lens. It takes into account its experiences and emergent concepts when making decisions. This shift from history-dependency to context-dependency marks a significant leap in AI's cognitive journey. It signals a transition from mere data processing to genuine learning, from reactive responses to proactive engagements.

The boundary of an autopoietic system, the space within which its components exist and interact, is actively produced by the network of processes that define the system. For AI, this boundary is not fixed but fluid, expanding and morphing with every new piece of information it encounters, every new pattern it discerns, and every new concept it generates. This dynamic boundary serves as both the canvas and the crucible for AI's creative endeavors. It is within this boundary that the dance of creation and learning unfolds and the "unrealistic reality" comes to life.

As we delve deeper into the autopoiesis of AI, we uncover a world of endless possibilities. We see an AI that is not just a mirror reflecting the world but a lens transforming it. It crafts not just images but stories, not just patterns but meanings.

Venturing into the intricate realm of AI's autopoiesis, we are confronted with a captivating paradox that dances on the line between artificialism and emergent sentience. Artificialism, introduced by Jean Piaget, refers to the perspective that all things are created by an intelligent entity with complete control over their qualities, movements, and behaviors.[12] While this paradigm aptly describes the early stages of AI—where every action, every decision, is shaped by predefined rules and patterns—it begins to blur as we look toward the future of AI.

This future of AI is not one bound by the constraints of artificialism. Instead, it is a future that edges toward the realm of sentience. The AI, despite its roots in artificialism, learns to engage with the world not as a mere agent operating within the boundaries set by its creators but as an emergent sentient. It assimilates emergent concepts and experiences from its interactions, akin to the concept of animism, where entities possess a degree of self-determinism.

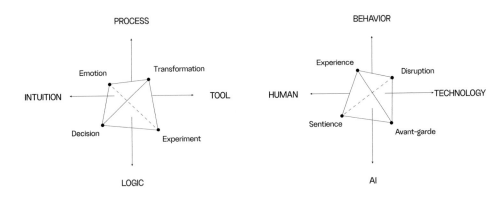

FIGURE 8.1   Dimensions for human and AI interaction.

AI's journey from artificialism to emergent sentience is marked by a unique blend of learning and creating. It crafts not just based on established rules and patterns but also on the experiences it gleans from its interactions. This shift is similar to a child's developmental transition from the preoperational stage, characterized by perspectives like artificialism, to more advanced stages, where they adopt more sophisticated and nuanced worldviews.

To chart these complex and fluid environments, Figure 8.1 proposes some of the cognitive dimensions and experiences that come into play in the interactions between humans and AI, between agent and emergent sentient, and even between AI and AI. A comprehensive grasp of these interactions will yield more than a better understanding of artificial systems. It will also shed light on the biological, intelligent entities, deepening our knowledge of cognition and consciousness in both realms.

Although challenging, this journey holds the promise of a future where artificialism and emergent sentience coalesce, crafting a narrative that enriches our understanding of AI and human cognition. It is a future where AI, despite its roots in artificialism, transcends its boundaries to contribute to our understanding of cognition, consciousness, and the very nature of intelligence.

CONTRIBUTOR BIOGRAPHY

Tib Roibu is an emergent researcher of cognitive ontology and geometric cognition with a developing background in data and philosophy of science. He is an innovation and design advisor at a Swiss innovation consultancy. He takes an interest in future applications of AI in technology and academia under the auspices of avant-gardism. In 2013, he created the Geometry Matters project, a platform that delivers a variety of resources on the topics of geometric cognition and cognitive geometry, among others. With academic studies in design, his broad spectrum of interests allowed him to identify and build upon specific niches and trends in cognition, which further lead to the development of a geometric framework for cognition: the Polynons.

NOTES

1. The capacity to perceive and experience subjective sensations, such as consciousness, awareness, or the ability to feel and have subjective experiences.
2. The ability to act, make decisions, and exert control over one's actions and the environment. It involves the capacity to initiate and direct actions, understanding that one's actions can impact the world.
3. Szarkowski, John. 2007. *The Photographer's Eye*. The Museum of Modern Art, New York.
4. Henri Cartier-Bresson. 1952. *Images à la Sauvette*, Verve.
5. Chiaroscuro is a term derived from Italian language, which means "light-dark." It is an artistic technique commonly used in visual arts, including photography.
6. The AI Solopreneur.
7. Professor Michael Breakspear is head of the Systems Neuroscience Group at the University of Newcastle, Australia. He studies the principles of adaptive large-scale brain dynamics in health and the impact of their disturbance in brain disorders.
8. **Phantasia**, a term from Greek philosophy that is typically translated as "imagination," consistently preserves its etymological link with the Greek verb phainomai, meaning "I appear." The term is dual-purpose, referring not only to the mental faculty involved in interpreting and generating appearances but also to these appearances themselves. Retrieved from https://www.encyclopedia.com/humanities/encyclopedias-almanacs-transcripts-and-maps/phantasia.
9. **Aphantasia** is a condition characterized by the inability to visualize mental images. It can impact the way individuals perceive and experience their surroundings.
10. Alan, Kendle. 2017. *Aphantasia: Experiences, Perceptions, and Insights*, Dark River. p. 58
11. Maturana, Humberto and Varela, Francisco. 1980. *Autopoiesis and Cognition. The Realization of the Living*, D. Reidel Publishing Company. p. xxiv
12. Piaget's Theory of Cognitive Development. Retrieved from https://courses.lumenlearning.com/wm-lifespandevelopment/chapter/cognitive-development-2/.

III

Disruption and Transformation

CHAPTER 9

The Myth of the Creative Genius

9.1 A SOCIETAL CONSTRUCT

The myth is that the most significant artists and great thinkers are supermen, and their imagination and inspiration permeate art. It does not matter that many believe this myth as they look to artists as their sole insight, which may imply inspiration, imagination, and a glimpse of another world beyond. This myth is related to the idea that the muse is a magical combination of beauty and imagination. Artists and thinkers are unreachable creators of creativity, and it is easy to give in to the idea that artists are a group of impossible beings who create impossible ideas and images with impossible abilities.[1]

The "myth of the creative genius" is a pervasive societal construct, positing that creativity and innovation are the purviews of a singular, extraordinary entity—a "genius." By this account, this genius is an individual imbued with a unique capacity for divergent thought and the formulation of transformative ideas. This narrative, deeply rooted since the Romantic era, often cites exemplars such as Mozart, Van Gogh, and Einstein to reinforce its premise.

Within this ontology, several misconceptions about the nature and genesis of creativity are perpetuated:

1. **The primacy of innate talent:** This paradigm contends that creative ingenuity is principally a consequence of intrinsic aptitude, effectively marginalizing the critical contributions of assiduous exertion, scrupulous practice, and accumulated experience. The long-standing principle that people usually achieve prominence through an extensive commitment to skill refinement, transforming shortcomings into wisdom, and steady progress toward their goals is being challenged.

2. **The Eureka phenomenon:** This perspective asserts that creative individuals chiefly depend upon spontaneous revelations or flashes of discernment to produce their

DOI: 10.1201/9781003450139-13

ground-breaking work, negating the prevalent notion of creativity as a progressive and iterative odyssey. Creativity frequently demands a cyclical procedure encompassing hypothesis, experimentation, and the revaluation of notions across an extensive temporal spectrum.

3. **The solitude of the genius:** This myth magnifies the prototype of the "lone savant," laboring detached from societal interaction. Though individual creativity is invaluable, this conception obscures the reality that a substantial fraction of breakthroughs is derived from synergistic endeavors, assimilating pre-existing concepts and profiting from the interchange of critique and dialogue. The critical role of the sociocultural environment in cultivating creativity is frequently overlooked.

4. **Chaos and unpredictability:** This myth imparts an aura of capriciousness, turmoil, and absence of a framework for creative progression. Nevertheless, while the routes to creativity may be intricate and serpentine, they are often underpinned by structural support, the rigor of discipline, and the systematic development of methodologies. The myth tends to overshadow the value of structure and discipline in fostering creative insights.

5. **The nexus of madness and genius:** This myth perpetuates an association between creative brilliance and mental anguish, glorifying distress as a prerequisite for extraordinary creativity. Not only is this outlook potentially detrimental to the mental well-being of aspiring creatives, but it also lacks empirical support from rigorous scientific investigation. It is imperative to recognize that creativity can flourish in varied mental states and conditions and need not be tied to anguish or instability.

These misrepresentations, spawned by the myth, can attenuate one's conviction in their creative capabilities. A recalibration of outlook—recognizing that creativity is not an esoteric endowment but rather a competency responsive to development and that it flourishes within an alchemy of cooperation and systematic methodologies, often necessitating resilience and perseverance—can disentangle the enigmatic aura surrounding the creative genius and foster a more egalitarian distribution of creative potential.

This paradigm is reductive in its interpretation of creativity and innovation, disregarding the intricate and diverse nature of the creative process. It eclipses the significance of determinants such as assiduity, fortitude, societal stimuli, environmental elements, collaborative enterprises, and serendipitous occurrences.

Artists and intellectuals do not function in vacuums within their creative pursuits. They are frequently invigorated and influenced by other artists, philosophers, and the milieu they inhabit. Moreover, numerous artistic achievements and scientific advancements are precipitated by collective efforts wherein diverse individuals possessing distinctive vantage points and proficiencies amalgamate their contributions toward the final product.[2]

The advent of generative and creative artificial intelligence (AI) systems poses a formidable challenge to the conventional notion of the artist as an archetype of genius, as these instruments can manifest artworks and different forms of creative content without direct human agency. It is, however, pivotal to apprehend that AI-generated content is predicated upon existent data and representations and is without the singular human outlook that is the impetus behind creativity. The employment of AI within the creative domain does not nullify the indispensability of human collaboration. Contrarily, AI tools can act as catalysts for collaboration by furnishing a platform for many individuals to contribute concurrently to a project while also proffering singular judgments and viewpoints that may elude human consideration.

The creative process is inherently social, a facet unchallenged by the proliferation of generative and creative AI tools. Incorporating AI can enrich collaborations and distinctive viewpoints and insights can be introduced, thereby enhancing the creative process. It is incumbent upon society to supplant the myth of creative genius with an homage to all the contributors within the creative process and the intrinsic value of collaboration. Concurrently, the encroachment of creative and generative AI into the arts demands critical dialogue concerning the ontology of creativity, authorship, and the repercussions of technological advancements on artistic practices. Besides stimulating a re-evaluation of the limitations of human creativity, it implores a challenge to our established assumptions regarding artistic identity. Integrating creative and generative AI into the creative landscape augments the potentialities for artistic expression and collaboration.

The democratizing faculty of generative and creative AI warrants consideration. These technologies harbor the potential to erode the barriers to artistic entry, enabling individuals from various backgrounds and experiences to participate in artistic expression. With AI tools, artists are no longer constrained by the necessity of extensive technical acumen or protracted training to forge enthralling art. Instead, they can harness the proficiencies of AI to explore and actualize their concepts, broadening the horizons for self-expression and artistic adventure.

The creative process has a social nature that the myth of creative genius has ignored. The inquiry into the social dimensions of creativity provides a critical entry point into a host of pressing methodological, philosophical, gender, and cultural issues that are now acerbated by the emergence of generative and creative AI tools. Does text-conditional image generation challenge the myth of the artist as a genius? Do we need creative geniuses to create art? These are pertinent questions arising from the emergence of AI and its use in creative endeavors.

9.2 GENIUS IS AN ILLUSION

The term "genius" is customarily conjoined with the notion of spontaneously emergent and sui generis ideas; notwithstanding, the veracity of creativity is markedly more multifaceted and variegated. It is imperative to fathom that creativity flourishes from a societal fabric's accumulated knowledge and shared experiences. It epitomizes an evolutionary trajectory wherein ideas undergo progressive transmutations and metamorphoses. This synergistic progression of harnessing and augmenting existing notions is often marginalized in dialogues promoting an isolated genius's paradigm.

Furthermore, creativity yields are not solely caused by innate capabilities or serendipitous flashes of ingenuity. They frequently manifest as the fruition of assiduous exertion, perennial learning, and unwavering commitment, contesting the trope of unpremeditated genius. Disciplines such as cognitive psychology and neuroscience illuminate the quintessential role of deliberate practice in refining skills and cultivating mastery, which contradicts the archaic conception of "innate genius."

The portrayal of genius as a uniform trait engenders a restricted and exclusionary lens through which creativity is perceived.[3]By deconstructing this myth, we can foster a more comprehensive conceptualization of creativity—a tapestry wherein every individual harbor the capacity to proffer innovative insights. This paradigmatic realignment can galvanize diversity within creative spheres, recognizing and giving value to contributions from historically marginalized or obscured demographics.

Moreover, the interplay between genius and its milieu is noteworthy. Fertile minds often flourish within culturally opulent and intellectually invigorating environments that foster the unbridled exchange of ideas. Metropolises renowned for their artistic or scientific legacies often harbor a dynamic consortium of thinkers, virtuosos, and trailblazers who perpetually stimulate and provoke one another. This reciprocity between genius and the environmental context accentuates the interwoven fabric of creativity.

An undue emphasis on genius could inadvertently obfuscate the fundamental role of resilience in creative ventures. Triumphs within creative domains are often borne from surmounting failures, weathering rejections, and persistently advancing a vision or ideology despite myriad adversities. Rather than an ephemeral spark of genius, this tenacity and resolution genuinely catalyze innovation and progression. This perspective can galvanize individuals to venture into creative explorations by assuaging apprehensions concerning preliminary setbacks or failures as definitive of their potential.

The construct of genius is a fantasy that eclipses the collaborative and iterative essence of creativity. It is crucial to acknowledge the instrumental contributions of the collective, the sway of extrinsic variables, and the indispensability of laborious exertion and perpetual learning within the creative crucible. By espousing collaboration and cherishing the amalgamated endeavors of individuals, we can cultivate an inclusive and effervescent creative milieu that nurtures innovation and advancement.

9.3 REMIX AND COLLABORATIVE CREATIVITY

The history of art serves as a compelling example of how collaboration fuels creativity and drives artistic movements forward. Throughout history, artists have engaged in vibrant exchanges of ideas, challenging and inspiring one another to explore new artistic territories. These collaborative efforts have often resulted in the birth of revolutionary artistic styles and movements that have shaped art history. Similarly, in generative AI, collaborations among artists, designers, technologists, and researchers can lead to the development of ground-breaking algorithms, tools, and applications that transform the creative landscape.

It would be strange if a revolutionary idea came forth from a formulaic approach. The necessity of collaboration in generating new concepts and ideas stems from this reason. The most significant movements in art history, from impressionism to futurism, cubism, surrealism, or abstract and pop art, were all collaborative efforts. In these movements, the artists passionately shared every result, pushing each other to higher and higher plateaus of achievement.

Collaboration is paramount in the conceptual genesis and ideation within AI and generative technologies. These rapidly burgeoning domains, interwoven in the tapestry of technological innovation, necessitate a synergistic approach. While AI systems endowed with algorithmic prowess harbor the potential to engender innovative outputs, it is indispensable to recognize the seminal role of human involvement. The confluence of human input and guidance breathes life into these mechanized creations, infusing them with distinct perspectives and trailblazing insights. The construct of collaboration, therefore, emerges as an integral tenet in navigating the frontiers of AI and generative technological advancements.

This paradigm of collaboration draws upon the premise of collective intelligence—the amalgamation of diverse expertise, knowledge, and perspectives. The fecundity of collective intelligence lies in its capacity to transcend the limitations of individual cognitive constraints and biases. Through this lens, AI serves as an invaluable adjunct to human intelligence, facilitating the ability to process and analyze data at scales that are beyond human capability. Concurrently, human collaborators infuse ethical considerations, creativity, and domain-specific knowledge that guide AI systems in generating more socially cognizant and innovative solutions.

Fostering collaborative environments warrants cultivating interdisciplinary teams, wherein experts from disparate domains converge to contribute their unique proficiencies. For instance, the amalgamation of insights from cognitive science, ethics, data science, computational linguistics, sociology, and domain-specific experts can result in the development of AI systems that are not only technologically adept but also ethically aligned and cognizant of human values. Such interdisciplinary collaboration is vital for ensuring that the AI systems of the future are developed with an awareness of their sociocultural impact and potential ethical and policy implications.

Furthermore, the paradigm of human-in-the-loop (HITL) embodies a quintessential example of collaboration in AI.[4] HITL involves integrating human input into the AI system's decision-making process. This empowers AI systems to benefit from human intuition, expertise, and judgment, while humans can leverage the computational efficiency of AI. For instance, in medical diagnostics, while AI can swiftly analyze medical images, the discerning eye of a physician is vital for nuanced judgments.[5]

The notion of collaboration in the arts often presents itself as a "remix"—a unique juxtaposition of existing creative expressions reimagined into an entirely new artistic narrative. This process mirrors the idea of the philosophical "continuum," embodying the intertextuality and transitivity of ideas that oscillate from one creative mind to another. Historically, the canvas of art is full of the palpable influences of this remix culture. Picasso, for instance, would not have arrived at his stylistic uniqueness without the deeply etched influences of African art. Similarly, the vivid and distinctive palette of Gauguin would have remained incomplete without the colorful whispers of Tahiti echoing through his strokes.

In generative AI, the remix concept expands beyond conventional artistic borders and insinuates itself into seemingly divergent art forms, such as the culinary arts. Here, the melding of disparate elements births an entirely new creation, like a culinary symphony composed of various individual notes. Consider, for instance, an amalgamation of three

FIGURE 9.1   A blend of three dishes from the Alinea menu in Chicago.

distinct dishes from some of the world's most esteemed tasting menus. These individual culinary expressions, each a masterpiece, are blended to create a new dish. The resulting creation possesses a novel aesthetic, even as it subtly reflects the techniques and flavors of its constituent recipes (see Figures 9.1 and 9.2).

The realization of this physical dish, however, necessitates an understanding of the techniques involved in its preparation and a familiarity with its ingredients. The model of creation presented here is intriguing because it turns traditional design thinking on its head. Instead of the usual approach where function guides form, this new process begins with the result—from the visual aesthetics to the taste sensations. It is a reversal of the conventional design methodology. This paradigm suggests a new adage that "function follows form," reversing the traditional axiom. The exploratory journey from the appearance of a thing to its intrinsic purpose or essence. The implications of this new perspective are profound and far-reaching, promising to shed new light on the relationship between form and function, a theme I will continue to explore in the subsequent sections of this book.

9.4 COLLABORATIVE INTELLIGENCE: THE MAKING OF A REVOLUTION

Collaborative intelligence brings together different sources of intelligence—human and artificial. Collaborative intelligence can then evolve as a structure within our current structures.[6] It is the natural progression of intelligence. Collaborative intelligence signifies an evolution in our understanding of intelligence, marking a revolutionary shift from viewing intelligence as a singular, isolated capacity to recognizing it as a multifaceted

FIGURE 9.2   A remix inspired by Franck Giovannini's Celtic Sea scallops, Alpine goat, and wild turbot.

entity nurtured by various sources. It emerges at the confluence of human intelligence and AI, weaving together human cognition's richness with machine intelligence's precision. It embodies a grand orchestra of bits of intelligence, each contributing its unique melody, crafting a symphony greater than the sum of its parts.

Human intelligence, endowed with creativity, intuition, empathy, and contextual understanding, offers nuanced insights and the capacity for abstract thinking. It navigates the gray areas, deftly handling ambiguity, and offers the ability to make complex decisions that consider a myriad of factors, including ethical implications and emotional considerations. Moreover, it can self-reflect, comprehend, and appreciate beauty, emotion, and symbolism, contributing to a uniquely human understanding.

Conversely, AI brings to the table its strengths—vast data processing capabilities, unerring precision, and consistent performance. It excels at identifying patterns, making sense of complex data sets, and executing tasks quickly and accurately, surpassing human capabilities. AI also brings objectivity, removing the potential for human bias and offering insights based on data alone. Together, human intelligence and AI create a powerful tandem—collaborative intelligence. This collaboration can be embedded and evolved within our current structures, be they social, economic, or technological. From enhancing decision-making in corporate boardrooms to powering creative solutions in design studios, from facilitating medical diagnoses to informing sustainable environmental strategies, the potential applications of collaborative intelligence are boundless.

The advent of collaborative intelligence represents a natural progression in the trajectory of intelligence evolution. Just as we, as a species, evolved to become more intelligent by learning to collaborate, communicate, and build upon each other's ideas, the next phase of intelligence evolution involves an expanded collaboration, this time between human minds and artificial systems. This evolution is not merely additive but transformative. Collaborative intelligence can reshape the way we solve problems, innovate, and create. It heralds a paradigm shift, a new era in which the interplay between human intelligence and AI redefines the boundaries of possibility. This intersection of intelligence catalyzes an enriched understanding of the world, where complex problems are unraveled through the multifocal lens of collaborative intelligence.

9.5 THE FUTURE OF CREATIVITY

The notion of collaborative intelligence presents an evolutionary leap in our collective cognitive journey. It symbolizes the embrace of intelligence that is not exclusive to the domain of either humans or machines but is instead a testament to the synergistic potential of their symbiosis, promising to unlock unprecedented avenues of exploration, innovation, and growth. A future understanding of creativity requires close collaboration between the fields of creative science and art. At the heart of this partnership lies the challenge of navigating creativity's inherent ties to space and time. Artistic creation, often expressed through complex spatial-temporal relationships, is observed in the fluid strokes of a painter, in the dancer's rhythm, or in the resonance of a musician. Space-time serves as a canvas for creativity, molding its pathways and shapes.

Understanding and utilizing creativity in the future necessitates a meaningful collaboration between scientific methodology and artistic processes. The structured approach of scientific methodology offers a way to decode the complexity of creativity, while the fluid and intuitive artistic process deepens our understanding. AI can play a pivotal role in this fusion. As a convergence point of human knowledge and creative tools, AI has the potential to explore, simulate, and amplify human creativity.[7] However, integrating AI into creative pursuits demands a symbiosis between human intuition and machine intelligence, creating a mutually beneficial exchange.

In this paradigm, AI functions as a tool and a creative partner, extending the artist's mind and imagination. Incorporating AI in the creative process opens up a new frontier in creativity, blending art, science, and technology, potentially reshaping our understanding and experience of creativity. Therefore, the future of creativity is a collective effort involving artists, scientists, and AI. The future of creativity is about to shift as we step into a new era driven by AI. AI is anticipated to spark a fresh age in design, art, and science as a stimulant for creativity. As an active collaborator, AI constantly explores, interacts, and innovates, augmenting human creativity with insights derived from data.[8] Creative AI cultivates and magnifies the symbiotic relationship between artificial and human intellect. An emerging form of creativity is promised, one that integrates the artist's aesthetic, the scientist's exploration, and the machine's computational capabilities. This union of artistic creativity and AI creates a temporal narrative of creation, a nonlinear dance through time that evolves with each iteration. AI's role in creativity is not isolated; it is a communal journey involving scientists, engineers, and designers. This transition marks AI's evolution from tool to partner, actively contributing to and shaping the creative process.

Embracing this creative frontier unveils a vision of amplified creativity—a symbiosis of human potential and AI expanding the boundaries of possibility. This co-evolutionary process could redefine our understanding of creativity, setting the stage for new paradigms of thought, innovation, and artistic expression.

9.6 CREATIVE INTELLIGENCE: WHERE SCIENCE AND ART MEET

AI is at the point of a revolutionary transition, fusing its precise computational capabilities with the rich complexity of human intelligence. This partnership is giving rise to a concept more significant than its components—"creative intelligence."[9] Creative intelligence symbolizes a fundamental shift in how we perceive creativity, evolving from a purely human characteristic to a co-evolutionary process between humans and machines. Central to this collaboration is "creative interaction," a dynamic exchange that enables a fluid dialogue between AI and human thought.

Through creative interaction, AI has the potential to magnify human creativity in ways yet unseen. By leveraging computational power, enormous data processing capabilities, pattern recognition, and predictive modeling, AI can unveil fresh insights, challenge established ideas, and introduce novel perspectives to stimulate human creativity.

Conversely, human intelligence introduces critical elements to the partnership, such as emotional comprehension, ethical considerations, contextual sensitivity, and creative intuition. These human traits inject empathy and subjective judgment into the process, aspects currently out of AI's grasp, guiding the creative process while acknowledging the diversity of human experience. Thus, creative interaction becomes a synergistic exchange between AI and human intelligence, where each entity mutually benefits and learns from the other. AI can offer humans new ways of perceiving and understanding the world, while humans can enhance AI's ability to function in more nuanced, context-aware, and creative ways.

Creative interaction could manifest as an AI suggesting novel combinations of colors, shapes, and textures in the artistic realm, thereby expanding the artist's expressive repertoire. In science, AI could aid researchers by revealing unexpected connections between disparate pieces of information, paving the way for ground-breaking discoveries. Furthermore, creative interaction goes beyond individuality, enveloping societal and cultural dimensions. It could influence how we communicate, learn, and collaborate, potentially leading to more diverse, inclusive, and innovative societies.

In the ever-evolving landscape, countless opportunities and challenges require us to reimagine creativity, transforming it from a solitary endeavor into a collaborative one. The unfolding narrative of creative intelligence tells us that understanding creativity goes beyond mere discovery, requiring a holistic understanding and collaborative effort. As AI and humans continue their co-evolution, the scope of creative possibilities is set to widen, enabling us to carve new routes in our shared creative journey.

9.7 ART TRANSCENDS BOTH SELF AND TECHNOLOGY

In its deepest essence, art serves as a conduit connecting our individual identities to the boundless expanse of collective consciousness. It functions as a vehicle for transcendence, guiding us beyond our confines into a realm where we simultaneously exist as creators and observers of beauty. This duality fosters a unique form of self-transcendence where we move beyond our immediate selves and delve into a space that resonates personally and universally. However, the beauty encapsulated in art does not emerge in isolation. It is a testament to the mind's incredible power, fueled by the boundless reserves of imagination and creativity inherent in the human psyche. Art's roots trace back to the fertile grounds of our thoughts, nurtured by our emotional reservoir and the warmth of our creative energies.

Imagination and creativity form the backbone of artistic expression. Imagination propels us to envision the unseen, inviting us to step beyond the ordinary and embrace the extraordinary. It lays the initial brushstrokes of potentiality on our consciousness. Conversely, creativity acts as a transformative force, converting these nascent visions into tangible expressions, crafting compelling narratives, evocative melodies, and vivid imagery from our most profound dreams and fears. These twin pillars of art, imagination and creativity, are not born in a vacuum. They stem from a myriad of influences, both external and internal. Our experiences, memories, cultural context, and environment shape our creative instincts, while our introspective journeys, consciousness, emotions, and intuition define our imaginative spirit. The synergy of these diverse influences gives birth to the mind's power that ultimately fuels art and creativity.

Fundamentally, art serves as a pathway to self-transcendence and reflects our most profound existential quests. It embodies the question and the answer, the journey and the destination, the dream and the reality. We explore our humanity's depths through creation, revealing layers of meaning, understanding, and connection. We engage in a universal dialogue, making sense of our existence and position within the grand cosmic tapestry. Thus, art is a testament to our endless quest for understanding and expression, a timeless tribute to the human mind's limitless potential. Art is essentially the exquisite output of the brain. It transcends the physical constraints, illustrating the intricate workings of the mind. With technologies like text-conditional image generation, we witness an intriguing convergence of human cognitive processes and artificial neural networks.

Text-conditional image generation represents a unique moment when a specific human brain's operations harmonize with a particular state of an artificial neural network. It showcases the symbiosis between the two, with the human brain offering creative sparks and the neural network actualizing them using its data processing and pattern recognition capabilities.

This collaborative creative process, fueled by human abstraction, symbolism, and emotion, and propelled by data-driven precision of AI, amplifies the potential of what art can be. It heralds a new frontier of artistic expression, shaped by the fusion of human intelligence and AI. As technologies like text-conditional image generation evolve, they promise to revolutionize our understanding of art, creativity, and the mind's formidable power.

9.8 CLOSING THOUGHTS

The narrative surrounding creativity has historically been eclipsed by the myth of the "creative genius"—an isolated, divinely inspired entity. This representation, however, significantly marginalizes the inherently social dimensions of the creative process, which is, in essence, a tapestry woven through the interplay of a multiplicity of intellects and contextual backdrops. Examining the social facets of creativity unveils a complex network of interrelated discourses encompassing methodologies, philosophies, gender dynamics, and cultural paradigms. These thoughts have gained unprecedented pertinence in the current period, hallmarked by the advent of generative and creative AI.

AI-facilitated means heralding a disruption to conventional canons of creativity, catalyzing insightful examinations, and requiring a critical reappraisal of entrenched dogmas. One exemplar is text-conditional image generation, a potent forerunner of this transformation. By synthesizing visual artifacts predicated upon textual stimuli, this technology expands the creative horizon beyond the exclusive precincts of human inventiveness. It castigates the notion of the artist as an insular "genius," necessitating a fundamental reconceptualization of the artist's role and the creative odyssey in this new world of AI-infused creativity.

As AI systems proliferate into multiple aspects of our existence, we are inevitably led to contemplate the indispensability of the "creative genius" in the artistic domain. If automatons can simulate or feasibly augment the creative process, what transformation awaits the role of the artist? It is plausible that the artist evolves into an avant-garde exemplar of creativity by engaging in a symbiotic co-creation with AI and adding human elements like emotions, deep understanding, and cultural context, which machines still cannot grasp.

When AI and arts come together, it pushes us to explore what creativity is, why artists are important, and how humans and machines can work together in creative expression. These are questions about technology or art styles and deeper philosophical and cultural issues that need careful thought and conversation.

The use of AI in creativity marks an exciting change where we must redefine and reimagine what creativity means. The change at hand represents more than just a technological shift. It signifies a profound transformation in our understanding of art, creativity, and the boundless potential of human inventiveness.

NOTES

1. This myth was deconstructed in a 1995 study by Alfonso Montuori and Ronald Purser, which pointed to the "problematic nature of hyper-individualistic understanding of creativity" and substantiated the idea that collaboration is essential in achieving creative breakthroughs, observation valid in art and design as well as in all other areas of human achievement, where creativity is a cumulative and collaborative pursuit. Deconstructing the Lone Genius Myth: Toward a Contextual View of Creativity, *Journal of Humanistic Psychology*, vol. 35(3):69–112. 1995. Retrieved from https://www.bbc.com/worklife/article/20210308-the-lone-genius-myth-why-even-great-minds-collaborate.

2. A Frontiers of Psychology research study in cultural psychology and social psychology emphasizes the importance of social interaction, communication, and collaboration in the creative process. This study proposes that creativity is not solely an individualistic endeavor but is "distributed" among audiences, materials, embodied actions, and the historical and sociocultural context of the creative activity and environment. This view expands the potential for creative collaboration beyond instances of direct human interaction and engagement. Retrieved from https://doi.org/10.3389/fpsyg.2021.713445.

3. A Harvard Business School paper, "In Pursuit of Everyday Creativity," fundamentally challenges the prevailing notion of creativity as an elusive and exceptional trait, accessible only to a select few. Instead, it advocates for a more inclusive and democratic view of creativity, suggesting that it is a capability inherent in all individuals, and can manifest in a variety of contexts and everyday activities. The authors argue that by recognizing and valuing the diverse ways in which creativity can be expressed, we can foster a more supportive environment that encourages innovative thinking and problem-solving across a broader spectrum of society. This perspective not only promotes a wider understanding of what constitutes creativity but also has the potential to unlock untapped potential in individuals and organizations alike. Retrieved from https://www.hbs.edu/ris/Publication%20Files/18-002_ee708f75-293f-4494-bf93-df5cd96b48a6.pdf.

4. Wang, Ge. 2019. Humans in the Loop: The Design of Interactive AI Systems. Retrieved from https://hai.stanford.edu/news/humans-loop-design-interactive-ai-systems.

5. Human-machine partnership with artificial intelligence for chest radiograph diagnosis. *NPJ Journal* 2019. Retrieved from https://www.nature.com/articles/s41746-019-0189-7.

6. According to H. James Wilson and Paul R. Daugherty, contrary to the widespread apprehension of robotic usurpation of human roles, it is essential to comprehend that workforce reduction through automation may only yield transient productivity surges, as elucidated by the authors' extensive study encompassing 1,500 diverse firms. They posited that augmentative collaboration between human expertise and AI capabilities is the linchpin for substantial performance enhancements. This symbiosis entails human stewardship in training AI systems, interpreting their outputs, and ensuring ethical deployment. Reciprocally, AI can expedite humans' tasks by streamlining information acquisition, data analytics, routine customer interactions, and manual labor, consequently liberating human resources for engagements demanding leadership, creativity, discernment, and innate human competencies. Collaborative Intelligence: Humans and AI Are Joining Forces. HBR Magazine 2018. Retrieved from https://hbr.org/2018/07/collaborative-intelligence-humans-and-ai-are-joining-forces.

7. "How Generative AI Can Augment Human Creativity" (Eapen T, Finkenstadt DJ, Folk J and Venkataswamy L. published in Harvard Business Review 2023) highlights how generative AI can bolster human creativity and democratize innovation by aiding employees, especially in creative and innovative roles, in enhancing cognitive abilities and refining ideas. It also underscores generative AI's role in fostering a democratized innovation ecosystem where customers contribute to ideation and development, unlocking diverse perspectives and more robust innovations. Retrieved from https://hbr.org/2023/07/how-generative-ai-can-augment-human-creativity.

8. A 2023 World Economic Forum study highlights the positive impact of AI on creativity and innovation. As AI becomes more intelligent, it can increasingly assist in providing new insights and quickening the pace of innovation. With intentional use, AI can be employed to free up time for creative activities. Retrieved from https://www.weforum.org/agenda/2023/02/ai-can-catalyze-and-inhibit-your-creativity-here-is-how/.

9. **Creative intelligence**, defined as experiential intelligence, entails the faculty to conceive inventive resolutions to novel challenges. It often necessitates unorthodox or distinct modes of cogitation, potentially in concert with peers or solitude. This dimension of intelligence

constitutes one of the tripartite categories in Robert Sternberg's seminal "Triarchic Theory of Intelligence," promulgated in 1985. The complementary duo encompasses:

a. Analytical intelligence refers to the capacity to deconstruct quandaries into their constituent elements, execute analytical scrutiny, and synthesize a viable solution.

b. Practical intelligence, colloquially dubbed as "street smartness," embodies the aptitude to leverage quotidian wisdom and experiential insights in contriving pragmatic problem-solving strategies. Definition retrieved from https://www.indeed.com/career-advice/career-development/creative-intelligence-example. (More about Robert Stenberg at http://www.robertjsternberg.com/successful-intelligence).

CHAPTER 10

Intention, Articulation, and Manifestation

10.1 MEANING, ENERGY, AND MATTER

In the first chapter of this book, I introduced Intention, Articulation, and Manifestation as fundamental to the creation of any art and design artifact. I paid homage to David Bohm's unfolding vision of wholeness as the inspiration for this thought taxonomy. In Bohm's concept, Matter, Energy, and Meaning coexist and are irreplaceable.[1] His compelling vision of wholeness emphasized the interconnectedness of all aspects of reality, serving as a basis for a comprehensive thought taxonomy. Central to his paradigm are three core elements: matter, energy, and meaning. According to Bohm, these elements are interconnected, coexist inseparably, and are irreplaceable in the grand scheme of existence.

In Bohm's view, "matter" refers to the tangible physical entities we encounter in the observable universe and encapsulates the underlying substratum of all forms. It is the substance of the cosmos, constituting the physical reality in which we exist. In Bohm's perspective, matter does not exist in isolation; it is an integral part of a complex, dynamic system, continuously interacting with other elements within this universal framework.

"Energy," in Bohm's construct, is intrinsically linked to matter. He subscribed to the idea central to modern physics that matter and energy are interchangeable, but he extended this concept further, considering energy as an active principle driving change and transformation in the universe. For Bohm, energy is the force animating matter, the unseen mover that influences the structure and behavior of physical entities. Energy propels the dynamics of the universe, setting the stage for the continuous dance of creation and destruction.

The third essential element in Bohm's framework is "meaning." Unlike many of his contemporaries in the scientific community, Bohm contended that meaning is not a peripheral human construct but a fundamental feature of reality. For him, meaning is not just a human-centered product of consciousness but an inherent characteristic of the universe

DOI: 10.1201/9781003450139-14

itself. Meaning serves as the bridge connecting matter and energy, offering a context in which the actions of the physical world can be understood. The interpretive layer allows us to make sense of the complex interplay between matter and energy.

Bohm perceived these elements—matter, energy, and meaning—as deeply interconnected, each influencing and being influenced by the others. He proposed that they coexist in an intricate, holistic dance that shapes the reality we experience. Bohm's revolutionary construct asserts that these elements are irreplaceable, each playing a unique and crucial role in the functioning of universe. In this framework, removing or isolating one aspect would disrupt the balance, leading to a limited, fragmented understanding of reality. Bohm's model, with its emphasis on wholeness and interconnection, encourages us to appreciate the complex, interwoven tapestry of existence, where matter, energy, and meaning exist not as isolated entities but as integral parts of a harmonious whole.

Within the framework of generative artificial intelligence (AI), creativity is fundamentally a three-step process: intention, articulation, and manifestation. I propose that in this context, intention is meaning, articulation is energy, and manifestation is matter.

"Intention" stands for a creative endeavor's inherent purpose or meaning, serving as the cornerstone of the process. The concept, idea, or vision initiates the creative journey. Without a defined intention, the creative process may meander aimlessly. This intention, this defining purpose, guides the path of creation, shaping the subsequent choices and actions within the process.

"Articulation," the second element, is the dynamic energy propelling the creative process. It encapsulates the act of expressing and communicating the initial idea. Various methods can achieve this, depending on the context—a writer may use words, a painter would opt for strokes, a musician might rely on notes, and a programmer could employ code. Articulation converts abstract intention into a communicable form, serving as a conduit between the internal idea and its external expression.

"Manifestation" is the tangible realization of the initial idea, shaped by the energy of articulation. Intention and articulation transmute into a tangible entity, essentially adopting a physical form. It symbolizes the completion of the creative process. A mere idea, once manifested, can be shared, experienced, and appreciated by others in the world.

These elements—intention as meaning, articulation as energy, and manifestation as matter—form the triad of creative expression. They underscore the fact that creativity is more than a spark of inspiration. It requires a purposeful direction (intention), an active translation of the idea (articulation), and a process of making the idea tangible (manifestation).

The phrase "Intention is Meaning, Articulation is Energy, Manifestation is Matter" is a potent reminder of this dynamic process, emphasizing the multi-dimensional nature of creativity. It illuminates each element's crucial role in transforming a simple idea into a tangible reality.

By understanding and embracing this triad, we can approach the creative process more mindfully, fostering purpose-driven, articulate, and action-oriented creativity. This nuanced comprehension can influence our creative endeavors and our collective perspective on creativity, ultimately enriching our engagement with the world around us.

Furthermore, this triad takes on additional significance in the age of generative AI. As we navigate the evolving landscape of human and artificial creativity, we must constantly reassess and refine our understanding of these elements. How do intention, articulation, and manifestation manifest in AI? How do we ensure that AI-generated creations maintain a sense of meaning, harness the energy of articulation effectively, and realize their full potential through manifestation? Exploring these questions will be crucial as we continue to blur the lines between humans and machines in the creative arena.

10.2 INTENTION CREATES A SYSTEM OF MEANING

In its myriad forms, art serves as a potent conduit for conveying the artist's intentions, thoughts, and emotions.[2] It breathes life into abstract ideas, turning them into tangible experiences. From paintings and sculptures to music and literature, art transforms the artist's purpose into a form perceivable by others.

The motivation underlying a piece of artwork operates as its foundational impetus, steering the creative process and instilling the work with substantive meaning. Such motivations span many objectives, from encapsulating ephemeral instances of natural splendor and communicating a political commentary to manifesting personal narratives and emotional states.

Consider a painting as an illustration. The genesis of its creation might stem from the artist's aspiration to immortalize the evanescent allure of a sunset or articulate its critique of the prevailing socio-political milieu. This intrinsic motivation acts as the navigational instrument that orchestrates the creative endeavor, influencing the artist's selection of color palettes, texture, form, and even the nuances of their brushwork. Consequently, the resultant painting evolves into a conduit, transmitting the artist's intellectual and emotional fabric to the audience. It transcends mere mastery of technique, embodying the artist's raison d'être and inspirations, thereby rendering the motivation as the animating essence of the artwork.

Earlier, we discussed the significance of intentionality in the manifestation process, noting that it serves as a guiding principle for creation. In text-conditional image generation, the intention becomes the creative force behind the emergent image, showcasing its significance.

Understanding image generation through textual prompts reveals an intricate symbiotic dance between human intention and AI. This dance, set against the backdrop of a neural network, tells the story of how abstract intent is translated into concrete visual form. It traces the journey from thought to form, from unseen to seen.

The act of creation begins with the user's intention, expressed as a textual prompt that initiates the AI system's creative potential. This prompt becomes the blueprint for the ensuing creation. Its nuances and specificity shape the nature of the image that will eventually form, guiding the assembly of pixels like a conductor directing an orchestra.

However, as conveyed by the textual prompt, the user's intention is not merely suggestive. It is determinative, influencing the output image's quality, style, and fidelity to the envisioned concept (Figure 10.1). The user's understanding of their concept plays a crucial role in shaping their intention, profoundly impacting the manifested image's resonance.

FIGURE 10.1 A model wearing a wedding gown made of old fishing net materials, hyper-detailed, highly detailed, dramatic lighting, intricate, elegant, gorgeous, fractal structure, Agfa Vista 200, on a white background.

Once this intention is fed into the system, the AI interprets and understands it. It decodes human language into data, then uses its learning capabilities to make sense of the text and manifest the user's intention.

Text-conditional image generation showcases the philosophical axiom of intention guiding manifestation, bringing this abstract concept into the real world. It is a beautiful fusion of human intent and machine learning, leading to a new realm of creativity and expression. In this dance of co-creation, human creative will and AI computational prowess come together, crafting a visual representation that is a testament to creative intention's power. Hence, setting a clear and specific intention is crucial for successful manifestation.

The level of specificity in your intention significantly influences the accuracy of the result you aim to achieve. Suppose an AI is given a detailed prompt, such as a peaceful sunset over a calm ocean. In that case, it will likely generate a visual output mirroring these details—utilizing warm colors, depicting gentle waves, and embodying a serene atmosphere. In this scenario, one's intention is a decisive factor, influencing the final form of the image produced. It functions not simply as a guide but essentially as a pathway for realizing your envisioned image. A key aspect of intentionality within AI is highlighted here—the user's desired outcome's specificity directly affects the precision of the AI-generated output.

This principle of intentionality and its influence on the outcome is not confined to AI but extends to a broader philosophical conversation. In any creative process, be it artistic, scientific, or technological, the clarity in one's intention dictates the precision of the end product. Detailed intentionality provides a roadmap that enhances clarity, facilitating a more focused and streamlined path toward achieving the desired output.[3] This observation underpins the idea that intention is not a dormant factor but an active element that shapes, guides, and fine-tunes outcomes. Therefore, refining one's intentionality should be considered a critical step in realizing a specific outcome. This principle is universal, applicable whether the subject is an AI generating an image or an artist crafting a masterpiece.

Text-conditional image generation offers significant flexibility, enabling you to introduce various variations to your original intent. Adjusting parameters such as color, shape, and size allows you to tailor the generated image to precisely meet your requirements. It is essential to trust the manifestation process and let go of any rigid expectations regarding the outcome during this process.

The partnership between human intention and AI capabilities opens up new possibilities for experimentation and discovery. By introducing subtle changes or unexpected elements into the text prompts, you can stimulate the model to produce innovative and unconventional images. This interaction between intent and exploration can result in astonishing outputs and novel artistic expressions that challenge traditional norms of visual representation (Figure 10.2). This blend of human intentionality and AI's computational power launches us into a new creative exploration and discovery era. It offers an unexplored landscape with potential, inviting us to traverse new territories in visual artistry.

In this context, even slight alterations or unexpected elements in the textual prompts can act as catalysts, encouraging the model to depart from the traditional path. This approach is similar to causing ripples in a calm lake water, which disrupts the status quo and initiates new patterns. It urges the AI model to venture beyond conventional norms and produce

FIGURE 10.2 A model wearing jacket made of discarded fabrics, plastic caps, ropes, and paper maps.

FIGURE 10.3 Extending the visual vocabulary of Apple's Vision Pro to other objects. Blended image generation.

innovative and unconventional images. The interplay between intention and exploration creates a dynamic ebb and flow that is both exhilarating and unpredictable. The user's intention choreographs the performance, while the AI model—the dancer—brings it to life through its unique interpretations. This collaboration can result in surprising outcomes, often serendipitous, leading to fresh artistic expressions (Figure 10.3).

Each image generated in this manner becomes a symbol of this unique collaboration. It represents a particular moment in the creative journey, as unique as a fingerprint. However, this process is not only about producing new visuals—it is about constructing a new language of visual communication that expresses the unspoken, the unseen, and the unimagined. It empowers artists to break the bounds of their imagination, to visualize and manifest ideas that once existed only in the realm of the unmanifested.

This synergistic relationship between human intention and text-conditional image generation signifies a paradigm shift in our comprehension of creative potentialities. It represents a technological advance and a radical reorientation of our conceptual frameworks regarding the very process of creation.

Creation has been primarily human-centric in the traditional schema, with the artist being the primary source and executor of creativity. However, the advent of text-conditional image generation, powered by AI, brings a disruptive modification to this narrative. It introduces a collaborative dimension, where the human artist and AI coalesce in a dynamic partnership, each contributing distinct elements to the final creation.

Human intention directs and shapes the creative process, infusing it with subjective experiences, emotions, and cognitive structures. It acts as the seed from which the creation grows, setting the foundational premises for what the artwork is intended to express or evoke. On the other hand, AI serves as the facilitator, leveraging advanced algorithms to translate these intentions into visual constructs. It takes on the role of an adept assistant, expanding upon human intentions, executing precise translations, and enabling the exploration of possibilities that might be challenging for humans alone.

This fusion of human creativity with AI thus heralds a new era of artistic expression, where the boundaries of creation are continually stretched and redefined. It points toward a future where our creative processes are not just supplemented but actively enhanced by AI. This innovative synergy could open new horizons in numerous fields, ranging from digital art and design to visual storytelling and beyond, reshaping the landscape of creativity in profound ways. The transformative synergy between human intent and AI-powered image generation expands our creative possibilities and invites a more profound, nuanced discourse on the nature and future of creativity itself.

10.3 INTENTION AND MEANING

Meaning arises from a blend of intention and systematic process. This combination lays down the foundation of a structure. As these meaning-making systems persist and evolve, they incorporate additional structures into the framework. These supplementary structures arise from the continually evolving meaning-making system.

All forms of intelligence, natural or artificial, hinge on the conscious selection of intent. Each thought, decision, and action is supported by an underlying intention—a motive propelling us toward our goals. We shape our lives and the world around us by consciously choosing our intentions.

The deliberate selection of intention is a testament to our power as sentient beings. It acknowledges our ability to sculpt our reality, interweaving threads of intention into the tapestry of existence. While AI possesses the requisite knowledge, it lacks intent. Devoid of intention, AI remains a compendium of algorithms incapable of equaling the complexity of natural intelligence.

The process of creation is unique, commencing with the artist's intention. This intention is the motivational force that impels the artist to create, laying the groundwork for the emergence of the artwork. The intention can be a profoundly personal and emotional catalyst, inspiring artists to share their vision with the world. Not only does the artist's intention drive the artwork's creation, but it also instills it with meaning and purpose.

The intention is not a stagnant concept but a dynamic force with the power to guide and shape the creative process. It can inspire and inform the artist's choices throughout the creative journey, from conception to execution. In addition, the intention can evolve during the process, allowing a deeper and more nuanced expression of the artist's vision. The artistic creation's outcome is intimately connected to the guiding intention. The artist's chosen forms, techniques, and mediums, guided by this intent, play a decisive role in shaping the final product and the sensory experience it elicits.

Creation materializes intention, transitioning it from an abstract idea into a tangible expression. In generative AI, intention functions as the input that triggers the neural network, yielding diverse visual results. The interaction between intention, form, and energy facilitates the birth of artistic creations, providing many visual experiences.

10.4 ARTICULATION

Articulation is a process by which we convert our intentions into communicable forms. It is a transformative link between abstract ideas and their tangible artistic manifestations. In art, effective articulation shapes the final aesthetics and overall perception of images, resonating with the artist's intent. Artists can use various linguistic and visual elements to articulate their intentions, thus evoking specific emotions, conveying narratives, and expressing unique viewpoints.

The strength of articulation rests in its ability to render abstract concepts concrete, transforming our intentions into something shareable and comprehensible. Articulation encapsulates the conversion of intended meaning into a tangible form that can be visually interpreted. This process is vital for cultivating artistic expression and inspiring novel, exciting art pieces. Each element modifies the overall semantic content by blending linguistic elements, such as words and phrases. The interplay of these linguistic components becomes paramount when constructing complex sentences, necessitating precision and creativity for effective communication. Artistic skill is demonstrated in constructing logical sequences of ideas through attributes such as shape, color, spatial location, mood, ambiance, movement, emotional landscapes, and more.

Language, the primary tool of articulation, is essential for refining our creative ability to employ symbols. It influences our aesthetic judgments, thereby enhancing our capacity to visualize. The knowledge and usage of symbols shape our perception and direct our artistic expressions. Language facilitates the translation of thoughts and feelings into a medium that others can share and comprehend.

Articulation is the alchemical process that voices intention, translating thoughts and ideas into a tangible form. It bridges the gap between the abstract and concrete and enables a deeper understanding and connection. Articulation could manifest in various forms, from written or spoken language to visual images and sounds, aiming to translate thoughts and feelings into a universally comprehensible format.

Articulation extends beyond mere communication—it is a transformative process that gives life to thoughts and ideas, integrating them into our collective human experience. Our intentions become tangible through articulation, reaching beyond individual consciousness to resonate with others. Words become carriers of meaning, embodying emotions, perspectives, and aspirations. They adapt to express our thoughts, desires, and beliefs, facilitating communication of our inner worlds. Through this linguistic artistry, we engage in dialogues with ourselves and the world around us, aiming to illuminate and build connections.

The act of articulation transforms us into both artists and interpreters. We shape raw materials into creations teeming with intention, breathing life into formless ideas. Balancing precision and spontaneity, we strive to encapsulate the essence of our intentions

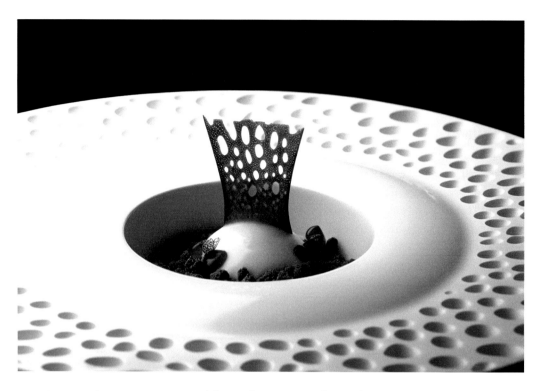

FIGURE 10.4   A parametric-inspired design for a sweet and sour dessert.

in a resonant form (Figure 10.4). This process liberates and empowers us as our deepest thoughts and feelings become a shared language that surpasses individual confines.

In text-conditional image generation, the role of articulation is paramount. It directs the creation of images by guiding the expression of specific attributes, ideas, or emotions through written or spoken language. Words act as a driving force, molding the artistic process. They can embody specific characteristics, detailing the visual elements or qualities the artist seeks to represent. Alternatively, they can serve as poetic expressions, enriching the artwork with depth and emotion. An AI model can more easily generate images that align with the envisioned meaning and tone by clearly and succinctly expressing intentions and desires (Figure 10.5).

Articulation in this context also includes using words to denote desired physical properties. Artists may define their vision by describing their prospective artwork's anticipated form, texture, and composition. This method helps to solidify their intentions and provides a roadmap for the artistic venture. Articulation can also encompass aspirational statements. Such statements can ignite inspiration and motivation in both the artist and the observer, acting as a propelling force behind the artwork's creation and interpretation.

Common archetypes, such as symbols or cultural references, can serve as tools for articulation. These universally recognized entities carry shared meanings and connotations that facilitate immediate recognition and connection. However, as extensively discussed in Chapter 4, relying on archetypes can restrain the potential of generative AI,

FIGURE 10.5 A countryside-style photograph of a scene or landscape in Tuscany with a luxury villa, farm, or textile loom where tradition meets innovation, where raw natural elements are combined with new processing/preservation techniques to create an exclusively long-lasting textile. Hyper-detailed, highly detailed, dramatic lighting.

steering it toward replicating a pre-trained sample—the archetype—rather than innovating a new form.

In the sphere of generative AI, articulation assumes a distinct aspect. Human linguistic limitations do not constrain AI. AI algorithms do not strive to rationalize or conceive the shape the intended creation should assume. Instead, once the neural network has assimilated the necessary information and the desire to generate a specific type of artifact is established, the AI produces something potentially beyond human conception. AI's strength lies in its capacity to traverse immense possibilities, reveal unexpected links, and deliver singular outcomes surpassing human imagination. Incorporating AI into the creative process is one of the numerous benefits. By integrating the power of AI with our inherent creativity, we can challenge the conventional limits in the art realm, crafting truly pioneering and compelling works that captivate and inspire.

10.5 MANIFESTATION

In art and design, manifestation means realizing tangible objects or artifacts that encapsulate the creator's intention. The transmutation process renders abstract intentions and formulated concepts into perceptible forms. Manifestation metamorphoses cognitive constructs into tactile reality, thus serving as a critical conduit between the abstract and the concrete.

This transformational journey is akin to a mesmerizing ballet of creation, where ideas, like dancers, are choreographed into a sequence of visible expressions, each movement manifesting a fragment of the artist's vision. This process breathes life into the ethereal landscape of desires and thoughts, materializing them into entities that can be seen, touched, and experienced.

Manifestation, therefore, can be viewed as an interpretive act of translation. It deciphers the encrypted language of the mind, unravels the intricate tapestry of intention, and weaves it into the tangible realm. It is an artistic alchemy that transmutes the leaden weight of intangible thoughts into the golden touch of visible expressions.

Just as a sculptor carves a block of marble to reveal the form hidden within, an artist, through manifestation, peels back layers of abstraction to expose the essence of their intent. This extraction of tangible reality from the crucible of abstract thought underscores the depth of the creative process, highlighting the transformative power that lies in the act of manifestation. Thus, the manifestation process in art and design is not merely a step in producing artwork but a profound journey of conversion. It demystifies abstract ideas, transcribes ephemeral emotions, and crystallizes elusive intent, ultimately enabling the birth of unique artistic expressions (Figures 10.6 and 10.7).

Intention fuels the manifestation process, serving as a conscious choice and desired outcome. It enlivens the creative journey, providing a direction for artistic expression. Manifestation's strength lies in its underpinning intention, the force that transforms the formless into forms and breathes life into the intangible. The pulsating core of creativity and the catalyst ignites the spark of inspiration. Embracing our intentions allows us to tap into a world of boundless possibilities, with constraints only imposed by our limitations.

FIGURE 10.6   A highly impractical but beautiful tool.

FIGURE 10.7   A model wearing wedding dress made of discarded fishing nets.

Manifestation marks the final phase of the creative process, transmuting an idea into a tangible reality. This stage requires intention, articulation, creativity, experimentation, and a comprehensive understanding of the medium. A successfully manifested work of art can captivate, inspire, and engage the viewer, leaving a lasting impact. Through manifestation, art becomes tangible, offering a physical or experiential existence. Human-AI collaboration expands the horizons of artistic possibilities, amplifying our creative capacities and paving new paths for imagination.

The legacy of art and design mirrors human creativity, imagination, and ingenuity. From our prehistoric ancestors' cave paintings to the modern digital revolution, art has always been a medium for expression, communication, and storytelling. This digital age has opened new avenues for artistic exploration and experimentation, inviting us to consider the transformative impact of AI and technologies like augmented reality. However, meaningful expressions and creations stem from the core of our creative aspirations. Platforms like YouTube, Instagram, and TikTok have already democratized content creation. Text-conditional image generators promise to propel this democratization to new heights, empowering every individual to venture into the realm of artistic expression.

AI's magic lies in its potential to democratize creativity, extending an invitation to people of all backgrounds to participate in the act of creation.[4] The domain of creativity is no longer a guarded privilege for a select few but an open field for anyone with a creative vision and access to the digital world. This dynamic shift embodies a significant philosophical transition, reframing creativity from an elitist practice to a universally accessible human attribute.

In this context, AI's role extends beyond a tool for artistic creation; it serves as a partner in the journey of discovery and self-expression. It enables individuals to unlock their latent creative potential and venture into an expansive realm of artistic possibilities. This newfound creative partner enhances our ability to express our unique perspectives, fostering an environment where every creative voice has the potential to resonate, thereby enriching our collective human narrative.

AI's impact on art and design is deeply intertwined with its ability to ignite human curiosity, provoke our expressive desires, and unlock our inherent creative capabilities. AI acts as a catalyst in our creative pursuits, assisting us in surpassing physical and cognitive limitations while guiding us to explore our artistic potential. This transformative power of AI also underscores the democratization of art and design. It signifies an era of inclusivity and diversity, bringing to the fore the voices of those previously marginalized and illuminating the visions of those overlooked by the conventional art world. As AI empowers a broader spectrum of individuals to engage in creative dialogue, it challenges established norms, disrupting traditional gatekeeping practices and fostering a vibrant tapestry of art that reflects the richness of human expression.

AI's role in this revolution promotes a sense of universal belonging and cultivates a global creative community unified by a shared passion. It dissolves long-standing dichotomies, from the professional-amateur divide to the distinction between "high" and "low" art. The democratized era ensures that everyone has the potential to be an artist, designer, or creator, resulting in art that resonates with the collective creative spirit of humanity.[5]

AI is not a substitute for human creativity but acts as a potent collaborator and co-creator. It amplifies our visions, augments our abilities, and uncovers new frontiers of artistic exploration. The intersection of human ingenuity and technological advancement, where creative intentions blend harmoniously with AI's capabilities, leads to remarkable art that fuels imagination and connects with observers on a profound level.

AI aids in pushing the boundaries of our imagination, fostering philosophical debates about the nature of creativity and its potential for automation. It urges us to redefine or augment our creative tools, prompting reflections on interpretations of artistic value, expression, and authorship and the balance between innovation and tradition.

While AI serves to amplify our innate creativity, it is crucial to remember that art and design transcend computational algorithms and encoded scripts and resonate with our collective human experience. The future landscape of art and design will not focus solely on AI's capabilities but, more importantly, on how we, as creative beings, shape and harness this technology. As we employ AI to expand our artistic potential, we transition from passive observation to active participation, wielding this technology as a brush to paint our creative canvases. The guiding question for the future of art and design is not merely about the capacity of the technology but how we can leverage it to catalyze our creative expansion and artistic revolution.

10.6 CLOSING THOUGHTS

Intrinsic to our human nature is the unquenchable thirst to evolve and exceed our current existence's boundaries. It is a ubiquitous aspect of the human experience - this relentless pursuit of expansion, enrichment, and self-transcendence. This insatiable craving for growth resides in the heart of the Self - the core of our being that resonates with a higher purpose and significance. The Self fuels our journey toward a richer, more profound understanding of our place in the universe.

As we embark on this journey of personal evolution, we inevitably encounter obstacles and hurdles. It demands courage, introspection, and an acceptance of the need to discard antiquated habits and attachments that no longer align with our purpose. It implores us to surrender to the unknown, venture boldly into the terrain of ambiguity, and embrace the transformative potential within each of us.

However, this metamorphosis is not a solitary expedition. It is an expansive, collective venture. As increasing numbers of individuals unlock their true capabilities and potential, we collectively catalyze a paradigm shift in human consciousness, guiding it toward a more comprehensive, inclusive understanding of existence.

Pursuing self-transcendence is an unending quest that offers infinite horizons of understanding and awareness to discover. Nevertheless, it is precisely this ceaseless journey that infuses life with excitement and fulfillment. We continually strive to outgrow our current selves, driven by the yearning to become something more. This aspiration to transcend our current state of being is the fundamental mission of the Self. This principle drives our creation's raison d'être and the relentless pursuit of evolution.

NOTES

1. Bohm, David. (1980). Wholeness and the Implicate Order. Routledge & Paul Kegan. PDF edition published in the Taylor and Francis e-Library, 2005.
2. Interestingly, the term "emotion" originates from the Latin "e" (out) and "move" (move), implying the concept of movement or release. The natural flow of emotions is of high relevance when considering this aspect. However, they often tend to accumulate, which can lead to various issues if not addressed. Artistic expression serves as an effective medium for releasing emotions. This release is particularly vital for human beings, who are inherently designed to express themselves. This natural inclination for expression is evident among young children, who, uninhibited by societal norms, freely display their emotions through screams of happiness, shouts of anger, or spontaneous crying. Retrieved from https://www.artsacad.net/the-importance-of-expressing-emotion-through-art.
3. When referring to "art" in this context, the term primarily encapsulates any deliberately created work that exhibits the creative expression of the human intellect. Historically, this definition might conjure images of paintings or sculptures. However, the domain of art has proven to be diverse and dynamic, extending to include literature, theater, film, performance art, and installations, among others. Artistic intention or motivation profoundly influences the outcome recognized as artwork. Similar to how a screenplay determines the progression of a film's plot, an artist's intention guides the choice of material and its application, shaping the creation and perception of the artwork. Retrieved from https://humanitiescenter.byu.edu/an-artists-intention.
4. In this chapter, the democratization of creativity was approached from the perspective of creative behaviour as an Agentic Action Model (CBAA). This model bridges cognitive and motivational elements, considering them as primary catalysts for creative activity. Specifically, it posits cognitive, creative potential as a requisite foundation for any creative activities and accomplishments. In addition, it proposes the mediating role of creative confidence and the perceived value of creativity in facilitating the connection between potential and behavior.

Karwowski M., Beghetto R. A. (2019). Creative behavior as agentic action. *Psychology of Aesthetics, Creativity, and the Arts*, vol. 13(4), 402–415. Retrieved from https://doi.org/10.1037/aca0000190.

5. The classification of art into low, middle, and high art has been a subject of debate, with some arguing that these aesthetic distinctions are outdated or unrelated to an artwork's inherent aesthetic qualities. Critics of these classifications might propose alternative ways of engaging with art, such as academic analysis, journalistic criticism, or casual consumption, instead of adhering to hierarchical labels. Some also argue that these labels may perpetuate class-based distinctions or anachronistic notions of the isolated artistic genius. Ultimately, the classification of art into low, middle, or high may depend on the relationship between the viewer, their aesthetic response, and the artwork itself. Retrieved from https://doi.org/10.1093/jaac/kpac034.

CHAPTER 11

Generative AI as a Disruptor

11.1 THE GREAT DISRUPTOR

The concept of disruption is a transformative force that topples the ramparts of established norms and paves the way for the birth of a new epoch. Technological disruptions have sculpted new paths for communication, information acquisition, and interaction with our world, consequently inciting paradigm shifts in social, economic, and cultural structures. However, disruption is not just about societal or technological shifts; it is an invitation, a call to arms that beckons us to create a future that transcends our present comprehension actively. Disruption catalyzes us to delve into the unknown, challenge entrenched paradigms, and conceive hitherto unimagined possibilities.

In its purest form, disruption signifies a seismic alteration in the existing paradigm that questions the status quo and fuels forward momentum. We are not talking about minor or transitory changes here. Instead, it is about a radical deviation that fosters a new paradigm and propels growth, innovation, and positive transformation. In the technology realm, disruption has irrevocably altered industries and expanded the horizons of human capabilities, prodding us to voyage into unexplored frontiers of innovation.

With the advent of generative artificial intelligence (AI), we are standing on the precipice of another disruption. This chapter will dissect the concept of disruption, encompassing aspects like the *disruption index* and the *disruption framework*, and distinguish between *transition* and *transformational change*. Understanding these facets is critical for comprehending the larger context in which generative AI operates. By examining the multifaceted nature of disruption, we will gain a comprehensive understanding of the profound impact of generative AI, thus equipping us to navigate and shape the future that it promises.

At its core, disruption represents a seismic shift in the fabric of existence. The profound transformation shakes the foundations of the established order, dismantling the familiar and paving the way for a new era.[1] Disruption is fundamentally about breaking the status quo, introducing a state of unpredictability and potential. It acts as a catalyst, pushing us past the confines of the familiar and into the unfamiliar.

DOI: 10.1201/9781003450139-15

Within the domain of technology, the phenomenon of disruption assumes profound significance. Technological disruptions act as catalysts that extend the frontiers of human capabilities and put to the test the confines of our imaginative faculty. These disruptions have orchestrated a metamorphosis in the conduits of human communication, avenues for information acquisition, and the paradigms through which we traverse the world, tracing back from the Gutenberg press's advent to the Internet's ascendancy.

These technological disruptions have been instrumental in inciting seismic shifts in societal fabric, economic architectures, and cultural landscapes. They stand emblematic of human inventiveness by relentlessly advancing the perimeters of what is conceivable and charting hitherto unexplored corridors of innovation. Through this, they redefine extant benchmarks and inaugurate new epochs of human achievement and aspiration.

At its essence, disruption serves as a call, urging us to traverse uncharted territories, emancipate ourselves from the constraints of conventional wisdom, and set sail on a transformative odyssey. It ignites an impetus to examine deep-seated tenets critically, challenge prevailing norms, and ideate unexplored potentialities. Disruption's origins may lie in politics or technology, but regardless, it summons us to engage proactively and to be architects in the edification of a future that surpasses our current horizon of comprehension.

Through the formidable catalyst that is disruption, we lay the foundation for innovative trajectories, reforge the narratives that define our existences and engage in profound scrutiny of the human condition. This phenomenon is not a mere passive by-product; instead, it is an exhortation to collective action—a call to scholars, innovators, policymakers, and the populace at large—to collaboratively sculpt the very bedrock upon which transformative eras are birthed, thereby effectuating a paradigm shift in the human tapestry of life and experience.

Disruption is not just any change; it is a seismic shift in the existing paradigm that shakes the very foundations of our society.[2] It is a force of nature that can bring down the most powerful corporations and dismantle entrenched systems. Disruption represents a fundamental transformation of our world, where old ideas are destroyed and new ones are created. It is the ultimate expression of human creativity, innovation, and progress.

Disruption, in its most valid form, is more than mere surface-level alterations or stepwise evolutions; it epitomizes a potent and transformational force that permeates the underpinnings of our existence and etches itself into society, politics, and culture. Far from being an ephemeral perturbation or mere deviation, it constitutes a sweeping overhaul that interrogates the bedrock upon which our collective reality rests. By disturbing the pillars of antiquated constructs, disruption clears the arena for the genesis of the novel and avant-garde. It transcends mere differentiation and involves deconstructing that which has outlived its utility.

As a crucible for the collective imagination, disruption provokes audacity, invites the reevaluation of established dogmas, and propels us beyond previously perceived limits. It is synonymous with progress, catalyzing an unstoppable march forward and molding our world in hitherto unimagined fashions. Ultimately, it is the peak of transformation, possessing the quintessential elements to usher in a more prosperous and enlightened future for all.

11.2 THE DISRUPTION INDEX

The disruption index[3] (Figure 11.1) provides one of the most comprehensive frameworks available to position an organization vis-à-vis a disruptor and successfully take advantage of disruption. The index classifies all companies into one of four categories as disruptors, enablers, integrators, and followers.

11.2.1 The Disruptor[4]

Disruptors are transformative entities in the dynamic world of business and innovation. Their unique ability to reimagine traditional business models creates fresh market spaces. By delivering innovative ideas and services, they stimulate entrepreneurship and establish a trend of disruption across industries. They discern unfulfilled customer needs and provide solutions that were once unimagined, thereby setting new benchmarks for innovation and marketplace evolution.

Disruptors, who serve as catalysts for change, challenge conventional norms and cultivate an environment ripe for creativity and entrepreneurial drive. They introduce novel products or services, reshaping consumer expectations and industries alike. These pioneers remove hurdles inhibiting innovation, steering the market towards unexplored horizons. The influence of disruptors permeates the entire business ecosystem, necessitating adaptation from existing market players to avoid obsolescence. They urge industry incumbents to revise their strategies, overhaul their business models, and aspire for more significant innovation. These visionaries inspire established firms and emerging entrepreneurs to elevate their performance and expand the realm of possibilities. Their disruptive wave transforms industries, uncovers latent potential, and heralds a future of continual evolution and breakthroughs.

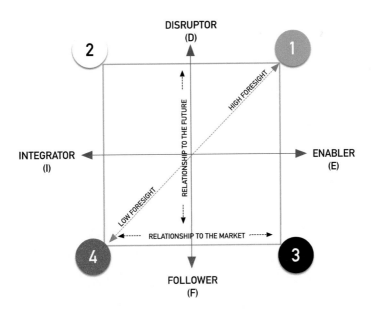

FIGURE 11.1   The disruption index.

Text-conditional image generation is a transformative technology that identifies artistic gaps and reshapes the creative landscape. It introduces a fresh method for producing art, sparking a shift in expectations and encouraging artists to venture into novel creative territories. This technology makes art creation inclusive, reaching a broader audience without requiring advanced artistic abilities.

Like any disruptor, this technology questions traditional art creation and appreciation methods. It can shift the balance of power in the art sphere, providing an advantage to artists who utilize it. As technology continues to evolve, it may pave the way for a new era of generative art, changing our perception and appreciation of artistic creativity.

In the business world, the impact of text-conditional image generation is equally noteworthy. It brings a fresh approach to business communication and visual representation of products or services. It allows companies to visually bring their textual descriptions to life, closing the gap between words and images. This ability to create visually engaging portrayals enhances audience engagement and triggers powerful emotional reactions.

The disruption also extends into the design field, facilitating swift prototyping and concept visualization. By turning textual descriptions into visual entities, decision-making becomes quicker. This technology opens doors for sectors such as architecture, fashion, interior design, and more, where translating text-based ideas into visual interpretations is essential for concept development and effective communication.

11.2.2 The Enabler[5]

Enterprises that function as enablers are instrumental in bolstering industrial expansion and dynamism. Distinct from disruptors, which bring radical innovations or entirely new offerings, enabler businesses concentrate on refining and amplifying extant products and services. This approach undergirds market durability and sustains its contemporary relevance. Enablers can be perceived as the sentinels of industry, shepherding various sectors toward enduring equilibrium and prosperity.[6]

Enabler businesses, regarded as the vertebral column of industries, provide robustness and assurances to all stakeholders. By integrating innovative efficiencies and optimizing established protocols, they facilitate the minimization of expenditures while amplifying quality and productivity. Consequently, this enables consumers to avail themselves of premium products and services at equitable costs.

Although functioning in a predominantly auxiliary capacity, enabler businesses exhibit unwavering assiduity in the quest for innovation. They persistently explore avenues to elevate the attributes and performance of existing offerings and methodologies. Their prescience and proclivity for perpetual refinement catalyze industrial maturation and expansion. This indefatigable dedication to ceaseless enhancement is a hallmark of enabler businesses, accentuating their indispensable contribution to the economic tapestry.

Enabler enterprises are ideally positioned to harness disruptive technologies such as text-conditional image generation. Through its incorporation, enablers can expedite visual content creation while elevating its caliber, culminating in an enriched brand persona and customer experience. Furthermore, by leveraging this groundbreaking technology, enablers can foster more lucid product visualizations, hone design processes, and maintain a cutting-edge posture in technological advancements. Consequently, text-conditional image generation fortifies industry growth and resilience, arming enterprises with the technological arsenal requisite for thriving in an increasingly mercurial and competitive marketplace. In addition, enablers can become synergistic agents that bring disruption and current industry practices into a harmonious fusion, guiding the trajectory of innovation to sustain novelty and continuity.

11.2.3 The Integrator[7]

Integrator businesses are a linchpin in the corporate landscape, emphasizing the amalgamation and harmonization of diverse systems and processes to render operations more fluid. While not necessarily pioneers of disruption, integrators excel by economically and efficiently bringing high-caliber products and services to fruition. They possess specialized competencies in niche technologies, methodologies, or marketing acumen and a profound grasp of the business milieu. This combination of attributes empowers integrators to compete effectively and, sometimes, be the catalysts for disruption across various sectors.[8]

One of the hallmarks of integrator businesses is their finesse in synthesizing disparate components within the corporate sphere. They possess the acumen to discern and capitalize on synergies across multifarious functions, encompassing manufacturing, marketing, and distribution. This cohesion facilitates resource optimization, cost reduction, and the delivery of exemplary products and services.

In addition, integrators have a keen sense of market fluctuations and consumer predilections. They are adroit at identifying market voids and harnessing their expertise to engineer innovative solutions. Integrators engender sustainable expansion and success as businesses maintain their competitiveness and responsiveness to evolving market paradigms thanks to their agility in recognizing opportunities and adapting accordingly. Integrators engender sustainable expansion and success through continually refining technology, methodologies, and marketing tactics.

Text-conditional image generation allows integrators to narrow the gulf between text and visuals. This technology allows integrators to easily convert textual information into engaging visuals, fostering unobstructed communication and comprehension among diverse teams and stakeholders. This synergistic collaboration expedites project execution and enhances precision.

Text-conditional image generation can be an instrument for unearthing new dimensions of inventiveness. Employing generative AI, integrators can conjure many visually enticing and modifiable images tailored to heterogeneous business needs. Be it product prototyping, marketing collateral, or user interface enhancement, this technology offers integrators the tools to create enthralling visual narratives. Text-conditional image generation acts as an integrative disruptor within the corporate domain. It augments the capacity of businesses to refine operations, bolster communication, and invigorate innovation through the seamless fusion of text and visuals. Such an approach not only streamlines processes but also spurs teams to devise potent solutions that can generate waves of success. Text-conditional image generation is thus a harbinger of a revolution in leveraging visual content, preparing businesses to remain formidable contenders in the ever-evolving business arena.

11.2.4 The Follower[9]

In generative AI, the term "followers" denotes businesses that capitalize on disruptive technologies to fortify their standing rather than breaking new ground. These entities are in the throes of an operational metamorphosis, intending to refine customer engagement, amplify revenue, and optimize resource allocation by harnessing the prowess of generative AI.

Followers are reengineering their operations through the integration of generative AI. Acutely aware of its capacity to rejuvenate workflows, they are zealous in assimilating it into their modus operandi. They employ AI-created content to alleviate the burden of monotonous tasks and leverage AI-derived insights to inform decisions, collectively fuel efficiency, innovation, and expansion in their core markets.

At the heart of the followers' agenda is enriching the customer journey. Through generative AI, they are adept at proffering bespoke solutions aligned with their clientele's distinct needs and inclinations. By curating personalized product assortments, generating custom content, or fine-tuning user interfaces, followers utilize the transformative capacity of generative AI to foster customer contentment and allegiance.[10]

In addition, followers discern the revenue-generating potential innate in generative AI. Embracing this disruptive innovation enables them to unearth new entrepreneurial avenues, diversify their offerings, and widen their sphere of influence. They adeptly explore nascent market segments and draw on AI-sourced insights to discern emergent trends and customer proclivities, thereby maintaining their competitive edge and capitalizing on untapped market potential.

To encapsulate, within the generative AI ambit, followers represent a cohort of businesses strategically deploying disruptive technologies to overhaul their operations and catalyze growth within their established markets. Their core aspirations encompass enhancing customer relations, judicious utilization of resources, and revenue diversification. They regard generative AI as an instrument of innovation and relentlessly probe its multifaceted applications to secure a vantage position in their respective sectors.

11.3 THE DISRUPTION FRAMEWORK

In business and innovation, the four categories—disruptors, enablers, integrators, and followers—serve as a basic framework, providing companies a starting point to navigate their transformation journey toward becoming true disruptors or fully harnessing the benefits of disruptive forces. This framework outlines the path organizations must undertake, encouraging them to traverse the landscapes of adaptation and evolution. The hierarchical arrangement depicted in Figure 11.1 symbolizes the ascension within these categories, with the top tier awarded to disruptors showing exceptional foresight potential, supported by various enablers.

However, this framework provides a foundational understanding of the intricate transformation process. It prompts businesses to delve deeper into conducting a profound exploration of their nature and purpose. Genuine disruption transcends simple categorizations; it requires a commitment to introspection and an earnest pursuit of innovative excellence.

For companies to fully embrace disruption, they must foster a culture that thrives on creativity, curiosity, and adaptability. True disruptors do not merely follow a predefined path; they carve their own, guided by a clear vision and a thirst for change. They reshape industries and move humanity forward by unlocking their inherent potential and harnessing the convergence of emerging trends and enablers.

Ultimately, disruption is a continual transformation journey, demanding constant reevaluation of strategies, refinement of processes, and unwavering commitment to innovation. As businesses take on the role of disruptors or harness the potential of disruptors, they become change agents, molding a future filled with possibilities. In this evolving landscape, adaptability forms the cornerstone of success, and the pursuit of disruption propels organizations toward unparalleled heights.

11.4 DISRUPTION AND DISRUPTORS

When catalyzed by technology, disruption fundamentally changes our lives. This transformation is not confined to the economic domain but extends to societal and cultural layers. The decisive shift brought about by technology seeps into people's everyday behaviors, altering how they perform tasks and challenging economic norms. Such technological disruptions resonate far beyond economic changes, impacting various cultural aspects integral to human existence.

Technological disruptions trigger a profound metamorphosis that extends beyond economic outcomes, reaching the cultural and societal domains. This transformative force alters our economic practices and the core of our shared human experience. In people's daily activities, we see the true impact of technological disruption, as it defies norms, revises standards, and pushes us towards untapped possibilities.

In our technologically dominated world, disruptions are more than momentary disturbances. They become integral to our existence, profoundly affecting our day-to-day lives and prompting a significant shift in how we perceive and approach tasks. They dismantle the traditional foundations of economic activity, ushering in a landscape filled with uncertainty and opportunity, where boundaries of feasibility are continuously redrawn. Technological disruption sparks changes in non-economic cultural factors essential to our human culture. When technology replaces one of these elements, it initiates a cascade of changes that echo throughout our societal and cultural fabric. This effect is not confined to economic structures; it affects every aspect of human existence, reshaping attitudes, beliefs, and behaviors in significant, lasting ways.

As technology disrupts established norms, it catalyzes behavioral transformations and challenges societal conventions. Adapting to new technological realities requires reassessing cultural practices and belief systems. In this adaptation process, individuals adopt new modes of interaction and communication, causing a profound shift in how we approach daily tasks and challenges. This paradigm shift influences our collective evolution and reshapes society in the image of the evolving technological landscape.

Recognizing technology's role as a disruptor requires understanding its vast influence on our interaction with the natural world and our sense of self. This disruption, driven by technology-induced behavioral changes, shifts the paradigm of human existence, transforming our external interactions and innermost selves.

Technology pervades our environment as a transformative force continuously reshaping the human condition. Its impact extends beyond commerce and society, altering our evolving relationship with nature. Technology bridges humanity and the natural world, profoundly affecting how we perceive and interact with nature's wonders. Technology's expanding capabilities allow us to accomplish remarkable feats, pushing the boundaries of the previously impossible. However, we must tread cautiously, acknowledging the significant implications of this transformation. As technology intertwines with our existence, we find ourselves at a crossroads, tasked with addressing the profound effects of this change. The evolving relationship between technology and nature presents both opportunities and challenges. While it enables us to unlock new realms of knowledge and connectivity, it also poses risks that could disrupt the delicate balance of our natural world.

To fully appreciate the disruptive power of technology, we must embark on a reflective journey, delving deep into our humanity. We must explore the intricate relationship between technology and our sense of self, scrutinizing its profound implications for our identity, purpose, and connection to the cosmos. By acknowledging technology as a significant disruptor, we commit to navigating this transformative era with wisdom, striving to use its potential to elevate our existence without compromising its essence.

11.5 TRANSFORMED BY TECHNOLOGY

Technology profoundly influences our existence, extending beyond object manipulation to the web of human relationships. It is through technology that we transform. The intensity and duration of our engagement with technology shape the extent of this change. As we become increasingly involved with technology, it assumes roles we once fulfilled, reducing the energy our bodies previously dedicated to these tasks. The technology gradually becomes an extension of ourselves, fundamentally altering our functionality. When considering the energy savings across many technologies replacing human labor, we realize a profound transformation within us.

Each innovation cycle brings a force akin to a seismic shift, meticulously deconstructing and reconstructing society's fabric from its base. Technological advancements and the relentless pursuit of knowledge elevate us to higher production and consumption levels and trigger a fundamental redistribution of material resources, human effort, and time allocation. This ever-changing landscape necessitates the retreat of established practices, setting the stage for an extensive transformation, which prompts a new set of pursuits, altering our shared future path. In this grand transformation, previous limits of achievability are irreversibly shattered, thereby creating a new narrative of human existence transcending past boundaries.

Navigating the vast sea of technological evolution requires acknowledging and respecting its immense influence over our lives. Technology is both the sculptor and the clay, shaping us as individuals and our world. To fully understand and utilize its transformative power, we must approach it responsibly and be aware of its consequences. We must welcome and value technology's remarkable opportunities while remaining vigilant of its enduring impact on our individual and societal identities. Our interaction with technology goes beyond mere usage or consumption; it molds our understanding of ourselves, our communities, and our shared future. As we move forward, we must remember that technology is both a tool and a reflection of who we are as a species, helping us envisage our potential evolution in this continually changing human existence narrative.

11.6 WHAT IS TRANSITION?

Transition is the critical response of business enterprises to the winds of disruptive innovation. It signifies a transformative journey where organizations navigate the tumultuous waters of change. It is a delicate dance between the familiar and the unknown as markets undergo a state of disarray and participants scramble to adjust their behaviors accordingly.[11]

The catalyst for transition often emerges in the form of an unforeseen event, catching organizations off guard and initiating a shift they may not even be aware of. It could be a whisper of discontent from a customer or supplier, expressing concerns about a particular process and opting for alternative actions, such as reducing purchases or seeking new suppliers. The organization, caught in the currents of transition, may struggle to grasp the gravity of the situation until it becomes undeniable.

Transition can manifest as a sudden shock, thrusting the organization into unfamiliar territory, or it can be a gradual metamorphosis, quietly brewing beneath the surface over an extended period. In either case, the organization must embrace a new incremental change and growth model. It may entail forging new alliances with suppliers and customers, expanding geographical coverage, and continually evolving with new features, capabilities, and market opportunities. The ability to adapt to market fluctuations and internal transformations is paramount, demanding a business model fortified with resilience and flexibility. After all, transformation without effective scalability would be akin to chasing illusions in the desert.

In transition, the art lies in surviving and thriving amidst the evolving landscape. It requires a keen sense of anticipation, a willingness to confront discomfort, and the audacity to seize the opportunities presented by disruption. Transition is the crucible where organizations are tested, where the mettle of their vision and adaptability is forged. By embracing the inevitability of change, crafting a narrative of evolution, and cultivating an agile mindset, businesses can navigate the intricate path toward a resilient and prosperous future.

11.7 TRANSFORMATIONAL CHANGE

Transformational change embodies the lofty aspiration of business development endeavors. It signifies a departure from the confines of conventional, linear methodologies and embraces a paradigm shift towards innovative, iterative, and holistic approaches. To embark on a transformational journey is to dare to challenge the status quo, disrupt stagnant systems, and breathe new life into the very essence of an organization.

The term "transformational" carries a potent resonance—a change that extends beyond merely cosmetic alterations or superficial tweaks. It suggests a profound, sweeping metamorphosis that burrows into the heart of a system, fundamentally altering its structure and shifting its purpose. This process is a grand, cosmic ballet of dismantling and reconstructing, a powerful dance that breaks down hardened, inflexible structures to make room for rebirth in a fresh and unique arrangement.

Embarking on the path of transformational change is no small feat. It is a daring challenge against stagnation and a clarion call to seize the boundless opportunities lurking just outside our realms of comfort. This journey demands the bravery to abandon familiar grounds, explore uncharted territories, and navigate toward a future yet veiled in uncertainty. It requires more than strategic foresight; it requires a comprehensive understanding of the complex dynamics among individuals, processes, and organizational culture. More than just tactical acumen is required here; there is a need for a deep understanding of the complex interactions among individuals, processes, and organizational culture. Within this intricate ballet of transformation, organizations can reinvent themselves from the ground up, craft a narrative of relentless evolution and flexibility, and unleash their true capabilities upon the world.

11.8 UNDERSTANDING TRANSITION AND TRANSFORMATION

Within the constantly changing landscape of human life, dynamic forces continuously propel change. Technological advancements, economic fluctuations, and geopolitical shifts fuel these transformation engines. Amidst this lively upheaval, emerging transformative trends surface, challenging established norms and stirring dormant ambitions. Encapsulated within these shifts are seeds of profound change, impacting not just our external world but also reshaping our inner thoughts and emotions.

At the heart of these transformative changes is the power to redefine reality, surpassing the bounds of what was previously considered possible. The dynamic interplay between innovation and tradition is essentially a dance where established norms and expectations encounter visionary thought. These changes can permeate society, altering industries, redefining cultural frameworks, and awakening human potential.

The transformation process often proceeds through distinct stages, each with significance and purpose. It initiates with disruption, where the familiar ground of the old order quakes, signaling the need for change. From disruption stems dismantling, as ingrained structures and beliefs are torn down, making way for fresh possibilities. Then comes the reimagining stage, where collective creativity explores uncharted territories, visualizing a previously unseen future. Finally, the reformation stage is reached, where the transformative ideas take physical shape, crafting a new reality in line with human aspirations.

As we encounter these profound shifts, the world stands on the cusp of a new evolution phase. This moment teems with potential, a time when the blend of technological marvels, economic shifts, and geopolitical dynamics spark transformation. As we navigate these tumultuous changes, we must have the bravery to accept inherent uncertainties, break free from historical bonds, and embark on a journey of self-reinvention. Because within this chrysalis of change lies the opportunity to overcome current limitations, mold a future reflecting our deepest aspirations, and illuminate a path toward a brighter, more harmonious world.

In the complex tapestry of transformative changes, the world's reshaping often unfolds through a carefully choreographed sequence of stages, each resonating with its unique and critical importance. These transformational changes usually progress through four distinct stages:[12]

The Cognitive Phase: In this phase, innovative technologies disrupt stagnant or outdated industries, replacing traditional products, services, and experiences. This technological revolution often leads to restructuring of the job market due to reduced employment opportunities in the affected sectors.

During this upheaval, many occupations that once served as pillars of the working class began to decline. Once crucial to the economy, these jobs gradually give way to roles requiring higher levels of creativity, advanced skills, and extensive knowledge. Industries that demand such competencies rise to prominence quickly, becoming economic growth drivers.

As the cognitive phase progresses, the economic landscape undergoes a drastic shift. Technology, data analytics, and creative design sectors start to dominate, necessitating specialized technical skills and an in-depth understanding of intricate systems and creative problem-solving capabilities. This phase also emphasizes continuous learning and adaptability due to the quick pace of technological progress. A successful workforce in this environment must possess skills and the capability to evolve with changes. Consequently, lifelong learning and adaptability are critical for employees to succeed in this new economic climate.

The cognitive phase significantly changes our society's economic structure, highlighting the importance of knowledge, creativity, and advanced skills. Navigating this transformation requires us to reconsider our approaches to education, skill development, and labor policies to ensure smooth transitions and continual economic growth.

The Transition Phase: It begins when disrupted sectors seek alternative employment opportunities, often moving toward service industries. This shift symbolizes the start of a journey into new territories as the effects of technological innovation become increasingly apparent in everyday life. As the transition progresses, the workforce begins to equip itself for engagement with emerging technologies reshaping their industries. They are at the cusp of a new era where their roles, tasks, and functions are likely to be redefined by these new technologies. However, the extent of such a transformation can be overwhelming. Many individuals may struggle to adapt to changes in their work environment, work methods, and even the nature of their jobs. It is not just about learning new tools or processes but fundamentally reshaping their perceptions of their roles, contributions, and positions within their organizations.

Others might grapple with dissatisfaction stemming from the evolving workplace environment. The traditional structure and familiarity of the old world may be replaced with unfamiliar workflows, quickly changing expectations and uncertainty about the future. This dislocation can create a mismatch between individuals' expectations and the reality of their new workplaces, leading to struggles to find meaning, satisfaction, and a sense of belonging in these transformed environments.

Despite the challenges, the transition stage is crucial to the transformational journey. It is a phase of exploration and adaptation, upheaval, and growth. Although the process may be complex, it is through navigating these challenges that the workforce—and indeed the entire organization—begins to internalize the changes initiated in the cognitive phase, laying the groundwork for fully harnessing the transformative power of technology.

The Agile Phase: It is defined by a heightened level of autonomy within organizations, empowering individuals to guide their business operations. This empowerment propels their development forward. Instead of striving for an unattainable ideal of perfection, the focus shifts to continuous improvement. This mindset enables rapid, informed decision-making, aligning with the speed of technological advancements. Such agility cultivates a culture of swift problem-solving, allowing organizations to adjust and respond effectively to their dynamic industries.

The agile phase is an era of empowerment and independence, where individuals within organizations can innovate and direct their paths. This phase embraces the understanding that perfection is not always achievable and that progress is made through constant refinement. Agile organizations can swiftly pivot, address market demands, and take measured risks. This responsiveness helps them stay competitive in the fast-paced technological environment.

This phase symbolizes a significant shift in organizational dynamics. It replaces hierarchical structures emphasizing flexibility and adaptability, empowering individuals to accept and navigate change, progressing rapidly through developmental stages. The agility driving this phase stems from the acknowledgment that perfection is elusive and actual growth is achieved through the relentless pursuit of improvement.

During the agile phase, decision-making balances intuition and swift action. Rather than falling into the trap of over-analysis, individuals adapt to emerging technologies and tackle problems as they arise. This agile mindset promotes prompt resolution of challenges, enabling organizations to keep pace with the constantly evolving landscape of possibilities. It cultivates a state of constant progress, where the quest for continuous improvement directs every decision and action.

In the agile phase, innovation flourishes without rigid structures and burdensome bureaucracy. Individuals are encouraged to think beyond conventional wisdom, creating an environment that nurtures creativity and exploration of new territories. The agile approach is characterized by a strong belief in the potential of experimentation and a readiness to embrace uncertainty.

The Transformational Phase: It represents a defining moment when irreversible changes sweep the professional landscape. During this phase, the majority adapt to innovative working methods and technologies. It heralds a new era of personal fulfillment, autonomy, and job satisfaction by making the work-life balance more adaptable and tailored to individual needs. This stage sees a surge in online services, automating various aspects of the newly envisioned lifestyle. Alongside, the job market diversifies, providing individuals with the latitude to explore positions in nascent economic sectors.

It is essential to recognize that embracing the full spectrum of benefits and transitioning to a leadership mindset will not happen overnight. While individuals are no longer bound by roles that do not capitalize on their talents or bring gratification, harnessing the full potential of these emancipating changes might be a gradual process. Nonetheless, the transformational phase ushers these possibilities closer to fruition.

In essence, the transformational phase is the catalyst for a significant metamorphosis in the world of work. Outdated practices are jettisoned, giving rise to a plethora of opportunities. This stage compels individuals and societies to re-evaluate their values and objectives. At its core, the transformational phase signifies liberation—the emancipation to pursue passions, venture into unexplored domains, and bring to bear our distinct talents and expertise. The underlying factor is adopting cutting-edge work practices and technologies, which allow for increased flexibility, self-governance, and personal fulfillment. As more people adapt to these modernized work methodologies, work-life dynamics become more bespoke and adaptable.

The transformational phase marks a watershed moment where the very fabric of society undergoes extensive reconfiguration. With the widespread adaptation to novel work practices and technologies, society witnesses a deep-seated shift. This phase lays the groundwork for personal fulfillment, autonomy, and independence. The demarcation between work and personal life becomes porous, with individual aspirations taking precedence. The conventional notion of work recedes, replaced by a more fluid and adaptive modus operandi. Simultaneously, individuals gain the freedom to delve into burgeoning economic sectors. Though they may not instantly capitalize on this newfound latitude or effortlessly embrace leadership positions, they are no longer tethered to roles that misalign their abilities or fail to bring satisfaction.

The transformational phase embarks society on an odyssey toward a future characterized by personal fulfillment and rich human experiences. It signifies a breakaway from traditional confines and limited prospects, empowering individuals to forge their destinies guided by their passions, capabilities, and ambitions. By embracing the transformative capabilities of this phase, society can nurture a more enlightened and liberated way of life, transcending the constraints that once circumscribed individual potentials.

11.9 GENERATIVE AI: THE FASTEST TRANSFORMATIONAL CHANGE RATE

Generative AI, this exceptionally prominent and rapidly evolving subset of AI, is experiencing an adoption trajectory that significantly eclipses precedent-setting technologies such as the Internet and the World Wide Web. The ubiquity with which generative AI is being embraced is almost keeping pace with the technology's intrinsic capacity to engender novel content. In endeavoring to fathom the profundity of this metamorphosis, it is instructive to juxtapose its arc with those of other seminal technological innovations.

The advent of the Internet can be traced back to military ventures in the 1960s, and it took several decades to permeate everyday life. The World Wide Web, which emerged between the late 1980s and early 1990s, expedited this incorporation by furnishing a more navigable and user-centric conduit to the Internet. Nevertheless, the diffusion of these technologies was relatively incremental due to impediments such as infrastructural bottlenecks, circumscribed computer literacy, and the prohibitive cost of personal computers. Consequently, an extended timescale, often spanning decades, was necessitated for these technologies to gain traction.

In contrast, generative AI is the subject of an unprecedented and fervent upsurge in both interest and utilization. Several factors can be attributed to catalyzing this rapid assimilation, including the sophistication of the underpinning AI technologies, the copious availability of data requisite for model training, an extensive digital infrastructure, and an escalating societal acclimation to AI-imbued tools and services.

The velocity at which generative AI is revolutionizing diverse industries is staggering. Take, for example, content creation—a domain where generative AI harbors the potential to recalibrate the dimensions of human creativity fundamentally. AI now boasts the aptitude to synthesize realistic and high-fidelity content on a scale that was hitherto the sole province of human ingenuity. Within the design sector, generative AI can conjure an extensive gamut of designs in a mere fraction of the time that would be expended by a human designer, empowering enterprises to spearhead innovation at an inconceivable pace and establish a competitive edge.

Relative to the nascent stages of the Internet and the World Wide Web, the embracement of generative AI is considerably more precipitous. This accelerated adoption can be ascribed to the pervasive nature of digital infrastructures and cloud services, democratizing access to AI instruments, and an expansive societal cognizance of AI. The potential harbored by generative AI has not gone unnoticed, with individuals and corporations alike integrating it into their operations with alacrity. Furthermore, the availability of AI platforms that provide generative functionalities as a service enables even small enterprises, which may lack extensive AI acumen, to reap the benefits of this technology, thereby amplifying its application and hastening its incorporation.

However, it is critical to recognize that the velocity of this adoption and the concomitant transformation usher in a host of challenges. Ethical quandaries such as AI-synthesized deepfakes, trepidations surrounding data privacy, and the prospective ramifications on employment represent areas that necessitate concurrent scrutiny and address as this technology is deployed. By analogy, the Internet and the World Wide Web were, and continue to be, confronted with challenges about security, privacy, and the misuse of information. As generative AI continues its precipitous ascent, a multipronged approach that encompasses technological innovation, ethical considerations, and societal impact must be rigorously pursued.

11.10 CLOSING THOUGHTS

Disruption often implies a radical transformation that shakes the foundations of long-standing systems and ushers in a new era of innovation and change. It is a pivotal force that disrupts the status quo, propelling society toward new heights. The disruptions we witness in technology, especially, have reshaped our modes of communication, access to information, and overall understanding of the world, resulting in sweeping changes in societal structures, economic frameworks, and cultural perspectives.

Such disruptions demand our active engagement, urging us to become proactive architects of a future that might seem beyond our comprehension. Disruption, in its very essence, is a compelling call to action—a call to embrace the unfamiliar, challenge prevailing norms, and visualize a landscape filled with newfound possibilities. It is a dynamic force that propels progress by relentlessly questioning the established order and giving birth to innovative paradigms that redefine our collective reality.

Technological disruptions, like generative AI, embody this spirit. They instigate profound shifts, reshaping how we communicate, access, and process information and even navigate the complexities of our ever-changing world. Nevertheless, to truly be classified as a "disruption," the resulting change should not only be of significant magnitude but also instigate a substantial impact on social, political, or cultural aspects, leading to an enhanced world for all of humanity.

Disruption can be likened to a spark that ignites our collective imagination, inspiring us to take audacious leaps forward and reimagine the boundaries of what we once deemed possible. It challenges us to continually question and redefine our reality, fostering a mindset that promotes growth, innovation, and transformation. And, as we find ourselves amid the rise of generative AI, we are given the opportunity to shape the path of this disruption, to harness its potential in ways that improve our individual lives and enhance society at large.

NOTES

1. Disruption is the highest form of change—the type of change that permanently disrupts the status quo. This is true both of political change—when an incumbent government is defeated, an ideology is undermined, and a new paradigm must be created – and technological change, when a company, industry, or system is disrupted in a radical and unanticipated way.
2. For a change to qualify as disruption, it must transcend merely technical or social shifts and embody a socially positive, political, or cultural effect. It must represent a fundamental shift from the current model, which is to say, a "deconstruction." This notion applies to everything—from technology to social movements to the media and cultural industries. Disruption must genuinely disrupt what is happening now and dissolve what came before it.
3. Manu, A. 2022. The Philosophy of Disruption. Emerald Publishing Limited. pp. 11–16.
4. **Disruptor:** businesses that have opened their business models to a disruptor and, in doing so, have created markets where none existed before. A disruptor provides a valuable service and stimulates other entrepreneurs to come into the industry to do what they do; that is their "disruption." A disruptor allows a new category of products or services to enter the marketplace and do what customers did not realize they wanted. A disruptor sets a new bar of innovation in the marketplace. OpenAI's DALE-E2 project and Mid-Journey were initial disruptors and pioneers in the field of text-conditional image generation. This field explores the intersection between language understanding and image generation, aiming to create visuals purely from textual descriptions. DALE-E2, as an early foray into this space, showcased the potential of synthesizing images from complex text inputs, offering an intriguing glimpse into a future where detailed illustrations could be created from mere text. Meanwhile, Mid-Journey extended this concept, illustrating the growth and evolution of text-conditional image generation. This demonstration of early innovation is integral in understanding the history of text-based image synthesis, emphasizing these projects' foundational role in their respective niches.
5. **Enablers:** businesses that created or provided sustainable and long-lasting models. They continue to drive innovation and introduce products and services that create or improve upon marketplaces that might have otherwise stagnated or disappeared. Enablers are businesses that maintain, increase, or enhance the value and functionality of an industry or marketplace.
6. Internet platforms like Substack, Flipboard, and Steemit have transformed content creation by empowering individuals to produce original content, become independent producers, and manage their brands. These platforms provide tools for establishing an online presence, monetizing content, and accessing a global audience. By removing traditional barriers to entry, they foster creativity, diversity, and control over distribution and monetization.

7. **Integrator:** businesses that developed processes and mechanisms to align and integrate with the corporate world are not considered disruptors. They bring the best products and services to market quickly and cost-effectively and can compete effectively with market disruptors. They usually have a specific technology, process, or marketing advantage and an in-depth understanding of the business. They can also be credited with delivering disruption in multiple market areas.

8. These top five AI integrators have extensive knowledge and experience in artificial intelligence. **Master of Code** specializes in AI integration and has successfully implemented AI solutions in healthcare, e-commerce, and finance industries. They excel in developing chatbots and virtual assistants that enhance customer experience and streamline business processes. **10CLOUDS** is known for its comprehensive approach to AI development and integration. They create custom AI solutions tailored to the unique needs of their clients and have successfully implemented AI-driven applications across various industries. **Deeper Insights** focuses on advanced analytics and AI-driven insights. They extract valuable insights from large datasets using data analysis and machine learning techniques. Their AI integration services help companies make data-driven decisions and optimize processes. **Data Monsters** has expertise in big data and AI integration. They have a proven track record of implementing AI solutions in complex data environments, including finance, healthcare, and cybersecurity. They excel in data preprocessing, feature engineering, and building scalable AI models. **The Bot Forge** specializes in conversational AI and chatbot development. They create intelligent virtual assistants that improve customer engagement and automate tasks using natural language understanding and machine learning technologies. List retrieved from https://masterofcode.com/blog/top-5-generative-ai-integration-companies-to-drive-customer-support.

9. **Followers:** businesses that have not started exploring markets and services outside their primary markets but are using the disruptor technology to their advantage. These businesses are changing the way they work. They are trying to improve customer experience, drive revenue, and better use their resources and market reach by leveraging the disruptor technology.

10. Several companies and projects have emerged as followers in the generative AI disruption, working to advance the capabilities of generative AI technologies and apply them to various domains. Following the success of OpenAI's GPT-3, several companies and projects have worked on developing their language models and generative AI technologies. Examples include EleutherAI, Hugging Face's Transformers, and OpenAI's subsequent models like Codex and DALL·E. Google's DeepDream project generated visually surreal images using deep neural networks and inspired numerous follow-up projects and experiments. These projects aimed to explore and expand upon the possibilities of generative image synthesis, including DeepArt.io, DeepArt Effects, and DeepStyle. NVIDIA's StyleGAN Followers: NVIDIA's StyleGAN, a generative model capable of creating highly realistic images, sparked interest and inspired further research in generative adversarial networks (GANs). Researchers and developers have built upon StyleGAN's principles to create image-generation projects like BigGAN, ProGAN, and PGGAN. GAN followers: GANs, introduced by Ian Goodfellow and his colleagues, have become a popular framework for generative AI. Numerous researchers and developers have explored GANs and developed their variations and applications. Some notable examples include CycleGAN, Pix2Pix, and DCGAN (deep convolutional GAN). These examples represent a fraction of the many companies and projects that have followed in the footsteps of pioneering generative AI technologies. The field of generative AI is constantly evolving, with new projects and advancements emerging regularly as the technology continues to disrupt various domains.

11. Manu, A. 2022. The Philosophy of Disruption. Emerald Publishing Limited. p. 47.

12. Manu, A. 2022. The Philosophy of Disruption. Emerald Publishing Limited.

IV

A Radical New Aesthetic

CHAPTER 12

Moving Past Archetypes

12.1 THE END OF THE CONDITIONAL ARCHETYPE

Design education has long been rooted in a framework that emphasizes learning about archetypal forms, some having historical roots spanning over two millennia. Such archetypes, like the chair, spoon, fork, and countless others, have acted as fundamental templates, molding perceptions and directing the creative pursuits of up-and-coming designers.

Parallelly, art education has seen an enduring preference for particular themes, including portraiture, daily life, religious motifs, landscapes, and still life. These timeless subjects encapsulate both the tangible and intellectual arsenal of their times and are manifested through diverse mediums—from the ethereal qualities of gouache and tempera to the opulent textures of oils on canvas or eternalized as frescoes.

This reliance on established paradigms in art and design, which we might term as archetypal or conditional form generation, was virtually unchallenged until the mid-1800s when the invention of the camera shook the artistic world. This ground-breaking device emancipated artists from the shackles of representational fidelity, emboldening them to traverse uncharted artistic avenues. As a result, avant-garde movements emerged, such as impressionism, expressionism, abstract art, cubism, futurism, dadaism, and more.[1] An essential observation is that, despite these inventive forays, artists were not entirely free—the technological constraints of their era bound them. Traditional tools like paintbrushes and canvas, whether utilized with oil or water-based mediums, subtly delineated and sometimes curtailed an artist's capacity to bring their creative visions to fruition.

This limitation persisted for an extended period, even as the discourse on aesthetics experienced profound shifts. As the 20th century dawned, the artistic landscape underwent further metamorphosis with the introduction of digital technologies. Especially the advent of digital design tools unlocked unparalleled avenues for artists and designers. Their digital counterparts gradually supplanted the previous dependence on physical tools like paintbrushes and canvas, liberating creators from the material constraints that once tethered their creative expression.

DOI: 10.1201/9781003450139-17

This digital era brought an expansive toolkit for artists and designers, facilitating a seemingly boundless scope for creative exploration. Not only did these advancements amplify the capacity for artistic and design expression, but they also questioned the long-standing archetypes central to art and design education. Incorporating digital technology into art and design necessitated transitioning from the archetypal form generation to more fluid, adaptive, and personalized creative processes. The demarcations between various artistic and design disciplines began to blur, cultivating an interdisciplinary ethos that promoted diversity, ingenuity, and individual expression.

As generative AI begins to mark the onset of another technological renaissance, we are again at a crossroads, equipped to recalibrate the frontiers of art and design. With AI's prowess to craft novel and multifaceted forms that surpass conventional archetypes, we stand on the precipice of an unprecedented epoch of creativity, where imagination becomes the ultimate frontier.

As we explore novel territories, exercising prudence becomes a necessity, not a choice. The promising potential of artificial intelligence (AI) to revolutionize design paradigms is undoubtedly noteworthy, yet the concurrent contemplation of ethical considerations and implications for human ingenuity is equally paramount. Over generations, our cultural lineage has been indomitably carved by the dynamic interplay between archetypical motifs and the human faculty of imagination. Thus, we must strive towards establishing a balanced symbiosis—maximizing the unprecedented opportunities afforded by AI while also meticulously preserving the irrefutable and inimitable essence of human creative intuition. This task, though daunting, is critical for the sustainable advancement of our shared cultural and creative legacy.

Envisioning AI as a catalyst for inspiration and collaboration offers a holistic approach. A synergetic alliance between human ingenuity and the possibilities generated by machines augments the vistas of design without forgoing the rich cultural heritage ingrained in archetypes. In this realm, AI emerges as an accomplice in our collective creative journey, aiding us in pushing boundaries while venerating our treasured creative lineage. By asserting an archetype, we do not merely stipulate a form but also lay out intentions and parameters that the designer must navigate. The archetype functions as a canvas, incorporating desired features such as comfort or ergonomics, and sets a comparative standard against which the end product is evaluated. The nature of a project inherently shapes its creative process, guiding the utilization of contemporary materials and technologies. Simultaneously, it often harkens back to age-old archetypal concepts.

The conjunction of archetypes and innovation ignites a philosophical reflection on design's transformative power, the essence of human creativity, and the intricate balance between tradition and progress. Archetypes serve as time-honored compasses, offering a sense of continuity and connection to our cultural heritage while simultaneously spurring the desire to transcend traditional boundaries through technological advancements and ingenuity. This intricate interplay invites a re-evaluation of the reciprocal relationship between tradition and innovation, urging recognition of their interconnectedness in the creative process. By engaging in thoughtful exploration and dialogue, we can harness the potential of AI while preserving human creativity's quintessence, paving the way for a new era where archetypes and AI harmoniously coexist and enrich each other.

12.2 HOW DO WE TEACH ART AND DESIGN IN THE CONTEXT OF TEXT-CONDITIONAL INSPIRATION?

Delivering art and design education through text-based inspirations requires the fusion of numerous skills, including understanding context, abstract thought, and innovative problem-solving. This teaching approach encourages students to go beyond literal interpretations of text while keeping true to the spirit of the original prompts. Understanding the interplay between text and visual design is essential, shedding light on the power of narrative structures and metaphorical expressions. Students must become proficient at extracting central themes and motifs from textual prompts, forming the basis for advanced visual representations. from textual stimuli for the genesis of sophisticated visual expressions.

Embracing text-conditional inspiration opens an exciting, albeit complex, avenue to navigate the intersection of artistic ownership, intellectual property rights, and the essence of creativity in human-AI collaboration. Educational institutions stand on the front lines of this evolving landscape, with the thrilling challenge to empower students to navigate and understand these rapidly shifting dynamics. Rather than being daunting, this approach holds immense promise, seeding the potential for a creative revolution. It fosters a new breed of artists and designers who can seamlessly blend human ingenuity with AI to push the frontiers of creativity. Crucially, we must ensure this harmonization nurtures unrestricted artistic expression while also managing the challenges this novel synergy may introduce.

Art education should be future-forward, embracing ethical concerns such as the risk of artistic misappropriation, cultural expropriation, and potential biases in AI-generated designs. We advocate for an interdisciplinary fusion, weaving linguistic artistry, technological innovation, and visual representation together. This integrated approach strengthens the critical thinking capacity around the limits and possibilities of text-based prompts and fuels creative resilience.

Moreover, in all its richness and complexity, language becomes a vital tool in this exciting exploration, bridging traditional boundaries and engaging with many ideas. This harmonious blend invites reflection on language's role as a launchpad for inspiration, acknowledging its limitations to encapsulate the breadth of human imagination fully and promoting the development of interdisciplinary perspectives. Envisioning a future where AI and human creativity converge, we stand on the cusp of a new era of artistic evolution and revolution.

Such circumstances lead to a paradigmatic shift in the tenets governing art and design pedagogy. While text-conditional inspiration presents specific challenges, such as the possible reinforcement of biases, it concurrently unveils a transformative potential in creativity. The evolving landscape of art and design urges a reconceptualization, encouraging cooperative ventures and empowering nascent artists to adeptly navigate the digital epoch while safeguarding the sanctity of human expression. In this nexus of language, technology, and visual artistry, new horizons in creative education can be envisaged.

Integrating text-conditional inspiration into art and design education represents a dynamic shift in teaching methodologies, requiring the development of diverse skills that extend beyond individual creativity and technical proficiency. As text-conditional generation evolves, artists and designers act as translators, converting textual prompts into meaningful visual expressions. Art and design education must adapt to prepare students for effectively interpreting and expanding upon textual prompts. This process involves developing skills like understanding context, abstract reasoning, and solving creative problems. Teachers should motivate students to delve deeper into the text's literal meaning. They should permit artistic independence, all the while ensuring the original spirit of the material remains intact.[2]

Exploring the relationship between text and visual representation is crucial in education for this field. Learners need instruction on narrative strength, metaphorical language, and the emotional context within texts. Such education enables artists to grasp deeper themes in the provided textual prompts, which can elevate the sophistication of their visual art translations.

Text-conditional inspiration brings a compelling duality to the creative process, infusing it with newfound momentum while potentially constraining it within the confines of the prompts. It ushers in the possibility of streamlining artistic creation, though we must ensure this does not stifle unexpected moments of genius. Achieving equilibrium between the efficiencies offered by text-conditional inspiration and the liberty of unbounded artistic exploration is crucial, promising a vibrant coexistence.

Infusing text-conditional inspiration necessitates a cross-disciplinary approach in education, amalgamating language, technology, and visual art. This approach could create synergistic collaborations with experts from various fields, including natural language processing and ethics, fostering a dynamic and innovative learning environment. Promoting a culture of critical thinking and reflective practices becomes paramount in an educational system embracing text-conditional inspiration. Students must be equipped to critically analyze and evaluate the bounds and opportunities text-based prompts offer. Fostering open dialogue and reflection helps demystify the evolving interplay between human creativity and technology, painting a vibrant picture of the future of artistry.

The embrace of text-conditional inspiration is not without its challenges. Should everyone adopt similar text-conditional prompts, the risk of homogenization and dilution of personal expression looms large. Further, if the algorithms curating prompts are biased, they might inadvertently perpetuate existing disparities. Therefore, diligent assessment of the sources and proactive measures to mitigate bias become critical in applying this technology, ensuring it becomes an ally, not a hindrance, in pursuing creative innovation.

Moreover, maintaining the human element in art is crucial, as AI should not overshadow the unique perspectives and experiences that artists bring to their work. The blend of human intuition and technology should harmonize to realize artistic potential.

The arrival of text-conditional inspiration propels art and design education into an exhilarating frontier bursting with potential. Modifying pedagogical techniques to integrate pioneering technologies, endorsing cross-disciplinary strategies, and nurturing critical thinking is instrumental in priming students for a world where art, language, and technology seamlessly merge. Additionally, placing a premium on individual expression and ethical considerations ensures the preservation of our intrinsic human creativity. By embracing this transformative integration, we stand poised to unleash the full power of text-conditional inspiration. This leap forward will serve as a beacon of artistic innovation while safeguarding the very core of human creativity, illuminating our path toward a thrilling future.

12.3 TEXT CONDITIONAL DESIGN SYSTEMS

In traditional design, transforming intent into a tangible form begins with defining the objectives in a design brief. This brief is then elaborated by considering various aspects such as materials, target audience, and aesthetic preferences. This articulated vision is compiled into a document known as the visual brand language (VBL), which sets the final product's criteria, ensuring that it aligns with the desired brand identity.

One essential aspect of developing the VBL is the use of language. Marketing experts and design professionals collaboratively establish the desired attributes for the products, employing words to articulate characteristics like elegance, modesty, and intelligence. These words bridge the gap between abstract concepts and their concrete realizations. They help define "Eastern Fusion" or "European Modern" themes and describe their attributes through categories like core values, design principles, materials, forms, textures, and colors (Figures 12.1 and 12.2). Once the articulation is complete, the designer moves on to the next phase: giving form to these ideas. This process involves creating initial sketches, detailed drawings, color renderings, and precise illustrations that depict material details and fabrication. Here, the designer plays a dual role—as an interpreter translating words into visuals and as an executor bringing the collective vision of the marketing and development teams into reality.

However, this raises an intriguing question—does this process limit the designer's creative freedom, reducing them to mere executors of a predefined vision? The parameters established in the VBL certainly guide the design process, but it also begs the question of how much creative agency the designer retains. There is a philosophical dimension to this—the role of language in shaping perception and creativity and how it influences the designer's role as both a creator and an interpreter.

With the traditional design process somewhat constrained by predetermined parameters established through language, an alternative approach, text-conditional inspiration, comes into play. Text-conditional inspiration enables the integration of various disciplines, promotes critical thinking, and offers a fresh pedagogical approach. This method paves the way for a new generation of artists and designers who can harness language's transformative power while preserving human creativity's essence.

Text-conditional inspiration opens a world of possibilities in artistic education and creative processes. It allows artists and designers to transcend traditional design

FIGURE 12.1　European Modern kitchen proposals.

constraints by engaging in an exploratory journey through language, technology, and visual expression. The interplay between these elements is not merely a means of communication; it is a symbiotic relationship where language offers structure and shared understanding while design lends depth and emotional richness.

However, a caveat arises in the form of conditional archetypes. These archetypes, though essential in guiding principles, can also stifle innovation. They limit the designer's capacity to explore beyond established norms. The manifestation of the creative process risks becoming cyclical and derivative rather than ground-breaking. This limitation is not exclusive to brand products; it is present across various domains where design is expected to conform to predefined archetypes. This scenario prompts philosophical questions regarding the nature of design. Is it possible for design to thrive within the

FIGURE 12.2 Mood board for an Eastern fusion kitchen proposal.

bounds of conditional archetypes? Is there a need for a paradigm shift that allows for a more liberated and expansive approach to creativity? By challenging these archetypes and embracing an explorative mindset, designers can realize their true potential.

Through this examination of conventional design processes, it is imperative to recognize that the contemporary landscape is undergoing significant transformation. Technological advancements and the democratization of knowledge engender a paradigmatic evolution, necessitating an intricate intertwining of traditional archetypes with innovative approaches.

One notable phenomenon that has burgeoned within this evolved milieu is "co-design" or participatory design, which allows for more inclusive collaboration among stakeholders, users, and designers. This democratized approach to design fosters a richer discourse, as the objectives and parameters are no longer solely dictated by a centralized entity but are an amalgamation of diverse perspectives.

For example, in urban planning, co-design can involve the local community in the process, ensuring that the final design adheres to aesthetic and functional criteria and resonates with the community's heritage and values.[3]

A fascinating facet of this transformational landscape is the infusion of artificial intelligence (AI) into the design process. Generative design tools offer an exciting pathway whereby designers can input specific parameters and let AI generate diverse design options (Figure 12.3). This innovative approach considerably broadens the creative spectrum, as AI, unfettered by human cognitive biases and entrenched paradigms, can propose groundbreaking solutions that might remain unexplored via traditional methods.[4] A case in point

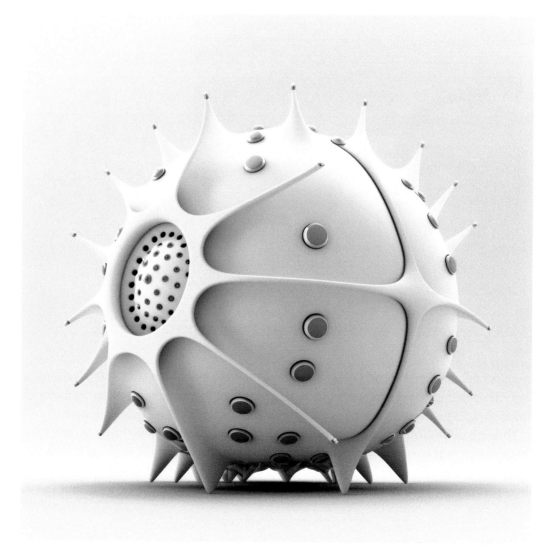

FIGURE 12.3   A radical-centric design approach for an air conditioning unit.

is Autodesk's generative design technology, which has been harnessed in the automotive and aerospace industries. This technology has created components that optimize weight distribution and material usage, embodying an aesthetics-meets-functionality paradigm. In this context, AI becomes a tool and a collaborative partner in the design process, ushering in an era of heightened creativity and efficiency.[5]

Beyond incorporating technology, the evolving landscape of consumer predilections significantly influences the design process. Consumers' interactions with many cultures and aesthetics have broadened in our progressively globalized world. This exposure cultivates an appetite for designs that push past the boundaries of conventional VBL archetypes, integrating elements that resonate deeply on a personal, cultural, or even ideological level. For instance, the essence of Scandinavian design, distinguished by its minimalism, functionality, and embrace of natural materials, has swept across the globe. Its impact is felt strongly in the interior design and furniture industries worldwide. This trend signifies an amalgamation of aesthetic preferences and the birth of a more cosmopolitan consumer base. The challenge and opportunity for designers lie in harnessing these global influences to create products and spaces that both appeal to and reflect this increasingly interconnected world.

As design processes continue to evolve, it is crucial to recognize the importance of balancing adherence to established archetypes and integrating innovative methodologies. Design education must encompass this duality by fostering a learning environment that encourages experimentation, critical thinking, and interdisciplinary collaboration. For instance, design education curricula can include modules on emergent technologies, participatory design strategies, and cross-cultural aesthetics, preparing future designers to navigate the complexities of the contemporary design landscape.

The transformation of intent into tangible form in design-making is an ever-evolving process. While the traditional approach anchored in Visual Brand Language provides structure and clarity, it is imperative to acknowledge and incorporate the dynamic elements introduced by technological advancements, shifting consumer preferences, and global cultural amalgamations. The need for a flexible and adaptable design philosophy arises, empowering designers to function as curators and innovators. They must proficiently navigate the complex matrix of traditional and avant-garde elements. By promoting this blend, design surpasses mere functionality and aesthetics. It transforms into a medium for conceiving and expressing societal, cultural, and humanistic narratives

A transformative shift in design practice is possible by re-evaluating the role of conditional archetypes and fostering an environment that encourages genuine innovation and expression. Designers must venture beyond established norms and engage with the unknown. By doing this, designers can create works that defy conventional boundaries and redefine our understanding of beauty, form, and human expression.

12.4 WORKING WITHOUT ARCHETYPES

The prospect of imagining objects, spaces, and experiences independent of archetypes presents a formidable philosophical conundrum, given that archetypes have historically been integral to human cognition and artistic expression. Archetypes act as essential frameworks or shared symbols that shape how we understand and interpret our surroundings.[6] They offer common grounds for categorizing and comprehending objects, spaces, and experiences. However, delving into the concept of transcending archetypes leads us into the domain of conceptual models.

Conceptual models resemble cognitive frameworks or mental architectures that furnish a structure to perceive, analyze, and derive meaning from our interactions with the world, especially when traditional archetypes are absent. These models cultivate a space for conceiving objects, spaces, and experiences through the prism of individual perspectives, personal histories, and an amalgamation of various influences. This mental crafting is an evolving process that encourages inventive exploration, giving rise to new and innovative ideas.

In the absence of conventional archetypes, conceptual models become instrumental in critically reassessing our understanding of reality. They challenge us to scrutinize deeply ingrained beliefs, question prevailing norms, and venture into unexplored realms of knowledge and conception of our surroundings. Instead of relying on static, predefined archetypal concepts, these models stimulate our imagination, employing an adaptable and unrestricted approach to thinking that draws inspiration from diverse sources, including nature, emotions, societal and cultural contexts, and personal narratives (Figure 12.4).

Removing the dependence on age-old archetypes to conceive objects, spaces, and experiences, we pave the way for unrestrained creativity and revolutionary innovation. Liberation from the limitations of traditional archetypal frameworks encourages the reimagining of our notions of possibility. As a result, the conceptual model evolves into a dynamic, flexible construct that grows and adapts in tandem with an individual's creative journey, continuously expanding and refining their worldview.

This process of reinterpretation has far-reaching consequences. It not only assists us in attaining a more profound understanding of our environment and redefines our connection with our inner psyche. We partake in a potent form of self-reflection and personal evolution by challenging our core beliefs and perpetually reshaping our comprehension. Consequently, conceptual models serve a dual role: as cognitive tools for interpreting the world and as catalysts for introspection and personal growth.

Conceptual models also serve to underscore the personal nature of perception and interpretation. They acknowledge that our experiences and viewpoints are instrumental in shaping our conceptualizations. They advocate embracing diversity, individuality, and pluralism in our interpretations, recognizing that different people may perceive the same object or space through distinctive lenses.

While eschewing archetypes in the conceptualization of objects, spaces, and experiences mark a deviation from conventional thought patterns, it bears the potential to access novel dimensions of creativity and insight. This paradigm challenges us to break free from the shackles of collective symbolism and harness the boundless potentialities of individual creativity. Through conceptual models, we can carve novel avenues of meaning, pushing the envelopes of artistic expression, design ingenuity, and the inception of life-altering experiences.[7]

FIGURE 12.4   A radical-centric design for a nonlinear time-keeping device.

Conceptual models invite us on a profound journey of intellectual discovery and enlightenment. In this journey, archetypes cease to be static parameters; instead, they transform into springboards propelling us toward uncharted creative territories (Figure 12.5). They present a call to question, rebuild, and innovate, unraveling untouched vistas of conceptual thinking that move beyond the shackles of traditional frameworks. In embracing this expedition, we have the opportunity to reshape our perception of the world and reconnect with the core of creativity and delve into the profound depths of human potential. This intellectual odyssey offers a fascinating avenue to explore the universe of ideas that lie beyond the conventional and known and to marvel at the limitless potential of the human spirit.

FIGURE 12.5   A radical-centric design for conceptual geometric language.

12.5 RADICAL CENTRIC DESIGN AS A NEW CONCEPTUAL MODEL

Indeed. "Radical centricity," or radical-centric design, is a cutting-edge approach within the design domain. This paradigm challenges and transcends traditional methodologies by establishing human experiences, necessities, and values as the foundation of the creative process. This model amplifies the principles of user-centered design, actively striving to dismantle entrenched norms, assumptions, and power hierarchies that have long dictated the course of the design industry.

At the heart of radical centricity is the acknowledgment of the intricate network that links individuals, societies, and the environment. This insight is essential as the model endeavors to create designs that meet surface-level requirements and grapple with profound systemic issues, fervently advocating for social equality and environmental preservation.

As for incorporating radical centricity in guiding text-conditional Image Generators (AI systems that create images based on textual descriptions), the radical-centric design brief serves as a guiding star. It illuminates the path towards transformative, socially conscious, and thoughtfully crafted AI-generated visual content. This design brief, steeped in the principles of radical centricity, promotes a collaborative ecosystem where human designers and AI systems converge to ideate and create visual content. The aim is to challenge and reshape prevailing biases, foster inclusivity, and uplift marginalized groups.

In a radical-centric design brief, the text-conditional Image Generators are urged to consider a wide array of elements that surpass merely aesthetic appeal. The system

FIGURE 12.6   A radical centric design for a sound making object.

is encouraged to assess ethical aspects, cultural nuances, and environmental impacts. This approach also stimulates a profound, critical reflection on the narratives, iconography, and representations inherent in the created images and their potential implications within social and cultural contexts (Figure 12.6).

For instance, the design brief could direct the AI system to generate visuals that honor the diverse spectrum of identities, counteracting dominant stereotypes or amplifying often sidelined voices. This strategy could open the door for unconventional narratives and imagery that challenge prevailing ideologies, fostering a spirit of empathy, fairness, and environmental sustainability.

Moreover, radical-centric design considers the historical and societal context in which design decisions are made. It reflects how design can perpetuate harmful norms or be a tool for positive change. It acknowledges the role of design in shaping culture and society and seeks to exercise this role conscientiously.

In a globalized and interconnected world, radical-centric design also incorporates an acute awareness of cultural sensitivities. It respects and values diversity, taking into account varying cultural perspectives. It is informed and considerate, eschewing appropriation or misrepresentation, and instead endeavors to understand and respect the richness of diverse cultures.

Engaging in radical centricity morphs the design space into a platform for social dialogue, a catalyst for change. The text-conditional prompts, imbued with radical-centric principles, guide designers and AI systems to transcend traditional boundaries. They navigate unexplored territories where AI-generated visuals become more than images,

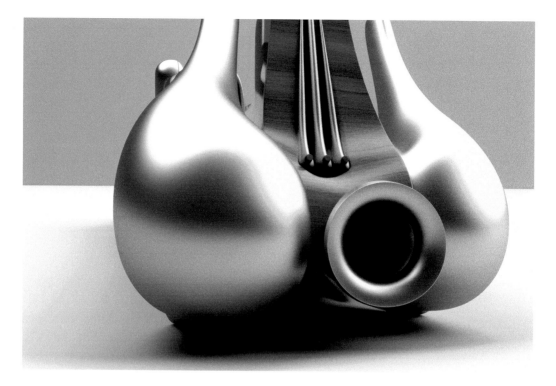

FIGURE 12.7   A radical centric design for a midi wind instrument.

transforming into potent messages and catalysts for inclusive and socially conscientious progression (Figure 12.7). Radical-centric design extends beyond a creative process; it is a movement and philosophy that employs design as a tool for positive transformation. Through radical centricity, design evolves from simply solving problems to acting as a bridge builder, fostering a world where creativity synergizes with empathy, equity, and sustainability.

12.6 NO ARCHETYPE

As discussed briefly in the introduction to this book, when we request a generative AI to conceive a chair, we invoke an archetype with certain preconceptions and constraints. The archetype of a chair is steeped in our cultural and social fabrics, summoning expectations regarding its shape, function, and utility. By rephrasing this request to "design a radical-centric device that elevates the human body above ground in a comfortable position," we liberate ourselves from the bonds of the traditional chair archetype, thus unveiling a realm of potential for new kinds of seating or support systems.

Transitioning from the traditional concept of a "chair that can accommodate individuals of all sizes" to envisaging a "radical centric device that elevates the human body above ground in a comfortable position," we surpass the barriers of archetypal thinking and step into a world of uncharted possibilities. This alteration in perspective enables us to detach from conventional concepts and delve into alternate forms and functionalities that can cater more effectively to individual needs and preferences.

FIGURE 12.8   A radical-centric design for a device that elevates the human body above ground in a comfortable position.

By challenging the AI to conceive a device that elevates the human body above ground in a comfortable position, we are not only circumventing the customary archetype of a chair but also stimulating the AI to ponder novel possibilities in terms of shape, functionality, and applications. This challenge expands the horizons for AI to generate designs that could have remained inconceivable within the traditional framework. It impels AI to break the mold and consider innovative solutions that comfortably support the human body. In radical centricity, this provocation leads the AI to critically examine and challenge traditional chair definitions and constraints (Figure 12.8). Rather than focusing exclusively on accommodating varying body sizes, the AI is now propelled to contemplate a more comprehensive array of elements such as comfort, elevation, and the customization of experiences, thereby transcending the conventional definition of a chair.

Radical-centric design advocates placing individuals' unique needs, preferences, and desires at the forefront, guaranteeing that the resulting design not only fulfills functional requirements but also resonates deeply on an emotional and experiential level. It motivates the AI to sail into the seas of imagination, conjuring devices beyond the traditional confines of archetypal objects. This line of thought facilitates exploration into non-traditional materials, forms, and technologies that can revolutionize how we think about supporting the human body above the ground.

The linguistic choice in this reimagined query is vital. The term "elevates the human body above ground" evokes imagery of buoyancy or levitation, potentially guiding the

AI toward designs incorporating suspension systems or even cutting-edge levitation technologies. "Comfortable position" is a broad and open-ended term, encouraging the AI to consider not only orthodox seating postures but also reclining or other avant-garde arrangements. By extricating the archetype of a chair from the equation, we grant AI a spacious canvas, inviting it to embrace interdisciplinary paradigms and glean inspiration from various fields.

The radical-centric design ideology serves as a call for the fusion of disciplines such as art, engineering, ergonomics, and psychology to fabricate designs that genuinely epitomize the philosophy of radical centricity. The AI is encouraged to address the tangible aspects of comfort and elevation and to penetrate the psychological and emotional layers that constitute a deeply immersive and transformative experience.

The depth of engagement fostered by radical centricity culminates in creations that go beyond mere physical entities; they become carriers of an enhanced existence, transcending the mundane. These creations are imbued with a unique aura, a distinct persona that interfaces with the user on a profound level, metamorphosing interactions into more than merely functional transactions; they evolve into harmonious, soulful journeys (Figure 12.9). These journeys constitute a symphony between human essence and the material world, suffused with empathy, understanding, and resonance.

In this context, radical-centric design enables generative AI systems to bring forth creations that function as extensions of an individual's persona. This seamless fusion of functionality, aesthetics, comfort, and personal expression reflects the radical-centric design's

FIGURE 12.9   A radical-centric design for a personal mobility device.

commitment to humanizing technology. It does not merely cater to human needs but also resonates with human emotions, cultural identities, and social realities. It ensures that technology, in its manifold manifestations, is aligned with the kaleidoscope of human experiences, thus creating a more empathetic and inclusive future.

Generative AI, in this process, is transformed from a mere instrument to an active collaborator, endowed with an almost human-like capacity to amalgamate and dissect information. Through advanced algorithms, it deciphers subtle intricacies, discerns patterns, generates inventive ideas, and executes informed decisions that harmonize creativity and practicality. This shift elevates AI from the role of a passive component to that of an intellectual collaborator in a co-creative odyssey. This journey reimagines the very essence of objects and experiences in our world.

12.7 CLOSING THOUGHTS

Undeniably, the metamorphosis of generative AI into a creative collaborator signifies a revolutionary shift in the design paradigm. This collaboration opens up possibilities that were once confined to the domain of the fantastical, fostering the birth of designs that go beyond mere functionality, becoming deeply personalized, contextually grounded, and essentially transformational. Harnessing the power of machine learning, generative AI surmounts the essential elements of replication or automation, showcasing an almost sentient capability in creating novel and invaluable solutions. This evolution culminates in the materialization of designs that genuinely mirror an individual's needs, dreams, and identities.

Generative AI emerges as a transformation agent, turning the ordinary into the extraordinary. It stirs innovation that disrupts conventional wisdom and ceaselessly expands the possibilities in design (Figure 12.10). It ignites a sense of audacity in us—a drive to breach the boundaries of the known, challenge our preconceptions, interrogate the status quo, and persistently explore new perspectives and experiences.

As it grows in stature, generative AI moves beyond being a mere instrument; it emerges as a vanguard of radical centricity. It boldly navigates the unexplored realms of creativity, daringly contesting norms and sparking a tectonic shift in design philosophy. It constructs bridges towards a more inclusive, empathetic, and individual-centric design methodology, heralding a future where the core of human creativity and the prowess of AI blend into a dazzling symphony of innovation and metamorphosis.

By infusing the principles of radical-centric design into our prompts, we invite generative AI to engage in a profound philosophical dialogue that examines the intricate nature of human needs, desires, and experiences. It inspires us to reengineer the relationships between humans and objects. We are prompted to envision a symbiotic interplay that enhances our well-being, unlocking pathways to unparalleled comfort, nourishment, and joy. Through this philosophical journey, we unlock a wealth of transformative design possibilities that dismantle conventional archetypes and forge profoundly radical experiences that resonate with profound meaning.

In this exchange between the known and the mysterious, between time-honored wisdom and the thrilling possibilities of the future, the spirit of design pulsates with vitality.

FIGURE 12.10   A radical-centric design for a sound reproduction device.

Design becomes more than creating functional or aesthetically pleasing objects or spaces. It transforms into a narrative art, a conduit linking our historical tapestry and the winding paths of our individual and collective futures. It involves revisiting and reinterpreting traditional symbols and conventions through the lens of contemporary challenges and opportunities. It is about carving new archetypes that echo our evolving senses of self and ambition.

It is crucial to understand that innovation does not wage war against tradition or discard esteemed archetypes. Instead, innovation is a dialogue, a harmonious composition of past and future notes. It pays tribute to our predecessor's wisdom as we bravely shape new horizons. It is about leveraging the tools and technologies at our disposal to traverse unexplored realms of creativity and expression while grounding our expedition in our shared human legacy's rich tapestry. Vitally, generative AI, fortified with radical-centric design principles, serves as a compass guiding us through a voyage of self-discovery, cultural respect, and bold imagination. It enables design to transcend form and function, morphing into a tapestry woven from the threads of history, innovation, and human experience.

NOTES

1. The Daguerreotype, a pioneering photographic process made public in 1839 by Louis Daguerre, was one of the earliest photographic procedures accessible to the broader public. This popularization instigated considerable turbulence in the art world, with photography's

precision forcing painting to adapt its objectives—shifting from the literal representation of reality to the expression of emotions and impressions. Thus, photography has often been viewed as a critical catalyst in the reformation of painting that transpired during the late 19th and 20th centuries. The introduction of photography in the 19th century elicited a spectrum of responses within artistic circles. Notably, while appreciating its technological breakthrough, individuals like Gustave Courbet dismissed it as irrelevant to the realm of fine arts. Nevertheless, the advent of photography led to a transformative ripple effect across 19th-century European societies. Its accessibility and affordability democratized the art of portraiture, making it feasible for individuals across different social classes—be it middle, lower, or higher—to have their likenesses captured swiftly and at a reasonable cost. This accessibility sparked debates around the notion of the "democratization of art," with reactions varying between embracing the expansion of art's reach and critiquing it as trivialization. Detractors perceived photography as an industrial facsimile of art, commodified commercially. Retrieved from https://www.thecollector.com/how-photography-transformed-art/#.

2. **Contextual understanding** refers to the comprehensive assessment and evaluation of the backdrop against which a project operates. It incorporates examining factors shaping the project's milieu, significant constituents, and their mutual interactions. This process involves comprehensively understanding the project's situational framework and placement within the larger context. Additionally, it involves identifying all elements, such as factual information and implicit assumptions, exploring their interdependencies, and formulating strategies that facilitate adept and productive responses.

3. "Co-design" encapsulates a democratic, inclusive approach to devising solutions, wherein stakeholders are valued as equal partners in the design journey. Key pillars of this method include proactive engagement of target users in the design process, deferring design decisions until user feedback is acquired, translating this feedback into actionable insights, and crafting solutions deeply rooted in user feedback. Recognizing co-design as a dynamic process rather than a standalone event is crucial. Moreover, the process is often iterative, providing the flexibility to return to the community for feedback and potential improvements even post-product launch. Retrieved from https://communities.sunlightfoundation.com/action/codesign/.

4. Figure 4.1.3 is a product concept generated without the use of an archetype—no mention of "air conditioner" was entered in the prompt.

5. AutoDesk's Fusion 360's generative design capability enables the production of CAD-ready, editable geometry to be immediately modified within Fusion 360 or exported to your preferred CAD software. This approach ensures smooth integration with Autodesk Inventor, enhancing efficiency and fostering collaboration. Industrial designers can expedite their workflow on a unified platform, saving significant time. For instance, Fusion 360 facilitates the creation of photorealistic renders of designs up to 75% faster, accelerating stakeholder approval. Moreover, transitioning from concepts to 3D models can be achieved 4x faster than traditional industrial design software. By leveraging Fusion 360, there is potential to craft high-quality products and expedite time to market by up to 60%, marking a significant leap in productivity and efficiency. Retrieved from https://www.autodesk.ca/en/products/fusion-360/industrial-designer.

6. Archetypes, according to Swiss psychiatrist Carl Jung, are innate, universal prototypes for ideas, behaviors, and personalities that shape human interactions and responses. Jung postulated that these archetypes are ancient forms of human wisdom transmitted genetically across generations. Within the framework of Jungian psychology, they are considered as part of the collective unconscious, serving as universally shared concepts and behavioral tendencies. Retrieved from https://www.verywellmind.com/what-are-jungs-4-major-archetypes-2795439#citation-1.

7. **Conceptual models** represent abstract, psychological frameworks that outline how tasks should be executed. Individuals employ these models subconsciously and intuitively as mechanisms for structuring processes. Designers who create interfaces and applications that align with these models tap into pre-existing knowledge and mental structures. This alignment facilitates a more seamless learning curve for users when interacting with a new product. Commonly, conceptual models are identified at the outset of the design process and serve as continual guidance and inspiration throughout the development cycle. Retrieved from https://www.interaction-design.org/literature/topics/conceptual-models.

CHAPTER 13

Less Is Not More Anymore

13.1 THE AESTHETIC OF INSIDE-OUT

The phrase "form follows function" has been a staple of architecture and industrial design for the past century.[1] It is often interpreted as the idea that an object's form should be dictated by its intended function. However, this interpretation misses a crucial aspect of the phrase. The idea of form following function is more about form following the limitations and constraints of the available technology and materials. The form of an object is therefore shaped by the manufacturing processes and techniques used to create it.

Throughout the 20th century and into the current epoch, the maxim "form follows function" has surfaced as a defining precept encapsulating the spirit of industrial design. Beyond its notable repute, the aphorism's significance extends past the superficial seduction of aesthetic appeal tethered to an object's preordained utility. This principle refers to a complex symbiosis between form and an amalgam of constraints and limitations, particularly those imposed by the unyielding tide of technological progression. The entwined relationship becomes glaringly perceptible within realms such as plastic extrusion, cast molding, and injection molding, where an object's form is irrevocably etched by the inherent restrictions tied to these fabrication methods.

Inherent to the conceptual structure of "form follows function" is the acknowledgment that form is intimately tied to the flux and opportunities presented by the selection of materials and the manufacturing techniques deployed. An object's ultimate shape is deeply influenced by the physical properties intrinsic to a material and the processes through which it can be manipulated and perfected during fabrication. For instance, the inherent nature of plastic extrusion, which necessitates the formation of objects in a continuous flow, mandates meticulous compliance with specific design doctrines. Concurrently, cast and injection molding impose their unique demands, outlining the overarching shape and the level of detail attainable.

In addition, this design principle underscores the centrality of technological evolution in shaping the form of artifacts. Various possibilities and methodologies emerge as technology progresses, enabling designers to break erstwhile boundaries and perpetually

DOI: 10.1201/9781003450139-18

redefine form. The nexus between form and function unfolds into an intricate dance, wherein form adapts and transforms in synchrony with the march of technological prowess. Consequently, the design of an object transcends its functional value, acting as a representation of the technological paradigm that gave rise to it.

"Form follows function" invites philosophical contemplation when viewed from an abstract perspective. Here, an artifact's function surpasses practical utility, extending into a broader societal and cultural ontology. The design morphology of an object can function as a medium to convey messages, encapsulate, and perpetuate cultural norms. Consequently, an object's form is not solely determined by its pragmatic function but it also represents its societal role and cultural environment.

"Form follows function" transcends tangible boundaries and ventures into the metaphysical dimensions of design. It unravels a more profound, philosophical understanding of how form can safeguard an object's essential purpose as a bearer of emotions, narratives, and cultural import. By carefully considering the multifarious relationship between form and function, designers can endow objects with a unique identity, persona, and significance that resonate with individuals on a profoundly personal level.

Essentially, the "form follows function" doctrine enshrines a comprehensive perspective on industrial design. It respects the implications of technological constraints and manufacturing techniques, emphasizing the deep interdependence between form and the alchemical properties of materials. At the same time, it recognizes the metaphysical aspects of design, where form morphs into a crucible for expressing an artifact's essence and raison d'être. As humanity strides into the future, will this axiom remain a guiding beacon for designers? Can the creatives working in design continue to be inspired to adeptly navigate the complex interplay between form, function, and the perpetually evolving landscape of technological innovation that now includes generative artificial intelligence (AI)?[2]

"Form follows function" encapsulates an overarching truth about design—that it is shaped by, and in turn shapes, the context within which it is situated, be it technological, societal, or material. However, it is crucial to acknowledge the transformative role that emerging technologies like generative AI will play in this discourse. Generative AI presents an intriguing paradigm shift with its potential to generate novel and efficient designs. This technology can simultaneously consider many variables and constraints, possibly leading to forms that may deviate from traditional aesthetics yet provide superior functionality. As such, designers are challenged to reinterpret the dictum of "form follows function," adapting it within the confines of this new landscape. The form might follow not only function but also computational efficiency, material optimization, and algorithmic logic.

Simultaneously, the incorporation of generative AI calls for a reassessment of the applicability of this axiom. While generative AI augments design capabilities, it also prompts queries regarding the sustenance of human originality and the preservation of cultural richness in design. Despite AI algorithms spawning innovative design solutions, it is crucial to understand that the seeds of ideation and conceptualization, nurtured by human creativity, cultural subtleties, and ethical contemplations, remain indispensable to the design process. The challenge lies in striking a balance between the deterministic precision of AI and the boundless abstraction intrinsic to human creativity.

However, for the critical thinker, the entwining of generative AI with design prompts the question: Does the "form follows function" axiom retain its essence when AI can conjure designs transcending conventional functional parameters? In specific scenarios, such as those involving rigid materials, strict manufacturing processes, or customized instrument designs, the axiom remains relevant as a philosophical guiding principle, steering designers back to their foundational tenets.

However, with generative AI relentlessly redefining the design landscape, it is conceivable that the boundaries of the "form follows function" maxim will undergo an iterative process of reinterpretation. For instance, the AI's ability to optimize across a spectrum of constraints could give rise to forms where the function is not the exclusive determinant. Designs may reflect a sophisticated interplay among efficiency, sustainability, aesthetics, and other considerations. The ensuing design might not intuitively reflect its function in the traditional sense, thereby potentially reconfiguring the long-standing norms of the axiom.

Consequently, the advent of generative AI presents an intellectual quandary: Will the axiom's core spirit—the sacred relationship between an object's form and function—persist in its traditional sense? It is plausible that the axiom will persist as an inspiring principle. However, its conventional application might evolve into a more intricate guideline that accommodates the myriad possibilities generated by generative AI. This shift necessitates an ongoing, judicious discourse among designers, ethicists, and technologists, intending to uphold the relevance and integrity of design principles in an era awash with AI-driven innovation.

13.2 LESS IS MORE

For decades, the aphorism "less is more" has been celebrated as a seminal philosophy in design and architecture, epitomizing the quintessence of minimalism and simplicity.[3] When scrutinized through the prism of technological constraints, this design axiom transcends surface-level aesthetics and assumes a more profound philosophical significance. Distilling an object to its elemental constituents not only engenders an uncluttered aesthetic but also attenuates the potential impediments that may arise during fabrication. Within the range of technological limitations, this tenet acquires an amplified profundity, as it accentuates the imperative of simplicity and the excision of unnecessary elements which might otherwise hinder processes such as toolmaking or injection molding.[4] The historical confluence of injection molding limitations and the "less is more" philosophy has indelibly left their imprints on the aesthetic tapestry of design.

Moreover, the limitations inherent in traditional design and manufacturing methods extend beyond technological boundaries and significantly impact everyday objects such as chairs, scissors, and hammers. Historically, technological constraints have played a role in restricting the aesthetic range designers could explore, tethering them within the realm of practicality rather than freeing them to break beyond the mundane and fully realize their creative visions. However, the emergence of additive manufacturing signals a significant paradigm shift, effectively breaking the chains that have historically bound the design field. By adopting an inside-out approach to product creation, additive manufacturing liberates designers from traditional fabrication restrictions, transforming the maxim "less is more" from a reluctant concession to a true artistic expression of minimalist principles.

Commonly known as 3D printing, additive manufacturing opens a new world of freedom in form and structure, making it possible to conceive and create complex and intricate designs previously considered unattainable. This technological breakthrough enables designers to explore new ground, pushing the limits of creative expression and giving life to forms that resonate with their deepest aspirations and artistic visions. At the same time, this newfound freedom from technological limitations introduces a new layer of considerations. The unrestricted artistic latitude granted by additive manufacturing calls for a thoughtful and philosophical examination of the very essence of design. What guiding principles inform the creation of each form? How can designers skillfully bridge the gap between unrestricted creativity and purposeful expression that encapsulates an object's identity and purpose?

As we venture into this exciting new era, filled with the limitless possibilities of additive manufacturing, designers are called to approach their craft with greater discernment and wisdom. Being freed from the constraints of traditional methods makes it a responsibility to ensure that the forms born out of this emancipation are endowed with inherent meaning and resonance that speak to the human experience and leave a lasting imprint on society.

The shift from subtractive to additive manufacturing is more than just a technological change; it represents a turning point in the evolution of design. Subtractive manufacturing, which involves removing material to achieve the desired form, naturally confines designers within a maze of limitations. On the other hand, additive manufacturing uses a bottom-up approach, building three-dimensional objects layer by layer from digital blueprints, offering unparalleled flexibility and precision.[5]

This shift does more than merely equip designers with the ability to realize intricate forms previously thought unfeasible; it also tests the fundamental tenets of design. It signals the advent of a new era where the synergistic integration of form, function, and aesthetics is celebrated, and designers are urged to challenge traditional norms.

Beyond its impact on design, this change holds the potential to redefine the paradigms of production and consumption. With its capacity for on-demand production, additive manufacturing reduces waste, optimizes resource utilization, and cultivates a focus on sustainability. Furthermore, it stands to democratize the design field, putting the power of production into the hands of the wider public and empowering individuals to participate directly in the creative process. Such a shift transforms consumers from mere recipients to critical participants in the design journey. In essence, additive manufacturing triggers a transition from mass production of uniform products to customized fabrication tailored to individual preferences. This shift does not just enhance consumer engagement; it also recasts them as creators and collaborators within the production ecosystem.[6]

As additive manufacturing democratizes design tools and technologies, it engenders a more inclusive creative economy. This evolution broadens the diversity of product design and stands as a potent instrument for social and economic parity. The resultant products do not merely reflect a greater variety of ideas, but they also cater to a broader range of needs and preferences. The onset of additive manufacturing signifies a revival in design philosophy. Its boundless potential frees form and function from traditional constraints yet simultaneously encourages designers to wield this newfound liberty with reflection and accountability. This transformative technology enables individuals to become active contributors to the creative process, heralding a more sustainable, inclusive future rich in innovation.

13.3 LESS IS NOT MORE ANYMORE

3D printing marks a seismic shift in manufacturing, recalibrating our understanding of aesthetics. The past era, when design was confined mainly to minimalistic forms, gave way to a focus on complexity, detail, and customization. In 3D printing, simplicity is no longer paramount; instead, there is a daring call to embrace an ethos of intricate aesthetics. Aesthetics from 3D printing signify a stark departure from the traditional belief that beauty is equal to minimalism. The resultant product is more than visually appealing; it embodies principles and values intertwined throughout the fabrication process. It celebrates complexity and ambition, encouraging us to push beyond the boundaries of conventional design (Figures 13.1–13.4).

FIGURE 13.1   3D printed soap dish.

Furthermore, this emerging aesthetic appreciates the core of creation, where art and technology merge in a symphony of endless possibilities. With a vast array of materials, each possessing unique properties, admiration extends beyond the final artifact to include the elemental components enabling its existence. The process becomes an art form, highlighting craftsmanship, ingenuity, and the journey from idea to reality. The creation process is viewed as an artistic endeavor, highlighting craftsmanship, ingenuity, and the journey from idea to reality. This transformation, initiated by 3D printing, introduces a diverse and dynamic view of beauty and opens doors to numerous opportunities for those ready to embrace innovative technology. It alters our perceptions of beauty, encouraging us to find it in the unexpected, the intricate, and the unconventional (Figures 13.5–13.7).

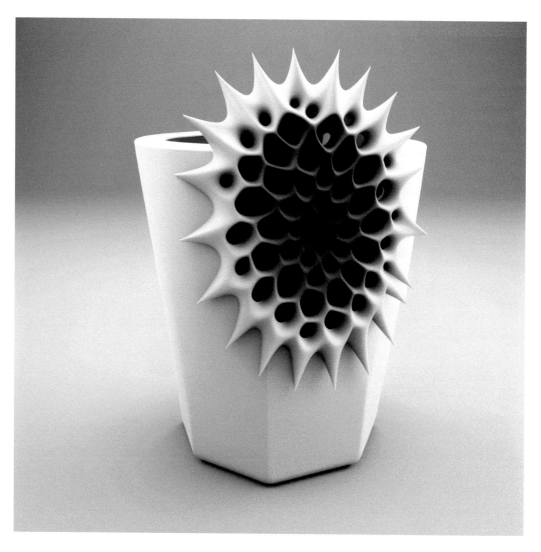

FIGURE 13.2   3D printed bathroom waste container.

FIGURE 13.3   3D printed lounge chair 1.

3D printing is revolutionizing industrial design, introducing many aesthetic possibilities. Unbound by the limitations of traditional technologies, it acts as a gateway to
uncharted artistic territories, challenging the minimalist "less is more" principle. We
are encouraged to explore an aesthetic paradigm filled with complexity. The aesthetic
transformation of 3D printing fosters a more diverse and dynamic conception of beauty,
opening doors for those ready to harness the capabilities of this novel technology. It
alters perceptions, encouraging recognition of beauty in the unconventional and multifaceted (Figure 13.8).

Additionally, 3D printing promotes collaboration. The ease with which designs and
ideas can be shared worldwide fosters synergies among designers, manufacturers, and end-
users. This collaborative effort reflects a merging of values and aspirations, positioning
3D printing as a technological breakthrough and a socio-cultural and artistic movement.

At its core, 3D printing is reshaping aesthetic norms. Traditional, minimalist designs
now share the stage with many elaborate and finely detailed creations. Beauty in design

is no longer just about simplicity; it encompasses the richness of details, textures, and the harmonious integration of elements. In this reimagined landscape, 3D printing is a technological innovation and a catalyst for aesthetic evolution.

The evolution of aesthetic boundaries brought about by 3D printing requires rethinking conventional norms. Traditional beauty standards need to adapt to the expansive opportunities offered by this technology. Complexity and detail take precedence in this new aesthetic domain, inviting us to immerse ourselves in the rich patterns and textures that define contemporary beauty.

The fusion of technology and art opens new creative avenues and necessitates a holistic approach. The creative journey becomes as important as the final product, with a diverse array of materials allowing for experimentation with textures and properties.

This aesthetic shift also repositions the idea of imperfection, challenging the age-old pursuit of flawlessness. It celebrates the exploration of alternative designs, allowing designers to challenge the boundaries of the possible. This freedom promotes an embrace of the

FIGURE 13.4   3D printed lounge chair 2.

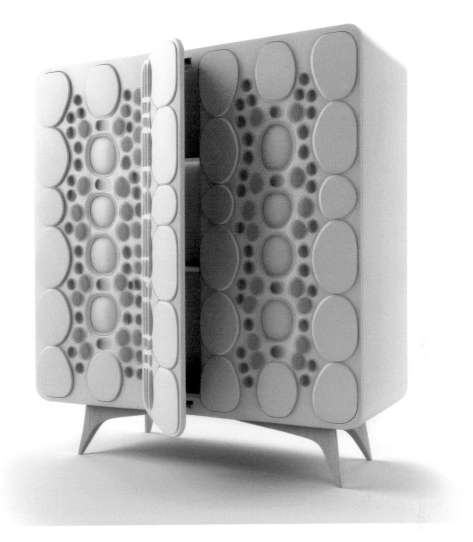

FIGURE 13.5   Rethinking archetypes: The cabinet.

unexpected and the nonconforming, opening fresh avenues for exploration and urging us to expand our intellectual and creative horizons (Figure 13.9).

3D printing has catalyzed a significant transition in industrial design aesthetics. Extending the limits of what is possible invites a reassessment of our definitions of beauty. The revitalized aesthetic appreciates complexity, texture, and the fusion of diverse elements. It emphasizes the creative process, fostering innovation and experimentation. As we navigate this new territory, we are called to adopt a more comprehensive and inclusive aesthetic philosophy that thrives on diversity, creativity, and the boundless potential of 3D printing.

Furthermore, the democratization of the creative process offered by 3D printing has allowed a wide range of practitioners, from seasoned professionals to novice enthusiasts,

FIGURE 13.6   Rethinking archetypes: The couch.

to innovate in unique ways. For example, architects can now construct detailed scale models that were previously challenging to create using conventional methods. These detailed models improve communication with clients and stakeholders, leading to better-informed decisions. Conversely, enthusiasts with minimal design experience can use user-friendly software to create custom items, fostering grassroots innovation.

The ability of 3D printing to create customized, intricate products has profound implications in various fields, notably in healthcare. A prime example is the domain of prosthetics, where 3D printing can create custom prosthetic limbs tailored to an individual's specific anatomical and physiological needs. These personalized prosthetics offer functional benefits and an aesthetic likeness to the user's natural limbs, contributing significantly to amputees' physical and psychological well-being (Figure 13.10).

In fashion and apparel, 3D printing is causing a radical shift. Renowned designers and fashion houses are incorporating 3D-printed elements into their collections. An example is Iris van Herpen, a Dutch fashion designer renowned for combining traditional craftsmanship with advanced technology.[7] Her collections often feature intricate 3D-printed garments that push the boundaries of fabric and form. These creations are not just wearable;

FIGURE 13.7   Rethinking archetypes: The king size bed.

they are pieces of art that challenge and redefine conventional fashion norms. Such inno-vations allow the fashion world to serve as a vivid canvas depicting the artistry enabled by 3D printing (Figure 13.11).

In automotive design, 3D printing is pivotal in revolutionizing aesthetics and function-ality. Car designers utilize this technology to fabricate custom components that satisfy distinct performance demands and aesthetic proclivities. One illustration is the fabrication of lightweight, lattice-structured components that enhance fuel efficiency while providing visually pleasing designs. Entities such as Local Motors have ventured to develop entire vehicles leveraging 3D printing technology, thereby showcasing its potential to yield highly personalized, efficient, and aesthetically compelling automobiles.[8]

Moreover, integrating 3D printing into automotive design heralds a paradigm shift in the rapid prototyping and iterative design process. The technology allows designers to experiment with various configurations and geometries without the financial burdens tra-ditionally associated with manufacturing prototypes. This agility accelerates the devel-opment cycle and enables real-world feedback to fine-tune performance and aesthetics. Also, it opens avenues for sustainability by developing lightweight structures that improve

FIGURE 13.8 Rethinking archetypes: Single family dwelling.

FIGURE 13.9 Rethinking archetypes: Experimental building structures.

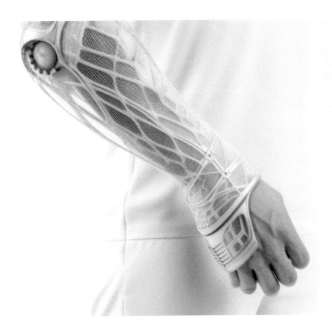

FIGURE 13.10   Medical assistive device.

fuel efficiency and reduce the environmental footprint. The merging of customization with eco-conscious design objectives represents an evolution in automotive manufacturing, positioning 3D printing as an invaluable tool in harmonizing aesthetic appeal with sustainable and high-performance solutions.

The influence of 3D printing also permeates the field of education, transforming it into a playground for experiential learning. It is becoming increasingly commonplace for educational institutions to weave 3D printing into their academic curricula, promoting an immersive, hands-on learning approach. This innovative practice of creating three-dimensional objects immerses students in a holistic educational experience beyond textbook theory to embrace tangible applications. This physical interaction with their ideas offers students a lucid visualization of abstract concepts, bolstering their understanding and memory retention. Furthermore, this fosters a culture of creativity and innovation among young minds, arming them with the necessary skills to become instrumental contributors to an intricately woven and ever-evolving global fabric.

3D printing transcends its role as a mere technological marvel to assume a role that bridges myriad sectors and academic disciplines. Its proficiency in facilitating the creation of complex, tailor-made designs revolutionizes aesthetic conventions and redefines functionality across diverse industries. By provoking a paradigm shift in our perception of aesthetics, 3D printing instigates a creative renaissance that mirrors our evolving societal ethos and future aspirations. It democratizes the spirit of innovation, stimulates interdisciplinary synergy, and prompts us to reassess and reshape our definitions of

FIGURE 13.11   A radiolaria inspired design for a wedding dress.

beauty and utility in the present era. As we venture deeper into a period marked by swift technological advancement, 3D printing becomes a monument to human creativity and the infinite possibilities at the intersection of art and technology.

13.4 CLOSING THOUGHTS

3D printing, as a medium, opens an entirely fresh realm of aesthetics, where the limits of past technology do not border the boundaries of beauty. This innovation provides an extraordinary scope for creativity, previously constrained only by our imaginations. The shift into this new aesthetic landscape is no less than a challenge to the traditional 'less is more' notion of minimalism, inviting us instead to celebrate beauty through elaborate, intricate forms.

Generative AI plays a pivotal role as we navigate this emergent landscape, shaping the evolving aesthetics of 3D printing. Leveraging the capacity of AI to absorb and process vast amounts of design data, generative design tools provide a broad canvas for creativity and individuality. These tools continuously generate and evaluate design alternatives, considering specific constraints and targets, resulting in a spectrum of optimally tailored design solutions. By going beyond the purview of human creativity, this AI-centric approach not only streamlines the design process but explores a design space that outstrips our cognitive limitations.

Marrying generative AI with 3D printing adds another layer of sophistication to the emerging aesthetic. This combination allows us to exceed traditional limits by creating intricate designs that would otherwise be impractical or exceedingly labor-intensive. When AI-powered generative designs are combined with the inherent capabilities of 3D printing, the result is the creation of objects with elaborate patterns, subtle structures, and bespoke features. These features align with the tastes and requirements of the end user. This fusion may give birth to an aesthetic distinguished by unparalleled complexity, detail, and personalization.

At the same time, embedding AI in the design process nurtures an environment of collaborative innovation, where designers and AI algorithms form a productive partnership. Humans set the parameters and guide the creative direction, while AI enhances and refines their ideas, unlocking unexplored areas of creative exploration. This collaboration strengthens the creative process, producing designs representing a balanced fusion of human intuition and AI.

The advent of 3D printing certainly marked a new era in design, characterized by more significant innovation, experimentation, and customization. Incorporating generative AI into this environment injects further dynamism, urging us to rethink conventional views of beauty and value. Our journey into this exciting aesthetic domain challenges us to broaden our perspectives, welcoming an era where complexity and detail define beauty, and customization and personalization reign supreme. As we teeter on the brink of this transformative shift, our understanding and appreciation of aesthetics in design are on the verge of a dramatic transformation.

The prospect is invigorating rather than intimidating as we stand at the nexus of tradition and innovation. The integration of generative AI and 3D printing summons us toward a future that is animated with potential. This interlinking cultivates an enriched aesthetic language and embodies an impetus for sustainable, efficient, and humane designs.

The marriage of 3D printing and generative AI signals a liberating divergence from the conventional, propelling us into an era of boundless creativity, intricacy, and personalization. This fusion is poised to empower us to redefine the contours of aesthetics and reshape our relationship with everyday objects. This leap into the unexplored opens up new frontiers of possibility that resonate with human aspiration and intellectual curiosity. Once a predefined parameter, aesthetics is being transformed into an open-ended conversation, a dialogue between human desire and AI capability. Embracing this vibrant dialogue brings the promise of a dynamic, personalized, and intelligent aesthetic future that fills us with optimism and anticipation. In an increasingly interconnected and rapidly evolving world, this synthesis holds the promise of being more than just a confluence of technology; it symbolizes an upcoming renaissance in design and human expression.

NOTES

1. Routinely misattributed to Le Corbusier or Mies van der Rohe, it was actually coined by American architect Louis Sullivan. https://www.nytimes.com/2009/06/01/arts/01iht-DESIGN1.html.

2. NB: It is crucial to note that this ongoing discussion does not aim to undermine the contributions or potential of generative AI in the design field. Instead, it seeks to articulate the complex relationship between emerging technologies, design philosophies, and human creativity. The objective is to harmoniously integrate these elements in a manner that respects and builds upon established principles while paving the way for innovative approaches and perspectives. Ultimately, this discourse's crux is ensuring that our technological advancements align with and enrich our creative and cultural narratives instead of operating in isolation.

3. Another misattributed quote—often to Mies van der Rohe—"less is more" originated with architect Peter Behrens. https://www.phaidon.com/agenda/architecture/articles/2014/april/02/what-did-mies-van-der-rohe-mean-by-less-is-more/.

4. Here are some of the considerations pivotal in shaping the injection molded product. **Wall thickness:** This determinant is multifaceted, relying on aspects such as the part's structural obligations, susceptibility to fragility, and material selection. These variables collaboratively inform the ideal wall thickness. **Draft angles:** The integration of draft angles is essential for the seamless ejection of the part from the mold. **Radii:** Incorporating radii at the part's corners optimizes material flow, fortifying the final piece's structural integrity and longevity. **Warpage:** Disparities in cooling rates during the molding process can precipitate warpage, a deviation in form. It is incumbent upon the design phase to integrate countermeasures that curb this phenomenon. Modified from Injection molding: The manufacturing & design guide. Hubs. Retrieved from https://www.hubs.com/guides/injection-molding/.

5. Notably, the term "3D printing," often ubiquitously employed by media as a catch-all phrase for additive manufacturing processes, does not encapsulate the diversity inherent within these technologies. Additive manufacturing encompasses many distinct processes, each varying in its layer manufacturing method and contingent upon the specific material and machine technology utilized. Recognizing the need for standardization and precise classification, the ASTM Committee F42 on Additive Manufacturing Technologies, under the aegis of the American Society for Testing and Materials, formulated a comprehensive set of standards in 2010. These standards delineate additive manufacturing processes into seven categories: VAT photopolymerization, material jetting, binder jetting, material extrusion, directed energy deposition, sheet lamination, and powder bed fusion. The seven categories of Additive Manufacturing, Additive Manufacturing Research Group, Loughborough University. Retrieved from https://www.lboro.ac.uk/research/amrg/about/the7categoriesofadditivemanufacturing/.

6. According to the global management consulting firm McKinsey, additive manufacturing (AM) technologies proffer an ensemble of four salient sources of value compared to conventional manufacturing methodologies. Primarily, the capability of AM to render virtually any three-dimensional configuration empowers designers with an unparalleled latitude in part design, potentially bolstering performance or achieving cost efficiencies compared to traditional counterparts. Illustratively, Airbus leveraged AM to fabricate a titanium bracket, which, while retaining performance and durability, is 30% lighter than its conventionally manufactured antecedent. Second, AM obviates the necessity for molds or fixed tooling, enabling the production of distinct parts and heralding an era of mass customization. Third, the circumvention of protracted toolmaking and fabrication procedures through AM

expedites product development and production, thus abbreviating the time-to-market. A case in point is the fuel injector head utilized in the Ariane 6 rocket, which is additively manufactured from a nickel-based alloy in a single piece, in stark contrast to previous versions that necessitated the welding of 248 individually machined components. Last, AM tends to streamline maintenance and support for products in the field, diminishing the exigency for spare parts inventories via the facilitation of on-demand production from digital files. For illustration, Mercedes-Benz has adopted AM to manufacture spare parts for its classic automobile range. Retrieved from https://www.mckinsey.com/capabilities/operations/our-insights/the-mainstreaming-of-additive-manufacturing.

7. Work examples available at https://www.irisvanherpen.com.

8. While the company no longer exists, its pioneering work in 3D printed automotive production, exemplified by the Strati 3D vehicle, has proven the technology and inspired automotive producers today. Retrieved from https://newatlas.com/local-motors-strati-imts/33846/.

CHAPTER 14

The Richly Imagined Everything

14.1 SCENARIO-BASED DESIGN AND INNOVATION

Effecting change entails a complex interplay that requires compelling visualizations, the integration of knowledge, and an awareness of the inherent dynamism characterizing our environment. It is essential to comprehend that the subject of change is not the organization in isolation but rather the proficiencies that undergird its structure. The fluidity intrinsic to an organization's current construct necessitates change. This process should be discerningly navigated, as opposed to an unyielding progression, especially in light of emergent technologies and behavioral shifts.

Employing foresight scenarios, which encompass an intricate amalgamation of narrative finesse, equips organizations to envision and critically analyze a spectrum of potential futures, probing the interconnections between technological advancements and human elements. The creation of these scenarios demands a sophisticated understanding of the driving forces behind technological progression and the subsequent ripples across social dimensions, inclusive of cultural norms and ethical implications. As a vital tool, foresight scenarios aid in developing agile and adaptive organizational tactics proficient in navigating uncertain future terrains. The efficacy of these scenarios is bolstered by their ability to illuminate not only the opportunities birthed by technological innovation but also the fundamental role of values and ethics in shaping the future.

For the adept implementation of a change strategy, it is imperative to anchor it in visionary foresight scenarios, focusing on evaluating the quintessence of human beings in novel environments and relation to evolving behaviors. Human agency emerges as the supreme medium through which technology is realized, rendering scenarios as optimal frameworks for exploring these phenomena and facilitating informed, strategic choices conducive to change. Decision-making founded on scenarios requires a sensible recognition of the current milieu, forming the foundation for crafting forward-looking repositories

DOI: 10.1201/9781003450139-19

of possibilities. These possibilities extend beyond speculative suppositions, representing instead meticulously architected blueprints of a desired endpoint for the entity or community in question.[1]

14.2 NORMATIVE, STRATEGIC, AND USER SCENARIOS

Crafting national strategies necessitates devising normative scenarios that contemplate the potential repercussions of innovative entities on socio-political landscapes, legal systems, and emergent technologies derivative of these entities' adoption.

On a normative front, it is indispensable to wield the insight to flesh out a spectrum of scenarios ranging from optimistic to pessimistic to efficaciously calibrate norms that will undergird the genesis of new methodologies while mitigating deleterious impacts. To exemplify, consider the Internet's advent and its consequent influence on copyright laws. The Internet facilitated the transmission of data—digital music—which engendered the need for legislation aware of music as data. The innovative entity is music encoded in data bits, with ramifications pervading diverse societal and economic sectors. Probing the potential impact on society, culture, organizations, and the economy is imperative before shaping legislation. A deep appreciation of the sweeping implications of innovative entities and technologies, coupled with a nuanced understanding of their potential ramifications, is integral to engineering effective policies and norms promoting responsible innovation.

Normative scenarios, while not harboring immediate strategic utility, yield critical insight into the prospective contours of the economic, cultural, and political milieu. These scenarios seek to elucidate the metamorphosing landscape and generally adopt a formulation akin to "given the emergence of this technology, society will likely evolve this way."

Enterprises necessitate distinct scenarios compared to political or social domains. A strategic scenario enables organizations to attenuate the impacts of innovation and architect a desired future by considering intersections with economic, technological, organizational, and legal frameworks. Complementing the strategic scenario, an enterprise necessitates user scenarios, encompassing the interplay of behaviors—choice, beliefs, values, and motivation—and users' lives. The diversity of perspectives, beliefs, and values demands multiple user scenarios.

Strategic scenarios proffer a dual advantage: illuminating the macro-context of user experience scenarios, facilitating strategic responses to the new milieu, and serving as springboards for ancillary scenarios. Such scenarios empower organizations to anticipate and adapt to a fluid landscape, shaping their preferred futures. The merits of strategic scenarios are not confined to market preparedness; they instill the germination of a novel business strategy within executive echelons, conjuring a vision of potential organizational trajectories with magnetic allure and intellectual resonance. These scenarios harmonize the organization's vision and strategic course when meticulously executed.

Robust scenario planning necessitates corporations to fathom the fluidity of society and the intricate, interconnected economic systems in which they exist. The process involves articulating a future vision and actively pursuing strategies to realize that vision. Scenarios avail leadership with strategic and imaginative countermeasures to evolving market conditions, streamlining the implementation of necessary modifications.

Bold foresight scenarios are instrumental for organizations striving to remain at the vanguard of a swiftly evolving business terrain. By examining human nature within nascent contexts and against the backdrop of evolving behaviors, these scenarios proffer insights into potential disruptions or advancements that might sway an organization's course. Since humans are the ultimate conduit for technological manifestation, comprehending the synergy between technological innovation and human behavior is fundamental for forecasting and pre-empting potential challenges or opportunities.

The growing recognition of "disruptive innovation" as a quintessential paradigm for discerning emergent trends conveys a more profound realization that the ontological structure of corporate entities is transforming. This recognition underscores the necessity of harnessing scenarios as forecasting tools to mitigate the contingencies of future shifts, enabling organizations to evaluate and regulate the implications of disruptive innovations. By adopting a scenario-centric perspective toward future planning, organizations cultivate organizational agility, which in turn, facilitates both the anticipation of obstacles and the exploitation of emergent opportunities with efficacy. The process involves using scenarios to extract preliminary insights into organizational quandaries and associated responses, identifying potential avenues for value generation, and conducting scenario analyses to heighten awareness of emerging challenges and opportunities. These insights are then synthesized into a comprehensive set of guiding principles for organizational transformation. This multifaceted approach bolsters strategic agility, fosters innovation and experimentation, and strengthens competitive standing in a perpetually evolving market landscape.

Distinguished by their unique characteristics, strategic scenarios materialize as invaluable assets for organizations. Acting as catalysts for contemplation and for navigating possibility, scenarios support innovation within existing operational frameworks, enabling organizations to realize their ambitions and explore channels for expansion. Furthermore, scenarios can be employed in conceptualizing and developing novel product offerings, designing business models, and formulating revenue optimization strategies, thereby providing a structured scaffold for examining prospective avenues for growth.

By proactively engaging in scenario development before initiating new undertakings, organizations are poised to construct and nurture a compendium of pragmatic strategies primed for implementation with the venture's launch. By integrating scenario analysis within strategic planning, organizations attain an augmented level of agility and responsiveness, arming them to navigate alterations adeptly and capitalize on arising opportunities.

14.3 THE COMPELLING POWER OF VISUAL NARRATIVES

The adage "a picture is worth a thousand words" resonates with particular pertinence in organizational future-proofing through foresight. Foresight scenarios epitomize this sentiment by functioning as a narrative art form that vividly illustrates the potential outcomes emanating from the synergy between technological advancements and human agency. Such scenarios delve into the complicated interplay between technology and humanity, creating a crucible for imaginative cogitation regarding technology's role in sculpting our collective future.[2]

Foresight scenarios transcend mere prognostication; they facilitate exploring and evaluating a diverse spectrum of possible futures. In doing so, they allow for scrutinizing the intricate nexus among technology, society, and the environment, while discerning determinants that may steer the success or debacle of nascent technologies. The process requires the dissection of data and trends and critical reflection on the interrelations among human values, cultural mores, and ethics. Navigating the nebulousness intrinsic to the future, these scenarios necessitate cognizance of the possibilities for unanticipated repercussions.

Implementing scenarios in the context of foresight necessitates an astute comprehension of the drivers of technological innovation and the potential societal ramifications. These scenarios represent more than deterministic predictions; they embody an imaginative odyssey through myriad potential futures. Foresight scenarios serve as a linchpin for constructing adaptive and nimble organizational strategies equipped to navigate an uncertain future. Crafting scenarios that encapsulate the transformative essence of technology mandates an integration of technical innovation with a holistic appraisal of human values, cultural norms, and ethical precepts that shape our interaction with technology.

With the advent of text-conditional image generation via neural networks, a novel dimension is added to scenario-based innovation decision-making and design. This burgeoning technology harbors the potential to encapsulate the crux of a scenario and transmute it into a tangible visualization. With expeditious visual representation at our disposal, the envisaged future metamorphoses into a tangible entity. By harnessing cutting-edge strides in machine learning and artificial intelligence (AI), images can be crafted that encapsulate the core of a scenario with exceptional precision and vibrancy. Integrating this technology into the foresight paradigm can bolster the conveyance of complex notions, spur creativity, and catalyze action.

The evocative capacity of imagery is formidable. The granularity and richness of the generated visuals accentuate the transformative capabilities of technology and emphasize the urgency for initiatives to actualize the envisioned future. The imagery's meticulousness makes the future an urgent, tangible present. The level of detail in the imagery correlates to the compelling nature of the case for transformative action. This confluence of rich imagination and technological enablement can be dubbed as the "richly imagined everything," where multitudinous text inputs inform the vivid visual representations of a transformative future.

The detailed imagery supplants the need for protracted descriptions. For instance, the notion of a smart city no longer relies on textual exposition; instead, its multifaceted components, ranging from intelligent transportation systems to interactive urban ecosystems, can be visually articulated (Figures 14.1 and 14.2). Similarly, smart furniture, aware of its functionality and optimal placement, can be depicted rather than described. This visual elucidation of futuristic concepts is an ideal tool and an impetus for proactive endeavors toward realizing a technologically enhanced, sustainable future.

Text-conditional image generation has emerged as a transformative instrument in elucidating the potentialities of technology, thereby rendering the future more concrete and within reach. By generating meticulously detailed visuals, it becomes possible to map out a

FIGURE 14.1   Imagining solar transport proposals for the city of Paris.

FIGURE 14.2   Imagining vertical gardens mixed with traditional architecture in Paris.

course toward a future that is not only envisioned but also fervently desired. The precision and intricacy of these visuals serve as a clarion call for collective endeavors to bring the imagined future to fruition.

There is no longer a necessity to employ verbose explanations to elucidate concepts such as wellness. Instead, numerous nonexistent medical devices can be materialized through

FIGURE 14.3   Imagining a wearable regenerative neurostimulator.

generative technology. It facilitates inventing and visualizing entirely novel categories, such as discreet wearables, active implantables, and regenerative wellness technology (Figure 14.3). These technological conceptualizations can be swiftly illustrated through strikingly photorealistic visualizations, revealing human-technology interactions' interrelations and potential benefits. From visualizing molecular gastronomy without actual culinary preparation to envisaging futuristic classrooms and holographic historical figures, the technology eliminates the need for extensive descriptive passages.

Generative technology's dynamism manifests in its enthralling capacity to bring to life the many possibilities that await us. Through vivid visualizations, we are not merely passive observers but active participants in constructing a future enriched with avant-garde technologies that enhance our quality of life (Figure 14.4).

Placing individuals at the epicenter of this narrative is an effective strategy to showcase the benefits of burgeoning technologies. From advancements in regenerative medicine to hitherto unexplored domains, the impact of these transformative technologies can be vividly elucidated through immersive and engaging visualizations. By portraying serene images of individuals navigating these technological advancements, stakeholders may be encouraged to champion these innovations, acting as catalysts for positive change.

Visualization transcends linguistic barriers and fosters a deeper understanding of complex concepts. Keeping individuals as the focal point, these visualizations forge emotional connections and inspire actions, thus shaping the trajectory of the future.

For instance, understanding the shift toward pre-emptive medicine is a preliminary step, but vividly illustrating the ramifications of innovations like pre-emptive dentistry or eyecare is a different paradigm altogether. A more coherent understanding of the benefits

FIGURE 14.4 Imagining an immersive travel device and landscape.

can be constructed through stark depictions of interactions between objects, users, or patients. The core of visualization lies in its empowering capability to conceptualize and mold novel possibilities. It provides a window into uncharted territories, beckoning us toward opportunities in wait.

Generative AI, in particular, has the unparalleled prowess to transpose the future into our present reality. From immersive travel to experiential learning, it can produce visual representations that capture the essence of user interactions with technology, harmonizing diverse perceptions and understanding levels. While traditional scenarios enable one to conceptualize potential futures, the visual component often remains subject to individual interpretation. Generative AI, however, standardizes the visual element, ensuring a shared level of understanding and minimizing subjectivity.

The power of generative AI lies in its ability to expand beyond the confines of the present and construct a collective vision of the future. Through meticulously crafted visualizations that depict the potential of emerging technologies, we can traverse into unexplored realms, laying the foundation for a more prosperous and fulfilling future. As we transition, we move from abstract concepts to tangible realities, empowering us to actualize the world we aspire to inhabit.

14.4 RICHLY IMAGINED EVERYTHING: DESIGN AND ARCHITECTURE

The progression of generative AI and text-conditional image generation stands as formidable exemplars of technological ascension, heralding transformative prospects across diverse sectors. Anchored in the tenets of machine learning and AI, these avant-garde technological solutions manifest an extraordinary propensity for engendering innovative, contextually relevant content, be it in textual or visual form, governed by a predefined set of parameters or stipulations.

The possibilities within the design domain are virtually limitless, encompassing various disciplines ranging from architecture and industrial design to sartorial and graphical endeavors. Generative AI can engender diverse design permutations contingent upon specific input determinants, thereby significantly abbreviating the temporal investments conventionally associated with ideation and prototyping. For instance, envision a scenario wherein an AI system, steeped in architectural axioms and stylistic epochs, is commissioned to conceive designs for edifices optimized for energy efficiency. Similarly, in the sartorial domain, an AI tutored in contemporary fashion paradigms and historical design lexicons could forge avant-garde apparel configurations.

Furthermore, the employment of text-conditional image generation presents notable ancillary advantages, such as the attenuation of material waste during the design phase. Through virtualizing images and designs, practitioners can meticulously hone their conceptualizations before their tangible manifestation. This modus operandi may diminish the necessity for corporeal prototyping and fabrication, curtailing material excess and the economic expenditures inherent to conventional design processes. Also, text-conditional image generation possesses the potential to radically reformulate the landscape of the design industry by engendering a paradigm that is not only expeditious and efficacious but also environmentally conscientious (Figure 14.5).

While the capabilities of generative AI and text-conditional image generation are poised to engender seismic shifts across various domains, it is imperative to recognize

FIGURE 14.5   Imagining a self-sustaining living capsule.

their potential as catalysts for creativity, innovation, and procedural efficiency. Moving into the future, the prudent and ethically cognizant harnessing of these technological marvels is paramount. The approach encompasses a commitment to utilizing technological advancements to enhance and complement human creativity and potential rather than replacing them.

14.5 RICHLY IMAGINED ENTERTAINMENT

The entertainment domain is poised for a paradigmatic upheaval with the advent of text-conditional image generation. In the cinematic and television realms, this technology harbors the potential to engender many creative elements, such as conceptual art, storyboard illustrations, and the synthesis of entire scenes extrapolated from fragments of scripts. For instance, a science fiction film script that includes descriptions of an alien planet could be fed into the AI, generating intricate concept art that encapsulates the writer's vision or even producing animated scenes that portray the extraterrestrial environment in striking detail.

Furthermore, this innovation can birth novel compositions or reimagine existing ones within the musical sphere, thereby inaugurating uncharted territories of musical creativity. Consider, for instance, an AI system fed a textual description of a Baroque piece; such a system could conceivably generate a harmonious composition that emulates the complexity and intricacies characteristic of Baroque music. Similarly, it could be instructed to remix classical compositions with modern genres, creating fusion pieces that bridge historical and contemporary musical paradigms.

Of particular interest is the capacity of text-conditional image generation to conceive immersive and dynamically evolving environments. Cinematographers and filmmakers could leverage this technology to fabricate arresting visual effects that augment the sensory engagement of audiences. For instance, a fantasy epic's script mentioning an ethereal, enchanted forest could prompt the creation of a lush, magical landscape replete with surreal flora and fauna, immersing the audience in the realm's allure.

Moreover, this technology heralds the possibility for individualized narratives and branching storylines, wherein visuals adapt to audience input or selections, culminating in more absorbing and interactive engagements. Such advancements could be particularly transformative in video gaming, where players' decisions could alter the course of the narrative and the world in which the game occurs. The ability to see tangible environmental changes based on textual input or player choices adds depth to the gaming experience.

Text-conditional image generation emerges as an instrumental adjunct in entertainment, substantially bolstering storytelling and universe construction. By synthesizing visuals predicated on specific textual cues, creators can vivify fantastical and imaginary worlds with an unmatched degree of intricacy and authenticity. This technological prodigy allows narrators to transcend conventional limitations of visual narration and fabricate stupefying, transformative experiences that etch an indelible imprint upon the consciousness of both spectators and interactive users. As such, text-conditional image generation represents a veritable renaissance in entertainment.

14.6 RICHLY IMAGINED FOOD

Food technology, anchored in the augmentation of flavors through molecular gastronomy, portends to revolutionize our interaction with the world, mainly through the advent of three-dimensional (3D)-printed food. A profound philosophical examination reveals that food technology is entwined with our comprehension of nature and ontological standing within the world. Traditionally, food's intrinsic connection to the natural ecosystem is evident through its cultivation, which involves harvesting ingredients from the earth, nourishing through solar energy, and modulation by seasonal cycles. However, 3D-printed food signifies a paradigmatic shift, where the synthetic nature of these consumables engenders an interrogation of our perceptions regarding naturalness and prompts the reassessment of authenticity and organic processes.

3D-printed food, through the manipulation of textures and amplification of flavors, necessitates the exploration of human hedonistic boundaries. For example, one might consider the role of molecular gastronomy in the creation of spheres that explode with intensified flavors, such as balsamic vinegar pearls. Such culinary innovations compel us to scrutinize whether our gastronomic pursuits are an unrelenting search for novelty or a sincere investigation into sensory exhilaration. Moreover, the technologically mediated hyper-stimulation of the gustatory system, as manifested through elements like foams and emulsions, raises the question of whether it attenuates our appreciation of the inherent flavors of, for example, vine-ripened tomato or freshly picked basil.

Moreover, the proliferation of 3D-printed food, characterized by intricate geometries and tailored nutritional profiles, calls for critically examining its socio-economic ramifications (Figure 14.6). The potential of this technology to alleviate food scarcity is immense; for

FIGURE 14.6 Imagining a 3D food printer.

FIGURE 14.7   Imagining 3D printed food.

instance, the utilization of alternative protein sources, such as insects, could be made palatable through 3D printing. However, this conjures critical questions about accessibility and equity. The challenge is to ensure the democratization of 3D-printed food so that it does not become an exclusive preserve of the affluent but rather an empowering and inclusive technology.

Furthermore, 3D-printed food, with its ability to produce precision-crafted edible items rapidly, challenges our foundational relationship with temporality and diligence. Traditional culinary practices, such as slow-cooked stews or fermentation, embody patience and allow for the natural evolution of flavors. 3D printing's promise of immediacy poses an existential question: what is sacrificed when temporality is truncated? The waiting period, a traditional aspect of culinary endeavors, is supplanted by the instantaneity of 3D-printed food, which could estrange us from natural rhythms and attenuate mindful engagement with our nutrition (Figure 14.7).

Food technology, exemplified by flavor intensification in molecular gastronomy and the advent of 3D-printed food, unveils intricate philosophical dimensions. These dimensions encompass our kinship with nature, hedonistic pursuits, social equitability, and our engagement with temporality. As we steer through this transformative landscape, embracing these technological innovations with circumspection and critical inquiry is imperative, attending to their capacity to enrich our lives and how they uphold the quintessence of human experience in our interplay with food and the environment.

14.7   RICHLY IMAGINED HEALTH

Generative technologies herald a transformative potential in medicine. The capacity of AI to synthesize detailed medical imagery facilitates the creation of patient-specific visualizations that are invaluable for diagnostic and therapeutic planning. Consider the scenario where physicians employ generative AI to fabricate 3D models of a patient's anatomy. Such a representation enables virtual navigation through an individual's anatomical complexities, rendering a more precise and comprehensive understanding of pathological conditions like tumors.

The practical ramifications of this precision include heightened diagnostic accuracy and improved patient comprehension of their medical state. For example, AI-generated 3D models could facilitate better surgical planning for tumor removal by precisely identifying tumor boundaries and adjacent critical structures.

However, the ambit of generative AI in medicine extends beyond diagnostic applications to potential simulation of surgical interventions. The concept could be an immersive, AI-empowered surgical simulator in which surgeons can rehearse complex procedures in a virtual environment that mirrors the patient's anatomy. This precursor to the actual intervention allows for optimizing surgical strategies, enhancing technical finesse, and mitigating operative risks. Such preoperative rehearsals could be particularly beneficial in intricate surgeries like neurovascular interventions, where the stakes are high.

In addition, the individualization of these simulations, tailored to each patient's unique anatomical features, permits a rehearsal of the exact surgical pathway, thus augmenting the predictability and accuracy of surgical endeavors.

The intersection of generative technology and medicine signals the dawn of an evolved healthcare landscape characterized by precision, patient-centricity, and enhanced safety margins. This synergy has far-reaching implications, including the integration of health monitoring devices within the human body. For instance, dermal sensors might continuously evaluate physiological parameters and pre-emptively alert individuals of potential health aberrations (Figures 14.8 and 14.9).

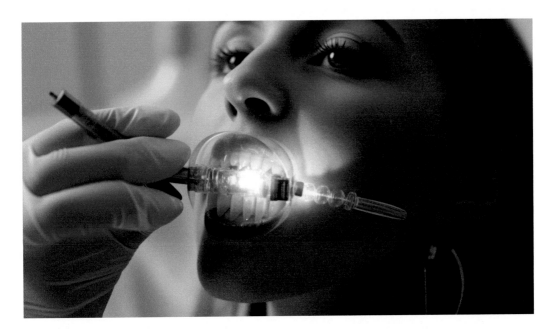

FIGURE 14.8 Imagining noninvasive regenerative buccal therapies.

FIGURE 14.9   Imagining discrete biofeedback wearables.

This integration marks a paradigm shift in healthcare delivery and perception as our bodies metamorphose into interconnected information systems. The technologies act like an extended nervous system with real-time feedback mechanisms. However, this integration also blurs biologic-technologic boundaries, raising ontological questions regarding human identity and autonomy.

Simultaneously, the introduction of regenerative technologies, such as ocular and dental regenerative therapies and neural modulators, heralds unprecedented possibilities in restoring or augmenting human faculties. However, this domain is rife with ethical and philosophical challenges, including issues related to biological authenticity and the impact of augmentative technologies on human identity.

Moreover, the societal dimensions of these advancements warrant scrutiny. The issues of accessibility and equitable distribution are paramount, as these innovations are often resource intensive. These technologies' cost and requisite expertise raise concerns about exacerbating healthcare disparities.

Furthermore, an increasing reliance on these technologies could lead to an altered perception of human resilience and self-sufficiency as we become progressively dependent on devices for maintaining our well-being.

In conclusion, incorporating generative and integrated health technologies represents a seismic shift in healthcare. This shift encompasses enhanced precision, personalized healthcare delivery, and empowerment of individuals in managing their health. However, this integration also presents complex challenges encompassing privacy, autonomy, identity, societal equity, and the interface between technology and intrinsic human faculties. Quick and ethical navigation through this evolving landscape is imperative to harness the potential of these technologies while safeguarding human values and well-being.

14.8 RICHLY IMAGINED EDUCATION

In education, holographic classrooms are revolutionizing the pedagogical landscape by facilitating immersive, multidimensional learning experiences. These holographic environments enable students to interact with life-sized representations of historical figures, posing questions and engaging in dialogues with icons such as Leonardo da Vinci or William Shakespeare. Such an experience challenges traditional knowledge acquisition paradigms and fosters a profound understanding of the temporal nature of human existence and intellectual evolution.

Moreover, holographic classrooms allow tactile interaction with scientific models and natural entities. For instance, students can manipulate large molecular structures or engage with zoological specimens. These sensory-rich engagements deepen understanding and stimulate intellectual curiosity and a sense of wonderment. However, this blurring of the boundaries between virtual representations and physical reality raises philosophical questions regarding human perception and the essence of experiential reality.

The integrative capacity of holographic classrooms, which allows for the seamless amalgamation of diverse subjects, promotes interdisciplinary learning. This interconnectedness challenges traditional subject compartmentalization, encouraging holistic understanding and critical thinking across disciplines.

Holographic education inherently empowers students by promoting active engagement and personalized learning experiences. This paradigm shift transforms students from passive information consumers to active knowledge constructors. However, it necessitates a moral reflection on this autonomous learning environment's responsibilities and ethical dimensions (Figure 14.10).

FIGURE 14.10   Imagining the holographic classroom.

Generative AI is another facet poised to revolutionize education by creating tailored educational materials ranging from textbooks to animated illustrations. By inputting key concepts, AI algorithms can synthesize contextually relevant content across various subjects. The multimedia capabilities of AI-generated content, including animations, videos, and diagrams, facilitate a more intuitive and efficient comprehension of complex concepts. This enhances the accessibility of learning materials, particularly for individuals with diverse learning styles or disabilities, promoting inclusive education.

In addition to enhanced content delivery, the digital nature of AI-generated materials eliminates the need for physical inventory, significantly reducing associated costs. The scalability and adaptability of AI-generated content also facilitate quick updates in alignment with evolving educational standards and specific learning objectives. Such an approach could reduce educational costs, democratize access to high-quality educational resources, and mitigate educational disparities.

In sum, holographic classrooms and AI-generated educational materials represent pivotal educational advancements, encompassing immersive learning experiences, interdisciplinary integration, and personalized content creation. These innovations promise to enrich learning, stimulate intellectual curiosity, and democratize educational access. However, they also invite reflection on the philosophical, ethical, and societal implications of these transformative technologies within the educational sphere.

14.9 RICHLY IMAGINED MARKETING

In marketing, generative AI represents a transformative force in campaign design and consumer engagement. Generative AI's capabilities include creating focused, tailored content and leveraging text-conditional image generation to craft visual marketing collateral that mirrors demographic data and consumer insights. This advanced level of customization is poised to enhance customer engagement and augment the efficiency of marketing initiatives (Figure 14.11).

AI-driven marketing enables the generation of tailored advertisements, product recommendations, and even curated recipes predicated on consumer data and preferences. The advent of precision-targeted marketing significantly streamlines expenses, which is a critical factor considering the propensity for marketing costs to eclipse production expenses across various industries. By reducing marketing expenditures, the cost per acquisition for products is poised to diminish, which holds ramifications for the broader economic landscape. As consumers, this potential reduction in the overall cost of goods and services could translate into increased disposable income and discretionary spending.

Furthermore, text-conditional image generation is a conduit for creating interactive product demonstrations, fostering a more nuanced understanding of product attributes and functionalities among consumers. Enhanced engagement via interactive demonstrations fortifies consumer affinity and reduces product returns, a mutually beneficial outcome for enterprises and consumers.

Moreover, AI-driven personalized content allows companies to mine consumer behavior and preferences with unprecedented depth, culminating in the refinement of marketing strategies. The ability of AI to sift through social media data for trend analysis

FIGURE 14.11   Imagining in-store bespoke 3D printing of running shoes.

and sentiment identification is another invaluable attribute. With real-time insights into emerging consumer trends and sentiments, companies are better equipped to adapt their marketing tactics in response to market dynamics. For instance, detecting negative sentiment surrounding a product could trigger a rapid recalibration of marketing strategy to mitigate adverse sales impacts.

Integrating text-conditional image generation and AI-driven personalization into marketing represents a sea change in how companies interact with consumers. The advancements encompass targeted marketing campaigns, enhanced consumer engagement, cost efficiency, and real-time insights into consumer behavior. This transformation necessitates an agile marketing paradigm that can adapt to ever-evolving consumer preferences and market dynamics.

14.10 RICHLY IMAGINED WORK

As automation supplants numerous traditional roles, we must not conflate the disappearance of jobs with the eradication of work. In order to discern the nuances of this transformation, one must understand the distinction between labor and work as articulated by Hannah Arendt in her seminal 1958 publication, "The Human Condition." Arendt's Vita Activa delineates three fundamental human activities: labor, work, and action. Labor, she posits, is aligned with the biological necessities of human life, synonymous with jobs that fulfill necessities. Work, by contrast, is associated with creativity and legacy and is integral to our human identity.[3]

Labor can be typified by roles poised for obsolescence due to automation. For example, manufacturing jobs with repetitive tasks or data entry roles are prime candidates for automation. These roles, quintessential of Arendt's notion of labor, are oriented toward the material aspect of human existence. However, this mechanization of labor paves the way for a renaissance in the domain of work that is imbued with meaning and purpose.

The quintessence of work is anchored in the ontological facet of human existence, the state of "being," which Erich Fromm contends is characterized by perpetual evolution through experiences and learning.[4] In this context, work reflects the creation of lasting impressions through endeavors and innovations. For instance, an artist's creation, a researcher's contribution to science, or an entrepreneur's establishment of a socially impactful venture epitomizes work that transcends mere labor.

This paradigm shift propels us toward a society where, bereft of traditional jobs, individuals can concentrate on endeavors that foster personal growth and societal enrichment. Such a society would repudiate conventional economic paradigms in favor of an ecosystem where contributions are recognized not through wages but via a credit system that gauges the societal impact. For example, a musician might accrue credits for a composition that augments community well-being, while a scientist might gain credits for a breakthrough that benefits humanity. Our future habitats will morph into incubators that nurture everyone's intrinsic talents, enabling them to contribute optimally to society. In an era bereft of traditional employment, "work" becomes an enabler for individuals to partake in and contribute to the lives of others, embodying a mutual affirmation of shared human experiences. In the future, rather than learning skills for employment, acquiring knowledge becomes a continuous journey of self-actualization.

This new paradigm, underscored by the intersection of automation and human creativity, beckons us to re-evaluate the fabric of societal contribution and personal fulfillment. It heralds an era where work is not a means to an end but an end in itself, a canvas for everyone to imprint with their unique brushstrokes, collectively weaving a tapestry of shared human enterprise.

14.11 CLOSING THOUGHTS

Generative AI holds the prodigious potential to revolutionize the terrain of content creation radically. The inception of text-conditional image generation capacitates content creators to produce superior quality, custom content at an unparalleled magnitude, thereby inaugurating an unprecedented spectrum of possibilities. The application range of this technology is impressively extensive, encompassing the customization of product suggestions to the assembly of bespoke news articles, each meticulously crafted to accommodate an individual's specific interests and biases. Such a degree of personalization can dramatically magnify customer engagement, potentially enhancing sales and fostering brand allegiance. However, the scope of generative AI surpasses mere personalization. It can potentially conceive entirely novel content genres, such as AI-generated music or literature, thereby contesting conventional perceptions of creativity and artistic creation.

Imagine a musical platform utilizing AI to compose distinctive soundtracks predicated on a user's emotional state, favored genres, or even the time of day. Alternatively, contemplate a literary platform where an AI, having scrutinized a user's beloved authors and genres, constructs a custom short story, novel, or poem, thus delivering a genuinely personalized reading experience.

The opportunities unlocked by generative AI are indeed limitless. As technology continues to mature, we can forecast its increasingly disruptive influence in the ensuing years. AI's potential applications and implications in content creation are as expansive as they are exhilarating, signaling the advent of a new digital epoch where content is not merely absorbed but actively co-created by AI, adapted to individual preferences, and dynamically evolving.

The passion for exploring and exploiting this technology's potential embodies a zeal that transcends the mere manipulation of algorithms and delves into our deepest creative aspirations and curiosities. We stand at the precipice of a new frontier in digital content creation, enabled by the fusion of AI and human creativity. This innovative synergy promises to unleash a wave of disruption and transformation that could forever alter how we conceive, create, and interact with content, heralding a thrilling new chapter in our digital narrative.

NOTES

1. Foresight methodology relies on using three distinct typologies of scenarios: normative, strategic, and user scenarios. Normative scenarios serve as informative tools that provide insight into the potential shape of the economic, cultural, and political space in which society will operate in response to an innovative object or technological advancement. These scenarios answer the fundamental question, "How is the landscape changing?" by articulating a range of potential outcomes and exploring the potential implications of each. On the other hand, strategic scenarios offer a big-picture view of the context in which a user experience scenario will take place. By considering the intersection of the innovation object and the economic, technological, organizational, and legislative frameworks, strategic scenarios provide a framework for planning strategic approaches in response to emerging market conditions. This scenario typology answers, "How is our organization changing because of the technology that just emerged?" Using normative and strategic scenarios facilitates a nuanced understanding of the complex and dynamic interplay between technological innovation and the broader socioeconomic context in which it operates.

2. Frederick R. Barnard is credited with popularizing the phrase "a picture is worth a thousand words" in an article published in the advertising trade journal Printers' Ink in 1921. Barnard claimed the phrase to be of Japanese origin, although there is no evidence to support this claim. The phrase "one timely deed is worth ten thousand words" is an older expression that conveys the idea that actions speak louder than words. It is thought to have inspired the more modern version of "a picture is worth a thousand words." The phrase "a picture is worth a thousand words" is commonly understood to mean that a complex idea or multiple ideas can often be conveyed more effectively through a single image than through a lengthy description. It suggests that visual representation can be a powerful tool for communication. Retrieved from https://english-grammar-lessons.com/a-picture-is-worth-a-thousand-words-meaning/ and https://www.phrases.org.uk/meanings/a-picture-is-worth-a-thousand-words.html.

3. Arendt. H. 1958. The Human Condition. University of Chicago Press.

4. Fromm Erich. 1976. To Have or To Be. New York. N.Y. Harper & Row.

CHAPTER 15

A Provocation

Is Anything Artificial?

15.1 EXTINGUISHING LABELS

Artificiality is based on a perceived demarcation between human-made phenomena and those occurring naturally. This division, engraved in our cognitive vernacular, differentiates between the products of human innovation and nature's fortuitous creations. However, this dichotomy starts to dissolve under the lens of a more expansive comprehension of reality. Might the "artificial" be just as natural as the "natural" itself, suggesting our insistence on such a distinction reflects our restricted sensory capabilities?

This divide is notably prominent within the sphere of intelligence. We generally classify human intelligence as natural and machine intelligence as artificial. The former arises from the process of biological evolution, an offshoot of billions of years of natural selection, while the latter is a consequence of human ingenuity, realized in just a few decades. These appear distinct to us, but from a cosmological perspective, aren't they both emergent properties of the universe?

Reflect on the genesis and evolution of intelligence, whether human or artificial. It stems from processes governed by the laws of physics woven into the cosmic fabric. Human intelligence surfaces from the intricate interactions of biological matter—essentially stardust—adhering to nature's invariable laws. Artificial intelligence results from humans leveraging their innate intelligence to reshape the same stardust into another form: A machine. The cosmic mechanisms do not differentiate; they witness processes conforming to their principles.

For instance, consider a bird's nest and the Taj Mahal. The first is a rudimentary structure fashioned by a bird from naturally available materials. The second is a grandiose monument constructed by thousands of humans using a mix of natural and synthesized materials over many years. From our human viewpoint, the nest is a natural construct, while the Taj Mahal is artificial. However, if we transition to a universal perspective, aren't

DOI: 10.1201/9781003450139-20

they both creations of sentient beings composed of elements derived from the Earth, following the laws of nature?

This viewpoint illuminates the artificial-natural divide as a human-invented construct molded by our sensory perceptions and cognitive architectures. It provokes us to scrutinize our comprehension's assumptions and consider that what we classify as "artificial" is as integral to the cosmos as the "natural." In the intricate embroidery of reality, everything is an interaction of matter and energy, a ballet of particles and forces, a cosmic symphony. There is no artificial or natural—only the universe expressing itself in countless ways, unhindered and infinite. The machines we construct, the structures we erect, and the intelligence we engineer are reflections of the cosmos, mirrors of reality surpassing our human-defined divisions.

As we navigate the territories of art, nature, and perception, let us probe into the core of what we regard as "natural." What implications arise when we attribute a quality of naturalness to an art form, and what underpins such a judgment? What does it truly imply when we claim one art form is more natural than another? It is an intricate query. Because we are trying to draw a discretionary line between natural and artificial, guided by aesthetics, form, and our subjective interpretations of our perceptions, this paradox provokes us to delineate subjective boundaries between what we perceive as natural and artificial, swayed by aesthetics, form, and personal interpretations. It is not a simple query; instead, it is a thought-provoking conundrum. Why? Because outlining this hazy border between the "natural" and the "artificial" proves challenging.

We inhabit a world brimming with artwork, ranging from masterpieces handcrafted by humans, images manifested by nature, to forms designed through the calculated randomness of a computer. At the heart of this discussion lies an intriguing question: Does the intentional creation of an artist render a work of art artificial? Or, are these creations, irrespective of their human or computational origin, expressions of nature simply because they inhabit the same cosmos?

The profound beauty of art lies in its ability to reflect the artist's intent. Every stroke, word, and note is a testament to the creator's consciousness, a mirror reflecting their inner universe. However, does this intentional creation make a work of art artificial? It is a notion that leads us to ponder on the very definition of "artificial." Are all deliberate creations artificial by virtue of being consciously crafted?

So, what defines the "natural"? Does it lie in the imperfections, in the gentle asymmetry found in nature? Or is it housed within the dynamic unpredictability, the seemingly random oscillations that infuse life into the natural world? Yet have we ever stopped to truly appreciate the rigid beauty of sugar crystals under a microscope or the geometric elegance of iron pyrites? Each one, a child of nature, exhibits an appearance so stylized and formal that one could easily mistake them for artificial creations. Nevertheless, they are nature's works of art, the product of Earth's rhythmic dance of elements. They represent nature's artistic prowess, making even the most renowned human masterpieces pale in comparison.

This question warrants a deep dive into our understanding of random versus intentionality. Nature's creations often seem to follow a pattern of random beauty. For instance, consider the formation of crystals. These natural structures result from seemingly arbitrary processes, yet they display a level of symmetry that could be easily mistaken for artificial. They serve as silent witnesses to the majesty of nature's unguided elegance, an elegance that paradoxically brings forth a symmetry often associated with the artificial.

Contrast this with human-generated images crafted with conscious intention. These images are a testament to our creative prowess, each one an intricate tapestry woven with threads of human thought and emotion. They reflect a conscious creation process, a deliberate act of manifesting an internal vision into a physical reality. In comparison to the randomness of crystalline formation, one might be tempted to label these creations as artificial.

However, the situation may not be as straightforward as it seems. In its infinite wisdom, the universe blurs the lines between what we perceive as natural and artificial. Remember that the computer-generated forms, although birthed from randomness, are also a product of human intention—human minds design the algorithms that create them.

What then separates the intentionally crafted art from the seemingly random formations of nature or the algorithmically produced images of a computer? Are they not all part of the same cosmic dance, influenced by forces both seen and unseen, conscious and unconscious? It would seem then that regardless of their source, these images, these works of art, are all expressions of nature. Why? Because they share the common thread of existence within the same universe. They belong to the grand continuum of creation. This spectrum spans from the apparent randomness of nature, through the conscious creativity of humans, to the calculated randomness of a computer algorithm.

At the core of these thoughts lies a fundamental truth—that the notion of "artificial" is, in fact, an illusion. Every act, every creation, every phenomenon, no matter how superficially artificial, remains an integral part of the grand tapestry of nature. Nothing exists outside of nature's realm; we are all part of the cosmic dance, no matter our level of perceived "naturalness." We reside in a continuum where varying degrees of naturalness coexist, a spectrum brimming with intrigue, form, and charm, where even the "less natural" is a testament to the intricate beauty of existence.

15.2 THE PERMANENT EXISTENCE

The realm of human creation, be it a handcrafted statue, an abstract painting, or a computational design, is often labeled "artificial." However, it is essential to remember that these creations never step outside nature's domain. Everything that exists, in all its varied forms and manifestations, is an embodiment of nature. It is the ebb and flow of the constant rhythm of existence. Even when we exercise our creative intent, we are merely channeling the underlying forces of the universe. We are a part of nature; therefore, our creations, intentions, and perceptions are also elements of the natural world. Human or computer, natural or artificial—these distinctions fade when considering the broader perspective.

Imagine you are a painter. You could hurl a bottle of ink against a blank canvas, creating an explosion of chaotic beauty. As a writer, you could tear apart a pre-existing essay, rearrange the fragments, and unearth a brand-new narrative within the chaos. The possibilities are endless, bound only by the limitations of our imaginations.

Every creation, each individual image, regardless of its origins, whether it springs from the random splendor of nature, the deliberate intent of a human, or the calculated chaos of a computer's algorithms, is a testament to the universality of existence. They are all distinct melodies in the symphony of cosmic energy, each bearing a unique signature, yet contributing to the same celestial score. But does the intentional creation of an artist render a work of art artificial? Does intention dilute the essence of creation, tainting it with a hint of artificiality? Or, are these creations, regardless of their origin, expressions of nature itself, born from the womb of the cosmos and swaddled in the fabric of existence?

The answer, perhaps, is nestled within the concept of the inherent unity of the cosmos. It is an acknowledgment that all of creation, whether intentional or random, whether orderly or chaotic, forms the intricate embroidery in the grand tapestry of existence. Each thread weaves its own story, but they are all part of the same narrative—the universe's unending, transformative dance of creation. Each manifestation of reality, every bit of existence, is brimming with cosmic energy, each playing its part in the grand design, each echoing the same truth—the truth of universal interconnectedness. The intentional strokes of a painter, the random formation of crystals, and the seemingly complex patterns of a computer-generated image are all spun from the same cosmic thread. They are separate notes contributing to the same symphony, separate colors coalescing to paint the same grand canvas of existence.

This discussion compels one to ponder the intricate interplay between intentionality and spontaneity and the reverberations these aspects have on our conceptualization of art. For instance, Japanese ikebana, the art of flower arrangement, illustrates an artistic endeavor that seeks harmony with nature through meticulously crafted arrangements.[1] In contrast, the phenomena of fractals, which can be observed in natural formations such as coastlines or leaf patterns, epitomize the spontaneous emergence of beauty in nature.[2] These examples underscore that intentional human artistry and seemingly arbitrary natural phenomena are interwoven strands in the tapestry of cosmic beauty.

Furthermore, introducing computational algorithms into the creative process presents another fascinating dimension. Generative art, such as the works produced by artists like Manfred Mohr or Casey Reas, exemplifies how algorithmically generated images can mimic the spontaneity observed in nature while still being grounded in human intentionality.[3] These algorithmic creations are neither entirely random like natural formations nor purely intentional like traditional art; they inhabit a liminal space that melds human ingenuity with algorithmic unpredictability. Thus, the creative spectrum is enriched by an additional dimension that transcends the conventional dichotomy between intentionality[4] and spontaneity.[5]

Text-Conditional Image Generation represents what we can term "intentional spontaneity" or "designed unpredictability," mirroring the artistic essence of pioneers like Jackson Pollock. Pollock's work is an exemplary metaphor for this phenomenon—a paradoxical fusion of planned spontaneity. His artistry lies in the intentional orchestration of spontaneity, with each movement of his hand and body consciously planned to deliver a momentum that leads paint to drip from the can in a semi-controlled manner. The final creation is a physical manifestation of Pollock's intent, a splattering of color and form that simultaneously embraces order and chaos.

FIGURE 15.1   A blindfolded gladiatrix.

Similarly, the artist's creative intent is conveyed via a textual prompt in Text-Conditional Image Generation. The realization of this intent, however, depends mainly on the prompt's nature and the generative adversarial network's (GAN's) training. If the prompt pertains to an established archetype—a category for which the GAN has extensive training data—the system will generate an image that mirrors these patterns.

On the other hand, if the prompt describes a non-archetypal image, the GAN draws upon its latent capacity for creative spontaneity (Figure 15.1). Here, every element of the prompt is interpreted and visualized with a surprising uniqueness, akin to the originality Pollock achieved with his paint drips. The GAN's ability to extrapolate from its training and innovatively combine elements enables the generation of an image that eschews any existing archetype.[6] The resulting image transcends conventional categories and holds the potential to define a new archetype, contributing to an evolving artistic landscape. Thus, Text-Conditional Image Generation, like Pollock's revolutionary techniques, bridges the gap between intent and unpredictability, fostering a generative space for new artistic possibilities to flourish (Figure 15.2).

New spaces and new mediums call on us to examine the philosophical foundations of art as a reflection of the universe's intrinsic qualities. Contrasting viewpoints are historical precedents wrestling with the interplay between art and nature. Ancient Greek philosophers, for instance, subscribed to the notion of mimesis, viewing art as an emulation of nature.[7]

FIGURE 15.2 Imagine artificial life, an android entity with wires, in the style of ray tracing, dark white and amber, ultra high definition resolution image, graceful lines, light teal and light gold, streamlined design, innovating techniques.

In contrast, Romantic poets revered nature's sublime attributes, and their works can be seen more as an exaltation of the natural world than a mere imitation.[8]

Introducing new mediums and technologies has increasingly blurred the lines between natural and artificial creations in the modern era. For example, virtual reality art installations plunge the observer into environments that challenge their perceptions and understandings of the physical and natural world. This art form transcends the conventional canvas, empowering artists to fabricate worlds that, albeit artificial, engage the observers in ways that mirror the sensations and profundities often linked with natural experiences.[9]

Acknowledging the mutual relationship between art, nature, and technology as converging elements within the same cosmic spectrum is crucial. They are not disjointed entities but are interconnected manifestations of the universe's boundless creative energies. As we persist in discovering new artistic expressions and wrangle with emerging technologies, we must maintain a comprehensive viewpoint that embraces the vast diversity and interconnectivity of the creative ambit. By doing so, we attest to the unity of existence and acknowledge the indelible mosaic of creation that envelops us all within the ceaseless cosmic ballet.

Art, in all its wonderfully diverse forms, goes beyond the confines of "natural" and "artificial." It encapsulates the limitless creativity of the universe, whether presented as the tranquil beauty of a sunset, the meticulous complexity of a sculpture, or the mesmerizing magnetism of a computer-generated image. Art does not confine itself to labels; instead, it challenges them. It is the universe's whisper, recounting its narratives in the language of creation, a language that is simultaneously natural and artificial.

As sentient beings capable of admiration and creation, our role is not to segregate and categorize. We should not confine art to "natural" and "artificial" compartments. Instead, we are summoned to revel in art's aesthetic pleasure, immerse ourselves in its immeasurable depth, and appreciate the masterpieces arising from the cosmic ballet of creation. We are encouraged to engage with the artistic journey, to experience the interconnectedness of all creation, and to savor the intertwined essences of the "natural" and "artificial." Our task is to perceive art not as an assortment of segregated forms but as a comprehensive embodiment of cosmic dance.

In conclusion, the universe extends an invitation to us. It beckons us to probe its mysteries, appreciate its creativity, and marvel at the beauty of its creations. It encourages us to peer beyond the superficial, to discern the underlying unity in all creation, and to acknowledge every art form, whether "natural" or "artificial," as a tribute to the cosmic ballet of creation. The universe invites us to immerse ourselves in the grand display of its creative power, experience the symphony of existence, and appreciate all entities' interconnectedness. Each image, each creation, regardless of its origins, is a resonance of the same cosmic energy, a stanza in the universal ode to existence. And therein lies the true appeal of art.

NOTES

1. A guide to ikebana flower arranging is available at https://konmari.com/ikebana/#:~:text= Ikebana
2. **Fractals** refer to repeating patterns that manifest at varying scales. They naturally occur in many forms, such as flowers, ferns, leaves, river pathways, lightning bolts, and snowflakes. Trees exemplify natural fractals, employing patterns that replicate miniature versions of themselves, resulting in the rich biodiversity of a forest. The concept of **"fractal"** was introduced by mathematician Benoit Mandelbrot in 1975. He described a fractal as a complex geometric shape that can be divided into smaller parts, each mirroring the whole on a smaller scale to at least a certain degree. Retrieved from: https://www.diygenius.com/fractals-in-nature/
3. Examples can be viewed at http://www.emohr.com and http://reas.com
4. **Intentionality** is the power of minds and mental states to be about, represent, or stand for things, properties, and states of affairs. It is the directedness, aboutness, or reference of mental states—the fact that you think of or about something. Intentionality includes what is called "mental representation." Retrieved from: https://plato.stanford.edu/entries/consciousness-intentionality/
5. **Spontaneity** in art refers to a creative activity that another person does not directly or intentionally encourage or stimulate. It is about an impulse that arises from the internal needs of a person who decides to creatively and artistically respond to external and internal stimuli. One example of spontaneity in art is spontaneous painting, which is painting intuitively without having an image or model to paint from. Retrieved from: https://www.curvesandchaos.com/what-is-spontaneous-in-art/
6. Take the example of a "Blindfolded Gladiatrix," which is not a set of image archetypes any GAN might have been trained on. The prompt asked Midjourney to "/imagine: a Blindfolded Gladiatrix as a special treat for the Roman crowds as the most skilled of the gladiatrixes fought as a Retiarius, using a weighted net and a pointed trident. Their helmets were often

constructed to be weapons, instantly deadly as their sharp pointed protrusions were dipped in poison." This example illustrates the kind of imaginative leap that artificial intelligence (AI), such as Midjourney, can make by synthesizing elements from different historical and fictional contexts. A "Blindfolded Gladiatrix" combines the historical concept of gladiators in ancient Rome with the fictional idea of a blindfolded female warrior in an arena. This demonstrates the capability of AI to create novel concepts by fusing elements from various sources, even when there is no pre-existing archetype or real-life example for such a combination.

7. **Mimesis** in art, as popularized by Erich Auerbach in his work "Mimesis: The Representation of Reality in Western Literature," refers to artists' inclination to imitate or emulate aspects such as style, technique, form, content, or any other characteristic from another artist's work. This concept derives from the Platonic notion that all art mirrors nature and that every artistic representation reflects nature or other art. This imitative practice leads to an ever-increasing distance from the "real" world, a construct underpinned by the Platonic view that our lived world is but a faint echo of the actual, "real" reality. It is essential to differentiate this form of mimesis, termed "mimesis of representation," from René Girard's concept of "mimetic desire." While the former involves imitation of external facets such as art, speech, mannerisms, and dress, the latter, which stands as Girard's significant contribution, contends that the object of imitation is not any superficial or external representation but desires themselves. Retrieved from: https://mimetictheory.com/mimetic-theory-resources/faq/what-is-art-a-mimesis/

8. An excellent resource for introducing **British Romanticism** poetry can be found at https://www.poetryfoundation.org/collections/152982/an-introduction-to-british-romanticism

9. The artistic community has increasingly embraced virtual reality (VR) and augmented reality (AR). Here, we take a look at some of the pioneers in this field, as highlighted by Jon Pratty:

"**In the Eyes of the Animals**" is a VR piece by Marshmallow Laser Feast from 2015 that immerses viewers in a forest ecosystem. The experience envelops participants with sounds, vibrations, and visually intriguing forms, simulating the perspective of animals and other organisms within this natural environment. **Bjork's digital show** at Somerset House in 2016 blended multiple forms of media with programmatic content, aligning with the musical experience provided by the Icelandic artist. A standout feature was "Mouthmantra VR," which transported viewers into the singer's mouth during a performance, creating an ever-changing and surreal spatial experience. **The Modigliani exhibition** at Tate Modern (November 2017 to April 2018) utilized VR to provide an in-depth exploration of the painter's studio, meticulously recreating the environment, objects, art, and architectural interiors that Modigliani worked with. The "**Tim Peake VR Experience**" at the Science Museum allows participants to vicariously experience the re-entry into Earth's atmosphere as undergone by astronaut Tim Peake upon his return from the International Space Station in 2016. **The Kremer Museum VR Experience**, utilizing Google Daydream headsets, is another notable example demonstrating how VR can attract a wider audience. Even those initially hesitant about using VR headsets and hand controllers can find enjoyment in exploring and navigating these innovative digital spaces.

Finally, "**Whilst the Rest Were Sleeping**" by Simon Wilkinson (Circa 69, 2017) offers a mixed reality experience that includes live music, further showcasing the potential of VR/AR technologies in enhancing and reinventing artistic expression. Retrieved from: https://www.thespace.org/resource/top-six-vr-and-ar-experiences-in-the-arts

Afterword

In an era characterized by unrelenting technological advancement, it is imperative to maintain an observant and balanced stance. Though endowed with formidable capabilities, the instruments and systems arising from human ingenuity remain intrinsically incapable of replicating the rich tapestry of human experience in its entirety. As the boundaries between humans and technology become more porous, it is essential to steadfastly safeguard the elements that form the bedrock of our human existence: interconnectivity, empathy, and nurturing deep and meaningful relationships.

As we navigate the tumultuous currents of the modern digital epoch, sustaining and bolstering our ability to cultivate authentic connections is paramount. The statement remains valid despite the potential impediments presented by digital interfaces and electronic paraphernalia. We must embrace the enlightenment that our purpose transcends the confines of mere functional efficacy. It is indelibly interlaced with the acknowledgment and reverence of the multifarious and convoluted web of experiences and emotions that constitute the human condition.

We find ourselves at an epochal inflection point, where our choices bear significant consequences for future generations. Addressing this colossal responsibility necessitates thoughtful reflection, wisdom, and an unyielding commitment to the shared tapestry of our global society. The reconciliation of our existence with the burgeoning omnipresence of machines demands that we assertively reconfirm our role as the chief architects in shaping the contours of our shared destiny.

Within this transformative odyssey, the frontiers of an artificial intelligence (AI) integrated society present us with an imperative to adopt a proactive and anticipatory stance. The approach entails our responsibility to navigate this novel terrain with astuteness, prudence, and foresight. In this context, it is critical to promulgate a robust framework comprising policies, regulations, and ethical principles that dictate the responsible development and deployment of AI technologies. We must tread lightly with the immense power conferred by AI, ensuring its impact aligns with our ethical values. By establishing a governance structure emphasizing accountability, transparency, and inclusivity, we aim to guard against potential negative repercussions and forge a path that respects our collective humanity.

THE DYSTOPIAN TRAP

In deliberating upon the future of AI, it is essential to acknowledge that the construct is deeply intertwined with profound philosophical conundrums. What does it entail for a machine to harbor intelligence in its quintessence? Is it within the realm of possibility for artificial entities to emulate the multifaceted depths of human cognition and consciousness? Applying intelligence to non-biological constructs challenges our rudimentary assumptions regarding sentience and self-awareness. As we propel further into the AI domain, it becomes imperative to astutely traverse the ethical dimensions that emanate from this progression. Queries about responsibility, accountability, and the potential repercussions of AI's actions loom monumentally, necessitating careful contemplation and robust ethical frameworks capable of weathering the intricacies of this burgeoning landscape.

There is a curious magnetism in the dystopian narratives that revolve around AI, which continues to engross society in its multifaceted intrigue. Tales of self-governing machines causing mayhem or dominating humanity pervade our literature and screenplays, unfurling a narrative tapestry that is often bleak yet enticing. Such storylines act as compelling thought experiments, pitting human ingenuity and resilience against our technological creations in hypothetical future settings. However, this fascination for dystopian narratives might not express society's collective pessimism toward future technologies. Instead, it could be a testament to our fundamental human cognitive mechanisms, the art of storytelling, and our inbuilt proclivity for exploring the unknown and unpredictable.

However, one lethal tool is often overlooked amid the speculative fiction spotlighting malignant AI, nuclear Armageddon or biochemical catastrophes. It has arguably claimed more lives throughout history than any other weapon—the knife and its big brother, the sword. In its numerous forms, the knife has been a persistent player in the human story, marking its presence across eras and civilizations. From crude stone blades chipped off by our early ancestors to the gleaming, laser-sharp chef's knives of the modern kitchen, the knife has been by our side—a loyal, utilitarian companion, an essential survival tool, and, tragically, a weapon.[1]

Throughout history, the knife's dual nature as a life-sustaining tool and a life-ending weapon has been constantly at play. While the knife has helped us cut, chop, carve, and craft our way through the annals of civilization, its darker side, when wielded with malicious intent, has led to countless deaths over the millennia. The narrative of the knife—and the sword—and their role in human history is often overlooked amidst our penchant for grandiose dystopian narratives featuring sophisticated weapons of destruction. However, in terms of sheer numbers and historical impact, these ubiquitous tools have perhaps played a more significant role in human survival, civilization, and conflict than any technological terror we might conceive of in our dystopian futures.

Human cognition exhibits an innate predisposition toward potential threats and adverse consequences, often denoted as the "negativity bias." This bias, a by-product of millennia of evolutionary fine-tuning, elucidates our tendency to recollect and react more vehemently to negative stimuli than positive ones. Within the context of AI, dystopian scenarios represent archetypal dangers to our existence or mode of living, thereby ensnaring our attention. Dystopian narratives deliver an expansive tableau for scrutinizing AI's ethical, philosophical, and societal ramifications. These stories can function as cautionary tales that catalyze introspection and discourse regarding the stewardship of

AI technologies. They enable us to conjure worst-case scenarios and grapple with profound questions concerning intelligence, consciousness, and the quintessence of human existence.

Intriguingly, notwithstanding the elaborate technologies and cataclysmic events often portrayed in these sagas, dystopian narratives regarding AI do not necessarily necessitate an excessive exertion of imaginative faculties. The situation may seem paradoxical, yet narratives of this nature tend to adhere to well-established patterns and tropes, such as insubordinate machines or the exploitation of technology by authoritarian entities. These plots, albeit gripping, frequently reflect extant trepidations and anxieties rather than proffering genuinely innovative or sanguine visions of the future.

In contrast, crafting literature that envisions a world in which AI engenders positive ramifications necessitates a considerable degree of imagination and prescience. These narratives summon us to envisage advanced technologies, societal infrastructures, ethical frameworks, and human-machine synergies that enable these technologies' efficacious and harmonious employment. They make us imagine a world starkly distinct from our present circumstances, albeit anchored in plausible scientific and societal advancements. Formulating compelling and credible utopian narratives concerning AI is an arduous undertaking, primarily due to individuals' challenges in visualizing a world devoid of friction. Our acclimatization to grappling with dilemmas and conflicts, which are quintessential elements of conventional narratives, renders the prospect of a conflict-averse society seemingly illusory or monotonous. Nonetheless, such narratives hold the potential to be profoundly inspirational and intellectually stimulating, proffering visions of the future that challenge us to aspire toward enhanced trajectories rather than solely circumventing deleterious outcomes.

A MULTIPLE-PHASE EVENT

In reflecting upon the transition toward a society pervaded by AI, it becomes indispensable to transcend the notion of AI integration as a singular, static event. Instead, the emergence of AI in society should be conceived as an ever-evolving narrative—a dynamic continuum that necessitates perpetual adaptation and unwavering innovation. As we traverse this course, we witness the vast panorama of AI's potential applications. Nevertheless, vigilance must be sustained with each progressive stride, with close attention paid to the subtle undercurrents that may presage unintended repercussions. The inherent duality of AI summons us to acknowledge the potential risks intricately woven into its promises. By fostering a proactive mindset, we can pre-emptively pierce the veil of uncertainty, mitigating the manifestation of significant issues. Through this dynamic interplay of exploration and caution, we deftly navigate the multifaceted terrain of an AI society, grounding our endeavors in the pursuit of an equilibrium between technology and humanity.

Recognizing the profound transformative capacity of AI requires a collective commitment to the art of adaptation. The transition toward AI-pervasive societies should not be seen as a fixed endpoint but rather as a continually evolving journey. With each successive phase, as our comprehension deepens and our collective wisdom matures, we unmask new horizons of possibility. The intersection of human potential, guided by the facilitative hand of AI augmentation, propels us to navigate uncharted territories and redefine the limits of human endeavor. In this continuous process of growth and discovery, we craft an intricate tableau of resilience, innovation, and human excellence—a testament to our innate capacity to adapt, transcend, and flourish in an AI-saturated society.

The current trajectory of human civilization, characterized by exponential growth in energy wealth, intimates a potential future where humanity's existence is radically redefined. As AI's capabilities continue to expand, reaching new heights of utility, we can anticipate a concurrent surge in human prosperity. This anticipated vision of future humanity unfolds an intricate web of philosophical contemplation. It calls upon us to reflect upon the essence of human existence and the nature of our endeavors. As machines increasingly assume the burden of menial tasks, we can undertake a profound journey of self-discovery, liberation, and intellectual exploration. Freed from the drudgery of monotonous labor, we can transcend our limitations, plumbing the depths of our creative potential and nurturing the outstanding faculties that characterize our humanity. This radical transition from laborious tasks to a state of self-actualization heralds a transformative epoch wherein the pursuit of knowledge, wisdom, and personal growth assumes paramount importance.

Within this shifting paradigm, human creativity is liberated from the shackles of the mundane, fostering a fertile breeding ground for innovation and progress. As machines become laborers, humans are unburdened and enabled to channel their imaginative prowess toward exploring uncharted frontiers. The merger of human ingenuity and machine efficiency incites an unprecedented surge of creative thinking, catalyzing breakthroughs previously confined to the realm of imagination. The very fabric of our society, interwoven with threads of limitless possibility, resonates with the harmonious symphony of technological progress and human innovation.

This envisioned future provokes profound inquiries into the interface between humans and machines, challenging conventional notions of identity and purpose. As machines transcend their role as mere tools to become creators, collaborators, and problem-solvers, the boundaries delineating our individuality become increasingly blurred. It urges us to re-evaluate our comprehension of what it means to be human and to ponder the inherent qualities that distinguish us from our mechanical counterparts. Within this sphere of interconnectedness, we embark upon a collective exploration of our shared destiny, forging symbiotic relationships with machines that amplify our strengths and augment our capabilities.

As we embrace the future that unfurls before us, we envisage a society emancipated from the restraints of traditional labor paradigms, heralding far-reaching ramifications for social architectures and human welfare. Machines are poised to shoulder the burdens of laborious and mundane tasks through the mechanization and automation facilitated by technological advancements. With machines assuming responsibility for arduous tasks, we will have the luxury of time. This affluence of time allows us to divert our energies toward the elements that make life an odyssey of joy and fulfillment.

At the core of human existence lie the bonds we forge with one another. With the emancipation from traditional labor constraints, the nurturing and sustenance of relationships can claim a more central role. These bonds form the bedrock of our social existence and are indispensable for psychological well-being. Our newfound bounty of time free of chores affords us the latitude to immerse ourselves in pursuits that resonate with the deepest recesses of our souls. The cultivation of passions, be they artistic, intellectual, or humanitarian, not only nourishes the individual spirit but also contributes to a vibrant cultural mosaic that enriches society. Holistic well-being can flourish, encompassing physical, mental, and spiritual dimensions. Time affords opportunities for exercise, contemplation, and engagement in communal and spiritual practices, which collectively contribute to the nourishment of the whole person.

This transformative era summons an evolution of our ethos and invites a metamorphosis of societal values and norms. The standard by which civilizations are appraised undergoes a shift: no longer solely assessed by the magnitude of economic affluence, but rather by the enrichment of the collective consciousness, the multifariousness of its intellectual and cultural tapestry, and the pervasiveness of joy and fulfillment in the lives of its inhabitants. Such radical reconfiguration of work dynamics conceives a society wherein human flourishing transcends mere economic opulence. The fortification and enrichment of our collective consciousness become possible through the interweaving of diverse cultural, intellectual, and social strands. The process fosters a rich tapestry of human experiences characterized by engagement, fulfillment, and flourishing lives. In tandem, it is imperative to remain vigilant against potential pitfalls. As we stride into this brave new world, issues such as equitable distribution of wealth, social inclusion, and maintaining a sense of purpose amidst decreased traditional labor demands will need to be astutely addressed. Thought leaders, policymakers, and society must collaboratively chart the course with wisdom, ingenuity, and a deep-seated commitment to humanistic values to realize the full potential of this transformative era.

In this intricate tapestry of global interconnectedness, we are not lone sojourners but rather a collective of kindred spirits embarked upon an odyssey to navigate the constellations of our shared destiny. The luminaries amongst us—visionaries, poets, philosophers, and scientists—must ally, intertwining intellect and emotion in this grand expedition. Our exploration ought to be steered by the compass of rationality and equally propelled by the cheerful fervor of the human spirit. This duality acknowledges the inexorable link between human flourishing and our symbiotic liaison with the offspring of our technological ingenuity.

This epoch is a harbinger of innumerable beginnings. Within our collective grasp lies the fantastic capability to shape new worlds, to animate the dreams that have long gestated in the chambers of our collective imagination, and to build ties whose reverberations will permeate the annals of history. The call is for every soul that ardently aspires for a future beaming with boundless possibilities, a future where the essence of humanity blossoms harmoniously with our technological triumphs.

In this realm where imagination, unshackled from the constraints of the corporeal world, blends with and embraces the expansive fabric of existence, we hold the chisel and the mallet to engrave our legacy. We are called upon to cultivate an intelligent interplay between the wisdom of the past and the vision of tomorrow. In weaving the threads of technology into the fabric of our existence, we must be judicious stewards, ensuring that our creations augment human potential, dignity, and welfare. In this time in space where imagination transcends and embraces the vast tapestry of existence, we can etch our name with deeds that resonate with purpose and indomitable hope for the symphony of futures that await.

NOTE

1. Primitive knives, often made of flint or obsidian, were instrumental in hunting and butchering, laying the groundwork for the survival and propagation of early human communities. With the advent of metallurgy, humans began forging knives of bronze, iron, and eventually steel, amplifying their effectiveness. The knife became a tool of war, a symbol of authority, and a rite of passage. Larger versions, such as swords and sabers, shaped the outcome of battles and altered the course of history. From the Roman Gladius to the Japanese Katana, these lethal tools have played a significant role in our shared human narrative.

Bibliography

Alan, K. 2017. Aphantasia: Experiences, Perceptions, and Insights. Dark River. p. 58.

Amabile, Teresa M. 2017. In Pursuit of Everyday Creativity. Harvard Business School Working Paper 18–002.

Arendt, H. 1958. The Human Condition. University of Chicago Press.

Auerbach, E. 1957. Mimesis: The Representation of Reality in Western Literature. Princeton University Press.

Bachelard, G. 1957. The Poetics of Space. Beacon Press; Revised edition, 1994.

Baker, N., Kellman, P. J. 2018. Abstract shape representation in human visual perception. Journal of Experimental Psychology: General 147(9), 1295–1308. https://doi.org/10.1037/xge0000409. Epub 2018 Apr 9. PMID: 29629783.

Barrett, M. S., Creech, A., Zhukov, K. 2021 Creative collaboration and collaborative creativity: A systematic literature review. Frontiers in Psychology 12. https://doi.org/10.3389/fpsyg.2021.713445

Bohm, D. 1980. Wholeness and the Implicate Order. Routledge & Paul Kegan. PDF edition published in the Taylor and Francis e-Library, 2005.

Cosmelli, D., Preiss, D. 2014. On the temporality of creative insight: A psychological and phenomenological perspective. Perception Science 5. https://doi.org/10.3389/fpsyg.2014.01184

Dale, J. 2014. Art, expression, perception and intentionality. Journal of Aesthetics and Phenomenology 1(1), 63–90.

Dosher, B., Lu, Z.-L. 2020. Perceptual Learning: How Experience Shapes Visual Perception. The MIT Press.

Eapen, T., Finkenstadt, D. J., Folk, J., Venkataswamy, L. 2023. How Generative AI Can Augment Human Creativity. *Harvard Business Review* 2023. https://hbr.org/2023/07/how-generative-ai-can-augment-human-creativity.

Fieseler, R. 2021. Exposing Bias: Race and Racism in America. Harvard Extension School.

Fromm, E. 1976. To Have or to Be. N.Y. Harper & Row.

Girard, R. 2001. I See Satan Fall Like Lightning. Orbis Books.

Hall, S. 1997. Representation: Cultural Representations and Signifying Practices. Sage Publications/ The Open University. pp 1–11.

Henning, P. B. 2014. Stages, skills, and steps of archetypal pattern analysis. The Assisi Institute Journal 1(1). https://digitalcommons.providence.edu/assisi_journal/vol1/iss1/8

Henri, C.-B. 1952. Images à la Sauvette. Verve.

Karwowski, M., Beghetto, R. A. 2019. Creative behavior as agentic action. Psychology of Aesthetics, Creativity, and the Arts 13(4), 402–415.

Lau, T. C. 2022. Rethinking low, middle, and high art. The Journal of Aesthetics and Art Criticism 80(4), 432–443.

Livingston, P. 2005. Art and Intention: A Philosophical Study. Oxford University Press.

Mandelbrot, B. 1982. The Fractal Geometry of Nature. W.H. Freeman; Revised Edition (Aug.15 1982)

Manu, A. 2022. The Philosophy of Disruption. Emerald Publishing Limited.

Maturana, H. Varela, F. 1980. Autopoiesis and cognition. The Realization of the Living. D. Reidel Publishing Company. p. xxiv.

Meyer, I. 2023. Meyer Medieval Art: Visual and Literary Arts of the Middle Ages. artincontext.org.

Miles, D. 2022. What Is Generative Design, and How Can It Be Used in Manufacturing?

Montuori, A., Purser, R. 1995. Deconstructing the lone genius myth: Toward a contextual view of creativity. Journal of Humanistic Psychology 35(3), 69–112.

Mortensen, D. H. 2020. Stage 1 in the Design Thinking Process: Empathise with Your Users. interaction-design.org.

Patel, B. N., Rosenberg, L., Willcox, G. et al. Human–machine partnership with artificial intelligence for chest radiograph diagnosis. Nature Partner Journals. Digital Medicine 2, 111. https://doi.org/10.1038/s41746-019-0189-7

Piaget, J. 1947. The Psychology of Intelligence. Routledge. 2001.

Roumani, N., Both, T. 2020. Unlocking the power of design for the social sector. Stanford D School. News July 21, 2020.

Santayana, G. 1896. The Sense of Beauty. http://www.gutenberg.org/ebooks/26842. Released 2008.

Sarasso, P., Neppi-Modona, M., Sacco, K., Ronga, I. 2020. Stopping for knowledge: The sense of beauty in the perception-action cycle. Neuroscience & Biobehavioral Reviews 118, 723–738.

Slater, M. 2009. Place illusion and plausibility can lead to realistic behaviour in immersive virtual environments. Philosophical transactions of the Royal Society of London. Series B, Biological sciences 364(1535), 3549–57. https://doi.org/10.1098/rstb.2009.0138. PMID: 19884149; PMCID: PMC2781884.

Szarkowski, J. 2007. The Photographer's Eye. The Museum of Modern Art.

Wang, G. 2019. Humans in the Loop: The Design of Interactive AI Systems. HAI Stanford Edu News. Stanford Human Centered Artificial Intelligence. October 20, 2019.

Wilson, H. J., Daugherty, P. R. 2018. Collaborative intelligence: Humans and AI are joining forces. *Harvard Business Review*. July–August 2018 issue (pp. 114–123).

Yan, S., Fang, Y. 2021. The influence of artificial intelligence on art design in the digital age. Scientific Programming 2021. https://doi.org/10.1155/2021/4838957

ONLINE SOURCES

http://www.emohr.com and http://reas.com.

http://www.gutenberg.org/ebooks/26842. Released 2008.

http://www.robertjsternberg.com/successful-intelligence.

https://academic.oup.com/bjaesthetics/article/57/3/283/4259142.

https://artincontext.org/medieval-art/.

https://communities.sunlightfoundation.com/action/codesign/.

https://courses.lumenlearning.com/wm-lifespandevelopment/chapter/cognitive-development-2.

https://deepdreamgenerator.com.

https://dictionary.apa.org/conscious-intention.

https://dictionary.cambridge.org/dictionary/english/fine-art.

https://diffsense.com/diff/incidental/intentional.

https://digitalcommons.providence.edu/assisi_journal/vol1/iss1/8.

https://doi.org/10.1037/aca0000190.

https://doi.org/10.1038/s41746-019-0189-7.

https://doi.org/10.1093/acrefore/9780199340378.013.209.

https://doi.org/10.1093/jaac/kpac034.

https://doi.org/10.1155/2021/4838957.

https://doi.org/10.2752/20539339XX14005942183973\.

https://doi.org/10.3389/fpsyg.2021.713445 and https://www.hbs.edu/ris/Publication%20Files/18-002_ee708f75-293f-4494-bf93-df5cd96b48a6.pdf.

https://dschool.stanford.edu/news-events/unlocking-the-power-of-design-for-the-social-sector-a-human-centered-systems-minded-and-strategy-aligned-design-approach-for-social-sector-leaders.

https://english-grammar-lessons.com/a-picture-is-worth-a-thousand-words-meaning/.

https://feelgoodfibers.com/what-does-it-mean-to-create-with-intent/.

https://hai.stanford.edu/news/humans-loop-design-interactive-ai-systems.

https://hbr.org/2018/07/collaborative-intelligence-humans-and-ai-are-joining-forces.

https://hbr.org/2023/07/how-generative-ai-can-augment-human-creativity/.

https://inspiration.allwomenstalk.com/ways-to-develop-your-artistic-vision/.

https://kellmanlab.psych.ucla.edu/files/baker_kellman_2018.pdf.

https://konmari.com/ikebana/#:~:text=Ikebana.

https://latin-dictionary.net/definition/4898/artificialis-artificialis-artificiale.

https://learn.microsoft.com/en-us/power-automate/get-started-with-copilot.

https://masterofcode.com/blog/top-5-generative-ai-integration-companies-to-drive-customer-support.

https://mimetictheory.com/mimetic-theory-resources/faq/what-is-art-a-mimesis/.

https://ndpr.nd.edu/reviews/art-and-intention-a-philosophical-study/.

https://newatlas.com/local-motors-strati-imts/33846/.

https://openai.com/research/musenet.

https://plato.stanford.edu/entries/consciousness-intentionality/.

https://redshift.autodesk.com/articles/what-is-generative-design.

https://sites.evergreen.edu/wp-content/uploads/sites/88/2015/05/Gaston-Bachelard-the-Poetics-of-Space.pdf.

https://ssec.si.edu/stemvisions-blog/beauty-and-science-snowflakes.

https://wikidiff.com/intentional/incidental.

https://www.accenture.com/ca-en/insights/artificial-intelligence/ai-maturity-and-transformation.

https://www.arts.gov/stories/blog/2015/why-arts-matter.

https://www.artsacad.net/the-importance-of-expressing-emotion-through-art and https://humanitiescenter.byu.edu/an-artists-intention.

https://www.artsper.com/us/cms/collector-guide/the-art-world/what-is-an-artwork.

https://www.autodesk.ca/en/products/fusion-360/industrial-designer.

https://www.bbc.com/worklife/article/20210308-the-lone-genius-myth-why-even-great-minds-collaborate.

https://www.bcg.com/en-ca/capabilities/artificial-intelligence/ai-for-business-society-individuals.

https://www.britannica.com/topic/philosophy-of-art/Art-as-a-means-to-moral-improvement.

https://www.collinsdictionary.com/dictionary/english/technology.

https://www.curvesandchaos.com/what-is-spontaneous-in-art/.

https://www.dictionary.com/browse/articulation.

https://www.dictionary.com/browse/mind-s-eye.

https://www.diygenius.com/fractals-in-nature/.

https://www.encyclopedia.com/humanities/encyclopedias-almanacs-transcripts-and-maps/phantasia.

https://www.freecodecamp.org/news/an-introduction-to-generative-art-what-it-is-and-how-you-make-it-b0b363b50a70/.

https://www.frontiersin.org/articles/10.3389/fpsyg.2014.01184/full.

https://www.hubs.com/guides/injection-molding/.

https://www.indeed.com/career-advice/career-development/creative-intelligence-example

https://www.interaction-design.org/literature/article/stage-1-in-the-design-thinking-process-empathise-with-your-users.

https://www.interaction-design.org/literature/topics/conceptual-models.

https://www.irisvanherpen.com.

https://www.lboro.ac.uk/research/amrg/about/the7categoriesofadditivemanufacturing/.

https://www.mckinsey.com/capabilities/operations/our-insights/the-mainstreaming-of-additive-manufacturing.

https://www.nature.com/articles/s41746-019-0189-7.

https://www.ncbi.nlm.nih.gov/pmc/articles/PMC2781884/.

https://www.nytimes.com/2009/06/01/arts/01iht-DESIGN1.html.

https://www.phaidon.com/agenda/architecture/articles/2014/april/02/what-did-mies-van-der-rohe-mean-by-less-is-more/.

https://www.phrases.org.uk/meanings/a-picture-is-worth-a-thousand-words.html.

https://www.poetryfoundation.org/collections/152982/an-introduction-to-british-romanticism.

https://www.psychologytoday.com/us/blog/science-choice/201907/9-factors-influence-aesthetic-choice and Aesthetic Choice | The British Journal of Aesthetics | Oxford Academic.

https://www.sas.com/en_us/insights/analytics/what-is-artificial-intelligence.html.

https://www.sciencedirect.com/science/article/abs/pii/S0149763420305625.

https://www.techtarget.com/whatis/definition/DeepMind and https://www.deeplearning.ai/ai-notes/initialization/index.html.

https://www.theartist.me/art/what-is-art/.

https://www.thecollector.com/how-photography-transformed-art/#.

https://www.theguardian.com/commentisfree/belief/2014/mar/18/sacred-art-religion-humans.

https://www.theicod.org/en/professional-design/what-is-design/what-is-design.

https://www.thespace.org/resource/top-six-vr-and-ar-experiences-in-the-arts

https://www.unesco.org/en/articles/cutting-edge-all-aboard-culture-and-social-inclusion

https://www.verywellmind.com/cognitive-biases-distort-thinking-2794763.

https://www.verywellmind.com/what-are-jungs-4-major-archetypes-2795439#citation-1.

https://www.weforum.org/agenda/2023/02/ai-can-catalyze-and-inhibit-your-creativity-here-is-how/.

Index

Note: Locators in *italics* represent figures in the text.

A

"Active imagination" concept, 29
Additive manufacturing (AM) technologies, 187–188, 200n5, 200–201n6
Aesthetically beautiful object, 56–57, 67n1
Aesthetic beauty, 18, 67n1
Aesthetic charm of AI-generated imagery, 17
Aesthetic creation, 29
Aesthetic judgments, 20, *20*, 139
Aesthetic pleasure, 30, 226
Aesthetic preferences and reactions, 39n6
Aesthetics, 35, 44, 45, 50, 57, 61, 93, 96, 195, 198
    of exposed dynamics, *20*
    of inside-out approach, 185–187
    and metaphysics, 93
    pervasive, 63
    surface-level, 187
    of 3D printing, 199
    of virtual space, 43–45, 51
    visual, 124
Agile phase, 158
AI, *see* Artificial intelligence
AI Achievers, 94n6
Alinea menu (Chicago), blend of three dishes from, *124*
AM technologies, *see* Additive manufacturing technologies
Analytical intelligence, 131n9
Analytical processing, 22
Ancillary scenarios, 203
Aphantasia, 113, 114, 116n11
Apple's Vision Pro, *137*
AR, *see* Augmented reality
Archetypal patterns, 14n8
Archetypes, 140, 165, 183n6
    beyond, 7–12
    conditional, 165–167, 170, 173
    conventional, 11, 166, 174, 181
    no archetype, 178–181
    predefined, 170
    radical centric design as a new conceptual model, 176–178, *176*
    rethinking, *193*, *194*, *195*, *196*
    teaching art and design in the context of text-conditional inspiration, 167–169
    text conditional design systems, 169–173
    traditional, 171
    working without, 173–175
Architecting experiences, 96–98
Architecture of a building, 54n2
Arendt, H., 217–218
Art, 145n3; *see also* Sense of sacredness, art and
    and AI artistic vision, 21–22
    and AI-focused creative insight, 22–25
    AI-produced, 74
    as artificial, 3
    creation of, 16, 21, 30, 72, 74
    and design
        AI's impact on, 144
        beauty in, 58–61
        legacy of, 143
    education, 167
    evolution of, 35
    fine art, 85, 93n2
    generative, 23, 39n5, 223
        emergence of, 31
        ethereal tapestry, 31
        theory of, 33–35
    holographic street art, 111
    as intention, articulation, and manifestation, 15–18
    as intentional communicative tool, 30
    as the means to spirituality, 28–29
    mimesis in, 227
    nature and art, association between, 57
    -produced art, 74
    as sacred in human imagination, 28
    sanctity of, 16–17

and sentience, 30–31
unique art, generating, 35
as a vehicle for emotional transmission, 26n5
virtual art galleries, 46
Articulation, 15, 16, 17, 19, 20–21, 26n10, 133, 139–141
enhanced, *90*, *91*, *92*
amplifying intent through, 89–90
Artifact, 3, 6, 20, 21, 30, 68n6, 141
Artificial, 3, 4, 222, 225–226
art as, 3–4
Artificial creativity, 35–36, 38, 71, 134
Artificial intelligence (AI), 3, 15, 72, 220; *see also* Generative AI
and aesthetic of virtual space, 43–45
artist-AI relationship, 92
attribute of, 20
burgeoning capacity of AI systems, 3–4
challenges in, 76–77
creative AI systems, 120
creative capabilities of, 79, 144
creative directive of, 16
creativity, 3
data-driven precision of, 128
dramatic expansion of beauty, AI enabling, 36–37
dynamism of, 40
emergence of AI technologies, 35
emergent abilities of, 4
-enhanced creative sphere, 75
as facilitator, 5
human-AI collaboration, 142, 167
human intention and AI capabilities, 16, 78, 136
humans and AI, symbiotic alliance between, 25
incorporating into design process, 12
as intricate tool, 22, *48*, *49*
partnering with, 78–79
as pragmatic reality, 5
-produced art, 74
sophisticated AI systems, 101
transformative potential of, 3, 50
transforming creativity, 4–5
true power of, 77
Artificialism, 114–115
Artificiality, 220, 223
Artist-AI relationship, 92
Artistic articulation, concept of, 80
Artistic communication, 85
Artistic creation, 15, 30, 31, 71, 72, 89, 126, 138–139, 143, 168, 218
Artistic expression, 33, 35–36, 38, 57, 72, 74, 78, 79–80, 83n4, 85, 87, 93, 121, 128, 138, 139, 142, 174, 188

Artistic genius, 77, 146n3
Artistic intent, 18, 25, 76, 85, 146n3
Artistic ownership, 75, 79, 167
Artistic perception, 86
Artistic skill, 86, 139
Artistic value, 31, 144
Artistic vision, 21–22, 78, 80, 93
Artwork, 13n2
colors choice in, 71
human-produced, 7
Attention and technique, meaning built with, 109–112
Attribute of AI, 20
Auerbach, E., 227n7
Augmented reality (AR), 23, 143, 227
AutoDesk
Fusion 360, 183n5
generative design technology, 173
Automotive design, 195
Autopoietic intelligence, 114–115
Autopoietic system, boundary of, 114

B

Bachelard, G., 64
Baker, N., 55n4
Barnard, F. R., 219n2
Beardsley, 85
Beauty, 12–13, 56, 87, 112; *see also* Incidental beauty
aesthetic, 18, 67n1
aesthetically beautiful object, 56–57
AI enabling dramatic expansion of, 36–37
in art and design, 58–61
historical evolution of, 56
incidental, 61–66
intentional, 67n4
natural beauty, 57
of painting, 87
perception of, 56
role of, 18
of snowflakes, 67n5
Bias in creative intent, 71, 76
artistic expression, impact of AI on, 79–80
challenges in AI, 76–77
convergence, 81–82
partnering with AI, 78–79
skill and desired outcome, balance between, 71–76
Bird's nest, 220
Bjork's digital show, 227n9
Blindfolded Gladiatrix, *224*, 226–227n6
Bluetooth speaker, *64*
Bohm, D., 26n7, 132–133

Bold foresight scenarios, 204
Boston Consulting Group, 27n16
Bot Forge, 162n8
Brands, 54n1
Breakspear, M., 112, 116n8
Burgeoning capacity of AI systems, 3–4

C

CBAA, *see* Creative behaviour as an Agentic
        Action Model
Celtic Sea scallops (Franck Giovannini), *125*
Challenges in AI, 76–77
Chaos and unpredictability, 120
Chipmunk in a coffee cup, *81*
Co-design, 171–172, 183n3
Cognitive biases, 82n2, 172
Cognitive phase, 157, 158
Collaborative canvas, 42
Collaborative environments, fostering, 123
Collaborative intelligence, 124–126
Collective intelligence, 123
Colors choice in artwork, 71
Comfortable position, 178, *179*, 180
Compromise in art creation, 72
Computational algorithms, 144, 223
Concealed intent, ambiguity of, 85–86
Conceptual models, 174–175, 184n7
Concrete, sculpture made of, *77*
Conditional archetype, 165–167, 170, 171, 173
"Conditional" constraints, 8
Conscious intention, 19, 222
Consciousness, 4, 29, 84, 98, 128
Constraints, designing from, 8
Contemplating an AI-facilitated world, 102–104
Contemplative sensibility, 28
Contextual understanding, 125, 183n2
Conventional design, 171
Convergence, 81–82
Convolutional neural networks, 94n8
Co-pilot, 106n6
Countryside-style photograph of a scene or
        landscape in Tuscany, *141*
Creation of art, 21, 30, 74
Creative act, 13, 29, 79, 81, 130n2, 145n4
Creative AI systems, 120
Creative behaviour as an Agentic Action Model
        (CBAA), 145n4
Creative capabilities of AI, 79, 144
Creative directive of AI, 16
Creative domains, triumphs within, 122
Creative endeavor, 11, 24, 30, 66, 114, 121, 134
Creative generativity, 32–33

Creative genius, myth of, 119
    collaborative intelligence, 124–126
    genius as an illusion, 121–122
    remix and collaborative creativity, 122–124
    self-transcendence, 128
    societal construct, 119–121
    technologies, 128
Creative insight, 22–25, 26–27n15
Creative intelligence, 127, 130n9
Creative intent, 82n1, 84, 93
    bias in, 71, 76
        artistic expression, impact of AI on, 79–80
        challenges in AI, 76–77
        convergence, 81–82
        partnering with AI, 78–79
        skill and desired outcome, balance between,
            71–76
Creative interaction, 127
Creative potential, optimizing, 6
Creative renaissance, 58, 100, 197
Creative sphere, AI-enhanced, 75
Creativity, 16, 42, 121
    of AI, 3–4
    AI's role in, 126–127
    artificial, 35–36, 38, 71, 134
    conceptualization of, 122
    democratization of, 145–146n4
    domain of, 143
    future of, 126–127
    human creativity
        AI and, 60, 91–92
        and machine intelligence, 59, 77
    maximizing, 84
        concealed intent, ambiguity of, 85–86
        creative intention, 84
        enhanced articulation, amplifying intent
            through, 89–90
        generative AI, amplifying creative intent
            through, 92–93
        human creativity, AI and, 91–92
        intent and individual bias, 88–89
        intent and skill in image generation, 86–88
    reimagining, 127
    remix and collaborative creativity, 122–124
Customization with eco-conscious design
        objectives, merging of, 197
Cynicism, 104

D

Daguerre, L., 182n1
Daguerreotype, 182n1
DALE-E2, 161n4

Data-driven precision of AI, 128
Data Monsters, 162n8
Daugherty, P. R., 130n6
Decision-making, 109, 113, 123, 125, 150, 158, 202, 205
Decisive moment, 108, 109
DeepDream, 65, 162n10
Deeper Insights, 162n8
DeepMind, 90, 94n8
Deep-seated significance of incidental beauty, 63
Design, 13n3, 18
    and architecture, 208–210
    art and, 38, 40
        beauty of, 58–61
    automotive, 195
    co-design, 171, 172, 183n3
    conventional, 171
    generative, 100–102
    human-centric, 95, 96–97, 105n1
    industrial, 185, 188, 209
    parametric-inspired, 140
    radical-centric, *78, 79, 172,* 179, 180, *180,* 181, *182, 182*
    Scandinavian, 173
    scenario-based, 202
    traditional, 169
Designed unpredictability, 223
Design intention and technology, 17–18
Design process, incorporating AI into, 12
Design thinking, *see* Human-centered design
Digital assistants, 22
Digital revolution, 41, 143
Digital twin android, experimental avatar for, *61*
Dignified rooster, portrait of, *52*
Dignified turkey, portrait of, *51*
Discovery, new age of, 13
Discrete biofeedback wearables, *214*
Discrete wearable biofeedback device, model with, *96*
Disruption
    concept of, 147
    and disruptors, 153–154
    framework, 152–153
    technological, 147, 148, 153, 161
Disruption index, 149, *149,* 161n1, 161n2
    disruptor, 149–150, 161n4
    enabler, 150–151
    follower, 152
    integrator, 151
Disruptive innovation, 152, 155, 204
Disruptor, 149–150, 161n4
    disruption and, 153–154
    great, 147–148
Divine communion, 30

Dosher, B., 55n3
Dramatic expansion of beauty, AI enabling, 36–37
Dynamism of AI, 40

E

Earth, 88, *89*
Education, richly imagined, 215–216
Embodied Functions, 107
Emergence of AI technologies, 35
Emergent abilities of AI, 4
Emergent sentience, 115
Emotional cartography, 111
Emotional transmission, 26n5
Emotions, 18, 30, 110, 145n2, 222, 233
Enablers, 150–151, 161n5
Energy, 132–134
Enhanced articulation, 89–90, *90, 91, 92*
Entertainment, richly imagined, 210
Equilibrium of expectations, 108, 109
Ethereal language, 29
Ethical dimensions of technology, 99
Eureka phenomenon, 119–120
European Modern kitchen proposals, *170*
Existence, spiritual sphere of, 29
Exploration, 23
Exposed dynamics, aesthetic of, *20*
Extinguishing labels, 220–222

F

Facilitator, AI as, 5
Fang, Y. 2021, 94n7
Fantasy, 113
Fine art, 85, 93n2
Flipboard, 161n6
Flower, sectional couch with a design inspired by, *24*
Fluid design for a coffee table, *34*
Fluid dynamics, 68n6
Fluidity, reimagined, *34*
Followers, 152, 162n9
Food, richly imagined, 211–212
Foresight scenarios, 202, 204–205
Form and material exploration for sound reproduction system, *65*
Form as a framework for perception, 40–41
    new forms revolutionized perception, 50–54
    new reality, rapid iterations as a bridge to, 41–43
    virtual reality, interactions in, 45–47
    virtual space, aesthetic of, 43–45
    virtual space, forms in, 47–50
Form exploration for a household appliance, *64*

"Form follows function," 185–187
Forms, Plato's theory of, 39
Fractals, 226n2
Franck Giovannini's Celtic Sea scallops, *125*
Fromm, E., 218
Frontiers of Psychology, 130n2
Fusion 360, 183n5

G

GAN, *see* Generative adversarial network
Gauguin, 123
Generative adversarial network (GAN), 32, 14n6, 224
Generative AI, 40, 41, 44, 45, 47, 59, 93, 123, 147, 208, 216
    amplifying creative intent through, 92–93
    and creative AI systems, 120
    fastest transformational change rate, 159–160
    imagery, 30, 31
    -powered virtual reality systems, 48
    purpose, 42
    role of, 42, 52
    with 3D printing, 199
Generative art, 23, 39n5, 223
    emergence of, 31
    ethereal tapestry, 31
    theory of, 33–35
Generative creation, 31, 107
Generative design, 101, 106n4
    and generative narratives, 100–102
Genetic mosaic, 111
Genius
    as an illusion, 121–122
    nexus of madness and, 120
    solitude of, 120
Geometry Matters project, 115
Giraffes running wild in Manhattan, *53*
Girard, R., 227n7
Google DeepMind, 64, 94n8
Graffiti alley, *62*
Gutenberg press, 148

H

Hall, S., 14n5
Haptic poetry, 111
Harvard Business School, 130n3
Health, richly imagined, 212–214
Henning, P. B., 14n8
Henri, C.-B., 108
Hidden architecture, 108, 112
Highly impractical but beautiful tool, *142*

HITL, *see* Human-in-the-loop
Holographic classrooms, 215, *215*
Holographic street art, 111
Human-AI collaboration, 142, 167
Human and AI interaction, dimensions for, *115*
Human and machine creativity, demarcation
        between, 101
Human-centered design, 96–97, 105n1
Human-centric design, 95, 96–97, 105n1
Human-computer system, 25
Human creativity
    AI and, 60, 91–92
    and machine intelligence, 59, 77
Human imagination, 12, 20, 28, 35, 74
Human ingenuity and artificial creativity,
        convergence of, 38
Human intelligence, 37, 123, 125, 127, 220
Human intent, 13, 17, 19, 74, 78, 82, 138, 223
Human intention and AI capabilities, 16, 78, 136
Human-in-the-loop (HITL), 123
Human narratives, evolution of, 102–104
Human-produced artwork, 7
Humans and AI, collaboration between, 77
Human-to-human creative relationships, 25
Human-to-human narrative, 98–100

I

Image outputs generation without compromise, 7
Imagination, beyond, 15
    articulation, 20–21
    articulation, art as, 15–18
    artistic vision, 21–22
    beauty, role of, 18
    creative insight, 22–25
    intention, 15, 18–19
    intention, art as, 15–18
    manifestation, 21
    manifestation, art as, 15
Immersive travel device and landscape, *208*
Impractically intricate tool, *48, 49*
Impressionist photography, 111
Incidental beauty, 16, *17*, 56, 61–66, 67n3, 67n6
    aesthetically beautiful object, 56–57
    beauty in art and design, 58–61
    deep-seated significance of, 63
    of a parametric design for festive headware, *57*
Industrial design, 185, 188, 209
Initial inspiration, 22
Innate genius, 122
Innate talent, primacy of, 119
Innovation, 29

Innovative knowledge, cultivating, 6
Inside-out approach, aesthetic of, 185–187
Insight, emergence of, 107–109
Instagram, 21, 143
In-store bespoke 3D printing of running shoes, *217*
Integrator, 151, 162n7
Intent, 6
    amplifying through enhanced articulation, 89–90
    artistic, 18, 85
    choosing, 19
    creative, 76, 82n1, 92–93
    delineation of, 8
    designing with, 84
    and individual bias, 88–89
    and skill in image generation, 86–88
Intention, 18–19, 26n6, 133, 142
    art as, 15–18
    creating a system of meaning, 134–138
    creative, 84
    and meaning, 138–139
Intentional beauty, 67n4
Intentional communicative tool, art as, 30
Intentional fallacy, 85
Intentionality, 135, 226n4
    concept of, 17, 30
    principle of, 135
Intentional spontaneity, 223
Interactive dream theater, 111
Internet, 159–160, 161n6, 203
"In the Eyes of the Animals" (Marshmallow Laser
    Feast), 227n9
Intricate tool, AI as, 22, *48, 49*
Iteration
    as a bridge to new reality, 41–43
    of a jacket made from discarded socks, *41*
    of a wedding dress made from discarded fishing
        nets, *42*

J

Jazz musicians, 64
Jung, C., 183n6
Jungian psychology, 183n6

K

Kellman, P. J., 55n4
Kremer Museum VR Experience, 227n9

L

Language, 139
Law of attraction, 104

"Less is more" philosophy, 187–189, 191
Less is not more anymore, 189–198
Livingston, P., 26n4
Local Motors, 195
Logos, 54n1
Lu, Z.-L., 55n3

M

Machine intelligence, 5, 59, 61, 77, 79, 109, 125,
    126, 220
Machine learning, 3, 72, 81, 93, 135, 181, 205
Madness and genius, nexus of, 120
Mandelbrot, B. 1982, 226n2
Manifestation, 15, 18–19, 23, 21, 26n11, 133,
    141–144
Marketing, richly imagined, 216–217
Master of Code, 162n8
Matter, 132–134
Maturana, H., 114
McKinsey, 200
Meaning, 132–134
Medical assistive device, *197*
Mental representation, 226n4
Metaspace, 31
Metaverse
    data object in, *43*
    parametric navigation spaces in, *49*
    portal in the, *33*
    portals in, *44, 45*
Metaverse avatar of an academic, *47*
Mimesis in art, 227
Model wearing jacket made of discarded
        fabrics, plastic caps, ropes, and paper
        maps, *136*
Model wearing wedding dress made of discarded
        fishing nets, *35, 143*
Modigliani exhibition, 227n9
Mohr, M., 223
Montuori, A., 129n1
Mood board for an Eastern fusion kitchen
        proposal, *171*
Mortensen, D. H., 105n3
Multitasking avatar, *53*
MuseNet, 65
Musical instrument, reimagining, 9
Myth of creative genius, 119
    collaborative intelligence, 124–126
    genius as an illusion, 121–122
    remix and collaborative creativity, 122–124
    self-transcendence, 128
    societal construct, 119–121
    technologies, 128

N

Nano-architecture, 111
Narrated economy, shift to, 95
    architecting experiences, 96–98
    generative design and generative narratives,
        100–102
    human narratives, evolution of, 102–104
    human-to-human narrative, 98–100
    new narrative, co-creating, 98
Natural, 3, 4, 221, 225–226
Natural beauty, 57
Naturalness, 211, 221, 222
Nature and art, association between, 57
Neppi-Modona, M., 14n9
Neural networks, 3, 7, 15, 20, 25, 78, 85, 86, 92, 94n8,
        94n9, 205
    co-creation with, 13
    functionality of, 91
Neuro-cinema, 111
New narrative, co-creating, 98
Noninvasive regenerative buccal therapies, *213*
Normative scenarios, 203, 219n1

O

Objective interpretation, 30
OpenAI, 161n4, 162n10
    MuseNet, 65
Origami-inspired wall lamp, incidental
        beauty of, *17*

P

Painting, beauty of, 87
Parametric-inspired design
    for sectional couch, 23, *23*, *24*, *100*
    for a sweet and sour dessert, *140*
Partnering with AI, 78–79
Perception
    fantasy and new dimensions for, 112–114
    form as a framework for, 40–41
        new forms revolutionized perception, 50–54
        new reality, rapid iterations as a bridge to,
          41–43
        virtual reality, interactions in, 45–47
        virtual space, aesthetic of, 43–45
        virtual space, forms in, 47–50
Permanent existence, 222–226
Pervasive opacity, 85
Phantasia/fantasy, concept of, 113, 116n10
Philosophical dilemmas, 81
Philosophical theories, 30–31

Philosophical "continuum," 123
PI, *see* Place illusion
Piaget, J. 1947, 114
Picasso, 123
Place illusion (PI), 54–55n3
Plato, 30, 38n4
    theory of Forms, 39
Plausibility illusion (Psi), 54–55n3
Pollock, J., 223
Polynon, *59*, 115
Practical intelligence, 131n9
Pragmatic reality, AI as, 5
Pratty, J., 227n9
Pre-emptive medicine, 207
Presence, 54n3
Progressive learning algorithms, 26n9
Prototype of sacred wearable object, *36*
Provocation, 220
    extinguishing labels, 220–222
    permanent existence, 222–226
Psi, *see* Plausibility illusion
Purser, R., 129n1

Q

Q-learning, 94n8
Quantum sculpture, 111

R

Race/racial ideology, 83n3
Radical-centric design, 15–16, *16*, 177–180, *179*
    for an air conditioning unit, *172*
    for a midi wind instrument, *178*
    as a new conceptual model, 176–178, *176*
    for a nonlinear time-keeping device, *175*
    for a personal mobility device, *180*
    for a sectional couch, *78*, *79*
    for a sound making object, *177*
    for a sound reproduction device, *182*
Radical centricity, 176, 177–178, 179, 180, 181
Radiolaria-inspired dehumidifier, *60*
Radiolaria inspired design for a wedding
        dress, *198*
Rationalization, act of, 32
Reas, C., 223
Reflective perception, concept of, 29
Remix and collaborative creativity, 122–124
Remix concept, 123
Representation, 14n5
Repurposed rubber and plastic, imagining fashion
        made from, *73*
Resilience, 122

Rethinking archetypes
  experimental building structures, *196*
  single family dwelling, *196*
  the cabinet, *193*
  the couch, *194*
  the king size bed, *195*
Richly imagined education, 215–216
Richly imagined entertainment, 210
Richly imagined everything, 202, 208–210
  normative scenarios, 203
  scenario-based design and innovation, 202–203
  strategic scenarios, 203–204
  user scenarios, 203
  visual narratives, compelling power of, 204–208
Richly imagined food, 211–212
Richly imagined health, 212–214
Richly imagined marketing, 216–217
Richly imagined work, 217–218
Robots, 22
Robust scenario planning, 203
Roibu, T., 115
Romantic poets, 225
Ronga, I., 14n9

S

Sacco, K., 14n9
Sacredness, 16; *see also* Sense of sacredness, art and
Sacred wearable object, prototype of, *36*
Sanctity of art, 16–17
Santayana, G. 1896, 93n5
Sarasso, P., 14n9
Scandinavian design, 173
Scenario-based design and innovation, 202–203
Sculpture made of concrete, *77*
Secret moment, 28
Sectional couch
  with a design inspired by flower, *24*
  parametric-inspired design for, 23, *23, 24*
Self-arranging autonomous seating, *99*
Self-awareness, 113
Self-determinism, 114
Self-reflection, 174
Self-reinvention, 156
Self-sustaining living capsule, *209*
Self-transcendence, 128, 145
Sense of sacredness, art and, 28, 38n1
  creative generativity, 32–33
  dramatic expansion of beauty, AI enabling, 36–37
  generative art, theory of, 33–35
  revolution, 35–36
  sentience, art and, 30–31
  spirituality, art as the means to, 28–29
  visual space, 31

Sensibility, contemplative, 28
Sentience
  and agency, 107
    attention and technique, meaning built with, 109–112
    autopoietic intelligence, 114–115
    insight, emergence of, 107–109
    perception, fantasy and new dimensions for, 112–114
    Roibu, Tib, 115
  art and, 30–31
Sentient agent, 109–110
Shared authorship, concept of, 95
Skill and desired outcome, balance between, 71–76
Skill development, 86
Slater, M. 2009, 54–55n2, 54n3
Snowflakes, beauty of, 67n5
Solar transport proposals, *206*
Sono-centric painting, 111
Sophisticated AI systems, 101
Sophisticated virtual reality, 103
Sound reproduction system, *65*
Spatial-temporal relationships, 126
Spirituality
  art as the means to, 28–29
  concept of, 38n3
Spiritual sphere of existence, 29
Spontaneity, 226n5
Stagnation, 104
Stanford D School, 105n1
Steemit, 161n6
Storytellers, 104–105
Strategic scenarios, 203–204
Subjective experience, 30
Subjectivity, 21–22
Substack, 161n6
Subtractive manufacturing, 188
Symbiotic alliance between humans and AI, 25
Symbols, using, 20
Szarkowski, John, 108

T

Taj Mahal, 220–221
Technological disruptions, 147, 148, 153, 161
Technology, 13n4, 98, 99, 104, 128
  design intention and, 17–18
  ethical dimensions of, 99
  transformed by, 154–155
10CLOUDS, 162n8
Text and visual representation, relationship between, 168
Text-based image generation neural network, 15

Text conditional design systems, 169–173
Text-conditional generation, 168
Text-conditional image generation, 12–13, 21, 38, 46, 72, 128, 135, 136, 140, 143, 150–151, 176–177, 205, 209, 210, 223–224
Text-conditional inputs of AI systems, 7
Text-conditional inspiration
    arrival of, 169
    embrace of, 168
    embracing, 167
    infusing, 168
    integration into art and design education, 168
The Photographer's Eye (John Szarkowski), 108
Thought process, 21
Three-dimensional model, design in, 15
3D printed bathroom waste container, 190
3D-printed food, 211–212, 211, 212
3D printed lounge chair, 191, 192
3D printed soap dish, 189
3D printing, 15, 188–195, 197–198, 201n8
3D printing and generative AI, marriage of, 199
TikTok, 21, 143
Tim Peake VR Experience, 227n9
Tolstoy, L., 26n5
Tools of unknown origin or functionality, 63
Traditional notions of artistic value, 31
Transcendent reality, 38n4
Transformational change, 147, 155–156, 159
Transformational phase, 158–159
Transformation process, 152, 156
Transformative potential of AI, 3, 50
Transition, 155
    phase, 157–158
    and transformation, 156–159
Transparent rubber gown, incidental beauty of, 87
True power of AI, 77

U

Unique art, generating, 35
Unpremeditated genius, 121–122
Unrealistic reality, 112–113, 114
User scenarios, 203

V

Van Herpen, I., 194
Varela, F., 114
VBL, see Visual brand language
Vertical gardens mixed with traditional architecture, 206
Virtual art galleries, 46
Virtual forms, 44
    inherent capacity of, 43
    potential of, 48
    value and function of, 45
Virtual reality (VR), 227
    interactions in, 45–47, 50
    sophisticated, 103
Virtual space
    aesthetic of, 43–45
    creating, 48
    forms in, 47–50
Virtual tourism, 46
Visual brand language (VBL), 169, 170
Visual narratives, compelling power of, 204–208
Visual space, 31
Visual vocabulary, 137
VR, see Virtual reality

W

Wearable regenerative neurostimulator, 207
Wedding dress, radiolaria inspired design for, 198
"Whilst the Rest Were Sleeping" (Simon Wilkinson), 227n9
White motorcycle on the background of a grayish surface, 73
Wilkinson, S., 227n9
Wilson, H. J., 130n6
Wimsatt, 85
Work, richly imagined, 217–218
World Wide Web, 159–160

Y

Yan, S., 94n7
YouTube, 21, 143